The Feral Classroom

Routledge Education Books

Advisory editor: John Eggleston
Professor of Education
University of Keele

The Feral Classroom

James Macpherson

Department of Education, Massey University
Palmerston North, New Zealand

Routledge & Kegan Paul
Melbourne, London, Boston and Henley

First published in 1983
by Routledge & Kegan Paul plc
464 St Kilda Road, Melbourne,
Victoria 3004, Australia,
39 Store Street, London WC1E 7DD, England,
9 Park Street, Boston, Mass. 02108, USA, and
Broadway House, Newtown Road,
Henley-on-Thames, Oxon RG9 1EN, England
Set by Columns, Reading
and printed in Great Britain by
Redwood Burn Ltd, Trowbridge, Wiltshire
© James Macpherson 1983

Library of Congress Cataloging in Publication Data

Macpherson, James, 1942-

The feral classroom.
(Routledge education books)
Bibliography: p.
Includes indexes.
1. High school students – Australia. 2. Classroom
environment – Australia – Case studies. 3. Social
interaction – Australia – Case studies. 4. Parsons,
Talcott, 1902-   I. Title.   II. Series.
LA2106.7.M22 1983   373.18'0973   83-13900

ISBN 0-7100-9514-7

Contents

Acknowledgments   xi

Introduction   1

1 School and peer group as agents of socialisation   6
2 The research population   20
3 Students' control systems   32
4 Mucking around   49
5 Intrusion of external statuses and associations   65
6 Stirrers and clowns   91
7 Teacher authority and student control   106
8 Diffuse relations with teachers   124
9 Students' construction and management of
   academic status   141
10 Teacher particularism   161
11 Students' evaluation of classroom seating position   178
12 Conclusions   191

Appendix A   Student interviews   207
Appendix B   Conditions and permit for research   218
Appendix C   A girls' classroom note   219

Bibliography   221

Index of students   230

Subject index   238

Figures

2.1 Physical features of Goldtown form rooms 26

4.1 Control and normative structure of competitive mucking around 53

7.1 Normative structure of dobbing 108

7.2 Flow chart of pressures on captain to control class 116

7.3 Captain's use of sanctions 119

8.1 Students' evaluation of classmates' helping teachers 129

8.2 Students' evaluation of classmates' talking to teachers 134

9.1 Management of high academic status 142

9.2 Management of low academic status 152

10.1 Teacher favouritism 162

10.2 Teachers' victimisation of students 169

Tables

2.1	Goldtown and Kimberley population cohorts in 1961 and 1971	21
2.2	Occupational status of Queensland, Goldtown and Kimberley work forces in 1971	22
2.3	Composition of Grade Nine classes by level and course	24
3.1	Model of controls	33
12.1	Boys' construction and use of power and success	193
12.2	Girls' particularism and use of influence	195

Acknowledgments

I am indebted to the principal, staff and students of Goldtown High School. The students spoke freely of how they saw classroom interaction. Teachers tacitly accepted an alternative definition of their classrooms. The principal supported and advised me through the year's fieldwork.

Professor J. Western, Dr R. Smith and Professor W.J. Campbell of the University of Queensland gave valuable direction and encouragement. Professor Eggleston, editor for Routledge & Kegan Paul, patiently read a series of drafts and provided helpful comments. Professor Scrupski of Rutgers' University saw this book in an early stage and was kind enough to praise its potential.

Some very good friends and my ward, Annette, have been companions while I worked, and kept some sanity in my life.

Miss Sue O'Regan and Mrs Nancy Woodward typed and retyped the manuscript. They worked with grace, care and accuracy.

I hope this book repays these people's confidence by making schools better places for students and teachers. This will happen if educators as a result of reading it cease to act against or ignore students' perceptions of classrooms. It will happen if educators, instead of blaming themselves for discipline and learning problems, look critically at the structure of schooling.

Introduction

High school students' classroom activities and concerns are in important respects unknown. Educators are usually too concerned with their own definitions of valued knowledge and proper social order to examine students' conceptions of valued knowledge and desired social order. Yet an understanding of students' classroom culture and social structure should be central to any analysis of the outcomes of schooling. This is true whether that analysis originates in a radical perspective which questions the function of schooling, or in a conventional teacher concern with pupil discipline and motivation to learn. The present study reports the results of investigations into 'the feral classroom', the untamed life of students in the supposedly domestic setting of the classroom.

Recent sociological studies of students' classroom life have been theoretically and methodologically limited. They have either lacked a developed model of schooling or have been dogmatically Marxist. Either their research methods have not had the depth and flexibility to explore adequately students' definitions of reality, or the research population has been too small to allow generalisation from findings.

Atheoretical studies long predominated. Descriptions of students' classroom life by Cusick (1973), Gordon (1957), Hargreaves (1967), Hollingshead (1949), Lacy (1970) and Woods (1979) all dispense with a developed theoretical statement. They contribute to an understanding of the consequences of academic streaming in the cases of Hargreaves and Lacey, and of the existence of separate student and teacher subcultures in the cases of Gordon, Cusick and Woods. None the less, such studies remain disappointing. Without a comprehensive theory of schooling, they cannot give an adequate account of classrooms and schools. There is a need for studies more solidly grounded in theory.

Two recent authors (Corrigan, 1977; Willis, 1977) combine Marxist theory with ethnographies of students' school and classroom life. Both depict interaction between an intrusive working class society and the dominant social classes represented by the school and its teachers. As a result of their theoretical and political commitments. Corrigan and Willis overemphasise working-class students' ideologically motivated resistance to schooling, and so underemphasise the independent origins of students' culture in the structure of schooling. Indeed, without a model of the structure of schooling, they cannot describe how an

1

intrusive working class culture intersects with an imposed schooling.

Most sociological studies of students' classroom life have only described the behaviour of boys (Deem, 1978; Llewellyn, 1980; Shaw, 1976). Hallworth (1953) in a brief journal article was the last to describe boys' and girls' classroom life. Later studies (Atkinson and Delamont, 1976; Bird, 1980; Furlong, 1976) have been small scale studies of single aspects of girls' classroom life. Further, both Hallworth's and these later studies lack a model of socio-sexual differences. They explain post facto socio-sexual differences uncovered by their research. Thomas (1981) is exceptional in using a sophisticated theory of socio-sexual roles to describe girls' classroom interaction, but has a very small research population. Thus, there is a need for a study which, informed by models of socio-sexual differences and of schooling, researches both sexes' classroom life.

A research emphasis on students' classroom interaction dictates use of 'school class' and 'school' as units of analysis (Galtung, 1967:37-48). Both compose a 'complex of units in interaction with definite boundaries distinguishing them from their environment' (Johnson, 1970:210), where a boundary is 'a theoretically and empirically significant difference between structures and processes internal to the system and those external to it (which) exists and tends to be maintained' (Parsons et al., 1961:36). Studies have often tacitly treated classrooms as aggregates of individuals by examining students' characteristics and values rather than interaction between students (Bossert, 1979). Studies such as Furlong's (1976) which have used the school class as a unit of analysis have not included a model of schooling to interpret their findings. There is thus need for a study which, using the school class as a unit of analysis, focuses on student interaction rather than on the aggregate qualities of students.

Dominant students have been shown to determine classmates' interpretations of the classroom setting and consequently to determine these classmates' behaviour (Cohen, 1973:488; Gnagey, 1961; Gorman, 1969:49; Polansky, 1954). How this is done has not been analysed (Meyenn, 1980). Even researchers who have reported that verbal and physical fights are rife have not analysed these fights and abuse in terms of the social construction of control. Despite concern with control in interpretive sociology, and the importance of interpretive sociology as a source of analysis and method in recent classroom studies, questions of how and by whom norms activated have been neglected. Willis (1977), whose Marxist model leads him to see teacher-student relations as marked by imposition of a normative system, does not describe control relations either within his groups of boys, or between them and others. Thus, there is a need for a study which analyses students' classroom interaction in terms of imposition and conflict.

Exigencies of time and resources have limited the value of

studies of students' perspectives on classroom interaction. Researchers have accommodated to these exigencies in one of two ways. They may, as Corrigan (1977) did, use a research method which allows quick and efficient gathering of data from a wide population. Use of such methods reduces the validity and types of data that can be collected (Zelditch, 1962). They may, as Willis (1977) and Cusick (1973) have done, reduce their sample size. This allows use of interviews and participant observation. These methods consume time but permit adequate qualitative research. A price has to be paid. This is the inability to generalise from a small research population which cannot be placed in the context of students' interaction in classroom and school. Thus, an adequate study must analyse a student population large enough to remove suspicion of arbitrariness of findings, and large enough to place each student clique within the wider context of school interaction. The method used to study this population must permit exploration of students' diverse subjective realities and allow questions to be focused on actual incidents and structures of students' classroom interaction.

The present study is designed to avoid the flaws of earlier studies. It has a comprehensive model of the structure of schooling. The model has been developed to allow second-order interpretation of students' subjective reality while minimising distortion of data by rigid imposition of categories of analysis (Sharp and Green, 1975:1-35). It incorporates a model of socio-sexual differences which has its roots in social structural considerations similar to those employed in the construction of models of the school and peer groups as agents of socialisation. It gives equal weight to analysis of girls' and boys' perspectives on classroom interaction. A model of control in students' interaction has been developed which takes into account how dominant students construct their positions of domination and determine the use of classroom norms. The research population includes a complete cohort of girls and boys in a high school. The research has been designed to explore students' constructions of classroom reality while focusing questions on classroom interaction.

Parsonian theory is used here to construct models of schooling, socio-sexual roles, the peer groups and controls. These models are constructed from analytic variables which have been related to central aspects of western industrial societies (Dreeben, 1968; Parsons, 1966, 1967, 1969, 1971a, 1971b; Parsons and Bales, 1955; Parsons and Smelser, 1956). Thus the study, though confined to analysis of classrooms, has obvious implications for socialisation into adult roles in these societies.

In the present research, voluntaristic rather than the better-known structural functional Parsonian theory (Menzies, 1977; Strasser, 1976:122-48) is used. This choice is compatible with Parsons' own preference. He terms structural functionalism 'a second best type of theory' (Parsons et al., 1961: 20) to be used only when there is comparatively little knowledge of a set of activities. Parsonian voluntarism analyses action in terms of meanings used by an actor to orient his actions. It does not, in the first instance, describe the action relative to its function in the social system of which it is part.

Parsons' models of schooling and peer groups as agents of socialisation have been merged in the present study's description of students' constructions of classroom reality. The model of schooling describes socialisation of students into values required by the dominant society as represented in the school. The model of peer groups as socialising agents asserts the importance of the independence of peer group interaction from adult control. Agreeing with Bernstein (1977: 188) that schools do not create 'a docile, deferential and subservient workforce', the models of school and peer group are conflated here to take into account students' frequent independence from teachers' control. Classroom norms are shown to be structured by schooling. However, it is also shown that the importance of each norm is related to creation of dominance among students and that the definition of conformity to norms is controlled by dominant students and imposed on subordinate classmates. The implications of these findings for functional theories of schooling are discussed in the concluding chapter.

Parsons' theoretical work is notoriously complex and often controversial. This book is primarily concerned with applying parts of his work to an analysis of classroom interaction. The book does not have as principal concerns the discussion of points of debate between Parsonian and other sociologists or the elaboration of theoretical issues which chiefly interest specialist Parsonian theorists.

A result of the substantive concern in the book with classroom interaction is that debatable interpretations of Parsons' theory have not been discussed in each instance nor has every departure from aspects of his theory been noted. The content and formulations of the book should interest the specialist systems theorist. However, the presentation of the content and formulations is designed for readers who have an interest in classroom interaction and the outcomes of schooling, and who have some knowledge of sociology but are not specialist systems sociologists.

There are three principal areas in which an extended discussion of nice points in Parsonian theory has been avoided. These relate to the sets of variables used to classify social roles, to the concept of 'norm', and to the analysis of control in social systems.

Parsons (1951: 58-67) originally distinguished five sets of 'pattern variables' which would be of general use in classifying roles. These pattern variables were self/collectivity orientation, performance/quality, specificity/diffuseness, affectivity/affective neutrality, and particularism/universalism. In his later work, Parsons (1967: 192-219) discarded the self/collectivity orientation variable. During early stages of the present research, one of the remaining pattern variables, affectivity/affective neutrality, was found to be largely irrelevant to the proposed analysis of classroom interaction. As a result, only three pattern variables, performance/quality, specificity/diffuseness, and universalism/quality have been used.

Münch (1981) has described the extent to which Parsons' use of the concept of a 'norm' emphasizes conformity to that norm. The use in the present research of the concept of norm preserves the emphasis on conformity, but makes definition of that conformity problematic. In doing this, tacit use is made of Parsons' theory of 'cybernetic hierarchy' (Parsons and Platt, 1973: 423-447) in which a model is presented of how the values and goals of actors help determine the operation of norms. The regard Parsons (1978: 433) has for aspects of action other than the narrowly social further limits the significance of conformity to norms. Conformity to norms, even in the modified sense employed in this book, is an important but limited part of Parsons' theory of action (DiTomaso, 1982).

In Chapter 3 of this book a model is presented of 'controls': inducement, power, influence, and the activation of commitments. These controls are called by Parsons either 'the categories of societal interchange' (Parsons and Platt, 1973: 432) or 'the symbolic media of interchange' (Parsons, 1978: 136-40). Parsons (1973: 423-447) in his discussion of symbolic media speak of their use as controls and sanctions. His terms are cumbersome and, for the general reader, uninformative. My term better expresses their use in this book.

This interpretation of 'norm', the use of 'the categories of societal interchange' as a taxonomy of types of control, together with the use of voluntaristic theory form a style of Parsonian theorising which refutes some of the conventional criticisms directed at Parsons by sociologists of education. This refutation is discussed briefly in the conclusions to the present research. The refutation does not take the form of an extended textual exegesis. Instead, it takes the form of a consideration of the use made of Parsonian theory in the present research.

Chapter 1

School and peer group as agents of socialisation

The aims of the investigations reported in 'The Feral Classroom' are empirical and theoretical. The empirical aim is to describe students' classroom interaction. The account outlines the interactive effects of teachers and peers on students, balances normative and control aspects of interaction, and includes an important intrusive element, socio-sexual roles. The theoretical aims are to illustrate the operation of normative and control aspects of Parsons' theory and to develop his model of schooling.

The present chapter uses models of schooling, peer groups and socio-sexual values to suggest likely patterns of student interaction. First, developing Parsons' model of schooling, it argues that students' acceptance of the values of schooling results in students rejecting the imposed authority of the school. Next, it is argued that values originating in peer interaction strengthen the acquisition of values associated with schooling and the rejection of the imposed authority of the school. Lastly, it is argued that socio-sexual values dispose boys to accept values implicit in schooling and girls to reject them.

Previous research is reviewed concurrently with the development of theory. Descriptions of boys' classroom interaction are included with the statement of the model of schooling with which boys' interaction is congruent. Descriptions of girls' classroom interaction are discussed under the topic of socio-sexual roles, as it is argued that female roles reinterpret rather than reinforce the structure of schooling.

PARSONS' MODELS OF SCHOOL AND PEER GROUP

Parsons' models of school and peer group compare them with the anterior and concurrent agent of socialisation, the family. In Parsons' analysis, the family encourages diffuse, particularistic and qualitative values in children, which tend to be replaced through socialisation into and by the school and peer group by their opposites, specific, universalistic and performance values.

The model of school
Particularism refers to the value of loyalty to friends and associates (Parsons, 1951: 61-62). Universalism refers to the value of treating others equally without regard to bonds of loyalty (Parsons, 1951: 62-63). Parsons (1959) says children tend to acquire universalistic values in school because parity of

age in teaching groups creates a rough equality of pupil capacities. This enables teachers to treat students as members of a category by assigning them similar tasks, privileges and obligations. This categorisation of pupils contrasts with the family where particularistic values are expressed in terms of loyalty to a person's children or parents.

A performance value is one where effectiveness or success in achieving goals is valued (Parsons, 1951:64). By contrast, the value of quality refers to an orientation towards others 'in terms of what they "are", of their qualities defined independently of performances' (Parsons, 1967: 201). Performance values tend to be learnt at school because classrooms are organised around core activities in which teachers assign tasks to pupils and compare and evaluate work. From this pupils learn the importance of success and failure and how to manage their social consequences. This emphasis on performance contrasts with the family where the child has no opportunity for prime identification as success or failure in the role of child (Parsons, 1959).

The diffuse/specific continuum refers to the scope of one person's interest in another. In the case of diffuseness, a broad range of interests in the other is valued (Parsons, 1951: 66). In the case of specificity, a narrow range of interest is valued (Parsons, 1951: 66). Specificity values are taught by the multiple specific relations which students encounter in primary school. These pressures are accentuated in high school. High school students often meet new teachers with each subject and learn that relations with each teacher have definite bounds (Parsons, 1959). This situation contrasts with the family where parents generally assume and are charged with a diffuse responsibility for their children. Reciprocally, the children usually have to argue strenuously for exclusion of any part of their life from parental supervision.

Parsons' model of schooling stresses students' acceptance of teachers' authority. He assumes that students are concerned with success in school subjects as defined and evaluated by teachers. Students, he assumes, accept the official school authority system.

However, Scrupski (1975: 175-176) has argued convincingly that contradictions in the process of schooling limit students' acceptance of teachers' authority. Acceptance of the value of performance means that the student will judge teachers by their performance and relevance to student concerns rather than acquiesce in an ascribed dependence of student on teacher. Acceptance of the value of specificity means that the student will question the pervasive teacher control of the classroom and restrict it to a specific focus of legitimate interest. Acceptance of the value of universalism leads the student to judge teachers' behaviour by consideration of equity.

The model of the peer group

The social and financial dependence of adolescents as pupils at
school and as children at home (Parsons and Platt, 1972:96)
contrasts with the situation in the peer group where relations
are free from ascribed status (Parsons and Bales, 1955: 21).
This freedom results in strong peer group orientation to performance which can be evaluated by universalistic standards
(Parsons, 1964: 104). Parsons distinguishes two types of
peer group performance. One is performance dimensions according to normative criteria (Parsons and Bales, 1955: 151) and
the other is the establishment of control within the peer group
(Parsons, 1964: 104). Evidence from Australia, the United
Kingdom, and the United States uniformly shows the importance
both of specific, universalistic performance dimensions in
children's games and of the use and construction of controls in
children's independent activities (Davey, 1981; Knapp and
Knapp, 1976; Sluckin, 1981). These games and activities differ
from academic attainment in not being contaminated by ascribed
dependence on teachers or other adults.

Conflation of the models of school and peer group: the evidence

Performance in students' classroom interaction Research has
shown that students do not completely or unconditionally accept
teachers' definitions of academic success. Academic success as
defined by teachers is too closely associated with ascribed
dependence of students on teachers (Marsh, Rosser and Harré,
1978; Young and Whitty, 1977). Kandel and Lesser (1972) found
that 'while the adolescent leaders do better in schoolwork than
nonleaders these leaders value schoolwork less, placing other
priorities ahead of schoolwork'. Kandel and Lesser explain these
findings in terms of high school students' identification of good
schoolwork with obedience and conformity to adult dictates.
Thus the leaders, as other students do, accept the importance of
schoolwork, but as leaders overtly deprecate such activity as
demeaning to their emancipated status.

The classroom offers conditions of independence and comparability of students' actions required for the growth of alternative
performance dimensions (Dreeben, 1976; McArthur, 1981).
Students are conscripted but teachers cannot, in state schools,
control their recruitment. Thus teachers cannot assume that
students do willingly what is legally required of them. In the
aggregate students have more control over the classroom than the
teachers who have only fragile coercive resources to enforce
their will. Therefore, teachers cannot enforce their order on
unwilling students.

Comparability of students' independent actions as a prerequisite
for their conversion to performance dimensions is ensured by
their homogeneity and public nature. The imposed physical and
social structure of the classroom limits the range of possible forms
of alternative action (Bycroft, 1973). The ease with which a

single student may disrupt the teacher-imposed order of a whole class renders many of these actions public. Thus, students are likely to be given the chance to compare and evaluate roughly similar forms of action. Research shows three alternative performance dimensions originating within the classroom: students' flouting of teachers' authority; students' independent classroom interaction unfocused on the teacher; and boys' use of power.

Researchers have paid considerable attention to students' challenges to teachers' authority. For instance, Stinchcombe (1964: 2) speaks of pupils '*flouting* rules rather than *evading* rules' and Woods (1976: 179) describes 'subversive laughter aimed . . . at undermining the authority structure of the school'. Such subversive behaviour occurs when students evaluate the performance of teachers and reject a normative definition of qualitative dependence on teachers. It occurs when the lesson is defined as a nonlearning situation because of teachers' failure to control the class (Davies, 1976: 41–48; Marsh, Rosser and Harré, 1978: 39–40; Musgrove and Taylor, 1969: 17–27; Nash, 1976: 60–69; Robinson, 1974: 263) or when the material of the lesson is defined as irrelevant or lacking status (Furlong, 1976; Hargreaves, 1967; Lacey, 1970; Stinchcombe, 1964; Woods, 1976).

Researchers have largely ignored students' behaviour which is not directly pertinent to teachers' goals of academic attainment and classroom order. Of researchers who have noted such behaviour (Campbell et al., 1976:345; Jackson, 1968: 60; Marsh, Rosser and Harré, 1978; Möhle, 1978; Sugarman, 1968: 56), only Woods (1976) has contributed to an analysis of its content, structure and significance. Its presence as a species of classroom interaction independent of teachers' control suggests that it may include performance dimensions. The ability to fight has been shown to be an important performance dimension in boys' classes (Gould, 1964; Pink, 1972; Sherif and Sherif, 1961: 57; Sugarman, 1968, 1973; Werthman, 1971), although fighting itself occurs more often outside than inside the classroom. Fighting and academic performance produce similar behaviour in male students' interaction (Zander and van Egmond, 1958). Hargreaves (1967) found the highest informal position among low academic status boys was gained by fighting. Sugarman (1968: 55; 1973: 176–177) shows boys' classroom sociometric cliques differentiated according to willingness to fight. Boys unwilling to fight under provocation were condemned by all other students.

Researchers have not examined whether male students' fighting ability is a basis for the construction of power. Hargreaves (1967) and Sugarman (1973) speak of students' use of power to obtain homework from classmates, and Werthman (1971) speaks of students' use of power to obtain information to validate perceptions of academic performance. However, they have not considered how fighting ability is used to construct power in boys' classroom interaction.

This omission has wide ramifications. If fighting has meaning, beyond being an end in itself, it is likely to be in terms of the control of the application, selection and activation of students' definitions of performance and conformity. As such it has implications for the whole student interpretation of schooling and the construction of relations between students.

Some writers have extracurricular activities and aspects of youth-culture as performance dimensions which intrude into classroom interaction and replace academic commitment. Reports that extracurricular activities afford each pupil clique in the school an informal status which then intrudes into the classroom come from American schools with extensive extracurricular activities (Coleman, 1961; Cusick, 1973; Gordon, 1957; Hollingshead, 1949; Stinchcombe, 1964). These reports contrast with reports from British schools where school hierarchy is more important perhaps because of less extracurricular activities (Blyth, 1960; Hallworth, 1954; Hargreaves, 1967). The best known American report, that by Coleman (1961), argues that high social participation and sporting performance become alternate sources of high status running counter to high academic attainment. Secondary analyses of Coleman's data largely refute his findings. Alexander and Campbell (1964) demonstrated that Coleman's 'leading crowd' were more likely to go to college than other students. Bernard (1971) suggested that school publicity rather than actual membership of the leading crowd determined whom Coleman nominated as members of the leading crowd. Other studies in America and the United Kingdom show correlations between academic and athletic commitment and prowess (Musgrave, 1964:39; Spreltzer and Pugh, 1973). The relation of extracurricular performance students' classroom interaction, however, has yet to be determined.

Participation in the teenage culture has also been seen to compete with academic attainment as a performance dimension. Murdoch and Phelps (1972) in the United Kingdom and Polk and Pink (1971) in the United States, argue that two principal life-styles are available to adolescents: the 'pupil' role accepting values and norms held by the school and the 'teenager' role – not enjoying school and doing badly in the schoolwork, and involved in the teenage culture. These writers, supported by the analyses of Stinchcombe (1964) and Hargreaves (1967) conclude that school is unpleasant and unrewarding for low academic status students. This leads to unrest in school and participation in the teenage culture. Teenage culture in its recruitment reflects school academic status even while the culture itself intrudes with these students into the school. Sugarman (1968) with different findings also argues for the unimportance of intrusive adolescent culture. He found among his population of schoolboys that interest in teenage culture was unrelated to classroom group membership or academic attainment.

Universalism in students' classroom interaction   Researchers
have shown that students apply universalistic values to the
classroom behaviour of teachers and students. Most often
mentioned in the literature is students' concern with the equity
of punishment. Students term 'good teachers' those who punish
equitably and they condemn those who favour or victimise students
(Davies, 1976: 41–48; Hargreaves, 1975: 131–133; Marsh, Rosser
and Harré, 1978: 39–40; Musgrove and Taylor, 1969: 17–27;
Nash, 1976: 68–69; Robinson, 1974: 263). Werthman (1971)
describes students' evaluation of the equity of the marks teachers
give students. He shows that students with universalistic values
are the 'delinquents who question school authority. The delinquents believe that marks are legitimately granted according
to specific, universalistic, performance criteria of "smartness"'
(Werthman, 1971: 40). They hypothesise that teachers try to
establish diffuse, particularistic relationships with certain
students by illegitimately awarding higher marks to the students
concerned or that teachers with diffuse, qualitative values
illegitimately penalise with lower marks students whom they dislike. The delinquents, having proved to their satisfaction that
a teacher's award of marks is inequitable, challenge that
teacher's authority. The students thus deny unconditional
ascribed dependence on teachers.

Students evaluate classmates' relations with teachers. They may
condemn classmates who try to establish particularistic relations
with teachers 'kissing ass' (Werthman, 1971: 41) or 'crawling'
(Macpherson, 1977). However, students sometimes give special
respect to students who establish diffuse and particularistic
relations with teachers. Gordon (1957: 47–48) demonstrates
how leading students benefit from intrusion into the classroom
of diffuse and particularistic relations of student and teacher
in extra-curricular activities. Researchers have not determined
when diffuse and particularistic relations between student and
teacher are a source of status for the student and when a
source of stigmatisation.

PARSONS' MODEL OF SEX DIFFERENCES

Parsons sees socialisation as systematic differentiation of the
personality structure, each division having implications for any
future subdivision. The first division involves sexual socialisation
in western nuclear families where children have prolonged contact with their mother but not with their father. Boys thus
experience different problems from girls in acquiring sexual
identities. The different identities thus received, and the
implications of the method of attainment, socialise each sex into
distinctive value orientations. These value orientations then
carry over into later positions which 'engage for most purposes
the whole personality' (Parsons and Bales, 1955: 100). According
to Parsons, the most fundamental difference between the sexes

is that, relative to the total culture, the masculine personality tends to be marked by universalistic, specific and performance values, and the female personality by particularistic, diffuse and qualitative values.

The difference between the masculine and feminine personalities parallels the distinct values taught in school and peer group when compared with those taught in the family. If prior values influence actors' perceptions of the structural demands of new settings, then girls are less likely than boys to express specific, universalistic and qualitative values in the classroom.

Female particularism
A long tradition of research has demonstrated strong female particularistic values (Berger and Bass, 1961; Lynn, 1962; Oetzel, 1966; Rosenberg, 1965). These particularistic values have been shown to be directed in the classroom to teachers, to female peers, and to boys.

Female students, rather than their male counterparts, tend to form solidary relations with teachers. High school girls have more favourable attitudes than high school boys to teachers (Gregersen and Travers, 1968; Leeds, 1947; Martin, 1972; McSweeney, 1971). Significantly Gregersen and Travers (1968) demonstrate that girls but not boys as they grow older increasingly transfer loyalties from teachers.

High school girls' attachment to teachers does not carry over into a desire for academic excellence (Keeling and Nuthall, 1969: 43). However, as with other dimensions which have been conventionally defined as performance dimensions, high attainment may occur when particularistic values are activated by a significant other (Atkinson and O'Connor, 1966; Atkinson and Raphaelson, 1956; Crandall et al., 1964; French, 1955; McClelland et al., 1953; Smith, 1969: 43-44; Tyler et al., 1962). In younger girls, high particularistic values often lead to higher academic attainment through the wish to please teachers by hard work and conformity (Hoffman, 1972; Sears, 1963).

There are suggestions that among older girls particularistic affiliation ceases to be related to high academic attainment. Coleman (1961) reports that high school boys named as 'best scholars' have higher IQ scores than girls so named, despite the girls' research population having, on average, the higher IQ scores. He explains these findings by suggesting that brighter and more mature girls as they grow older become sooner indifferent to pleasing teachers. Shaw and McCuen (1960) found that girls who later become low achievers in secondary school have higher marks until Grade Five than secondary school high achievers. At Grade Six, secondary school high achievers first attain a higher grade point average, and the differences increase every year until Grade Ten. The drop for the secondary school low achieving group coincides roughly with the beginning of puberty (vide Holter, 1970: 165; Milner, 1949). Llewellyn (1980) and Stinchcombe (1964: 126) found that girls' low academic attainment is related to their orientation to marriage and their entry into dating relationships. Another sign of decreasing significance of teacher relations for girls is the tendency to finish school earlier than boys despite more harmonious relations with teachers and higher academic attainment (Holly, 1965; Kolesnik, 1969: 138-141).

Parallel to changes in academic attainment are sociometric and cultural changes in girls' classroom interaction which lead to the formation of groups reflecting orientations either to boys or to teachers. Gordon (1957: 16-17) shows in his sample that by Grade Ten two cliques dominated the cohort of girls. These were a social elite influencing dress and dating culture and somewhat in conflict with school authority, and an intellectual elite highly approved by teachers and administration. Influence lines following low to high sociometric choices operated through both popular and marginal clique members to those of similar values not in the group.

Realisation of particularistic values varies with the context of schooling. Hallworth (1953) shows that in the first year of high school, the sociometric structure of girls' but not boys' classes was determined by ascribed attributes, notably socioeconomic status. This suggests that the qualitative orientation may dominate where not enough time has elapsed to establish particularistic ties with classmates. The second year, the girls were competing for a limited number of high stream places in the following academic year, and valued academic attainment so highly that sociometric rank was a better predictor of academic attainment than intelligence. The only girl to choose a boy was the girls' sociometric star, a forerunner of girls' higher sociometric status associated with sexual maturity. The following year, academic attainment was less of a determinant of informal status and sexual interests became more important. The most influential body of opinion had anti-school values and comprised a group of six girls each friendly with older boys, while of the other girls in the class only one had a boyfriend. In the fourth year there were again two groups. The larger group was well-groomed, using cosmetics, outside the school associating easily with boys, and inside the school able to express sociometric rejection. The smaller group had the opposite characteristics and acted defensively.

Thomas (1981) shows strong particularistic values shaping the school behaviour of low stream, anti-academic Grade Ten girls. She describes these girls forming cliques based on caring relations between girls and on shared knowledge of boyfriends. Status of cliques was determined by level of sexual maturity. School subjects were judged according to their relevance to achievement of traditional female roles: marriage and motherhood. The girls did what they saw as proper for sexually mature girls of their age and resisted and avoided teacher authority which countered expressions of this maturity.

Other evidence shows girls' particularism directed towards

classmates. In high school, girls responding to sociometrics have
'a consistently higher percentage of mutual choices than males'
(Gronlund, 1959: 110). In a study of high school students, far
more girls than boys listed their greatest abilities as getting on
with others, fitting in, and making friends easily. Despite this,
it was girls, and not boys, who wished to improve themselves
in this area (Edgar, 1974: 36-40). Girls' levels of anxiety and
the number of sociometric rejections received were significantly
correlated.

The focus of particularistic values on female peers may also
lead to higher academic attainment through student co-operation.
Girls tend to co-operate with each other and thereby gain higher
marks where boys tend to compete to the detriment of their
average score (Boocock and Coleman, 1970).

Socio-sexual roles and performance values
Until recently it was generally agreed that boys were more
performance oriented than girls (O'Leary, 1977: 81) and more
likely than girls to see academic attainment as a performance
dimension (Campbell, 1964:4). Male but not female performance
orientation and academic attainment are positively correlated
(Klinger, 1966; Veroff et al., 1953). The greater importance of
academic attainment for boys is shown by correlations of
leadership and self-esteem with academic status. Low academic
status boys tend to have low self-esteem but with girls the
correlation between self-esteem and academic attainment is
lower and often insignificant (Bledsoe, 1964; Klinger, 1966;
Veroff et al., 1953). Among boys, more than girls, peer status
correlates with academic attainment and ability, and when class
leaders are compared with nonleaders of equivalent ability, the
male leaders tend to have higher academic attainment (Kandel
and Lesser, 1972: 34).

Recent writers have cast doubt on this research and deny the
sex specialisation of male performance and female particularistic
dimensions. Maccoby and Jacklin (1974) believe that activities
usually associated with males have been too easily interpreted
as reflecting performance values. Similarly activities usually
associated with females have been too easily interpreted as
reflecting particularistic values. The research which has claimed
to show that male performance dimensions are stronger than
those of females has been criticised because of its neglect of
female dimensions of performance (Bardwick, 1971; O'Leary,
1977). Many women believe that social skills are an important
dimension of female achievement (Stein and Bailey, 1973). When
scoring of projective tests of achievement motivation includes
these dimensions of female achievement, a close relationship is
found between women's performance orientation and performance.
Thus, it would be a mistake to assume with earlier writers such
as Ausubel (1970: 407), Bakan (1966), and Garai and Scheinfeld
(1968), the empirical identity of the universalism/particularism
and performance/quality dimensions. Instead, it needs to be

asked whether success and effectiveness in performance may
not be the requisite of the establishment of particularistic goals,
and whether loyalties are manifest in what are, like academic
attainment, conventionally taken as performance dimensions of
classroom activity.

Socio-sexual roles and diffuse/specific orientations
Research generally indicates that girls' values are more diffuse
than those of boys in schools. Boys' academic interests tend to
be specific to individual school subjects whereas girls' interests
tend to transcend individual school subjects. Coleman (1961)
found that boys are likely to do well in school subjects that
interest them and poorly in subjects that bore them, but that
girls' attainment in school subjects is independent of interest
in them. This suggests a specificity of male academic interests
combined with a performance definition of student-teacher
interaction, and a diffuse female academic interest combined with
a qualitative definition of student-teacher interaction. Mancini
(1972) shows that, independent of academic attainment, boys'
verbal behaviour in science and their perception of how they are
succeeding in science correlate more highly than their verbal
behaviour in science and their general self-concept. Among girls
the reverse is true. The correlations between verbal behaviour
in science and general self-concept are higher than correlations
between verbal behaviour in science and perceptions of success
in science. Findings may be different in school subjects tra-
ditionally associated with a female image, but these findings
show, in science at least, a greater male than female orientation
to specific performance values in the classroom.

Some measures of specific/diffuse orientations relate to
extensions of legitimate school authority from an assumed
academic core. Stinchcombe (1964) found that girls are more
likely than boys to agree that students' neatness in written
work should be taken into account in assessment, but boys more
often than girls agree that teachers have a right to enforce
dress standards by partly basing assessment on them. However,
Hibbins (1974) found, in a slightly older population, girls were
twice as likely as boys to agree that the school should set dress
standards. These findings illustrate some problems of testing
for specific/diffuse values. Extensions of legitimate school
authority may be in different directions for male and female
students. The legitimate scope of teachers' authority also
depends on which interaction system the student is oriented to.
If, for example, the dominant female orientation compared with
the male orientation is not to academic life, then girls may reject
teachers' dress authority not because of a specific academic
orientation but because of diffuse concern with another
social system.

Other research has tended to show girls' diffuse values.
Stinchcombe (1964) found the closer the informal status system
of the school to the school's academic core, the greater the

alienation from school of boys, but not girls, with low status
in that system. Conversely, girls were more likely than boys to
be alienated from the school as a result of their low status in a
diffuse status system based on involvement in extracurricular
activities, students' informal life, and parents' occupation and
income (cf. Brown and Bond, 1955; Jones, 1943). However,
sometimes even qualitative diffuse status systems such as
parental socio-economic status are more relevant for male than
female self-esteem (Rosenberg, 1965: 40-41).

In short, there is some evidence for male specific orientations
in a movement from a core of single school subjects to school
subjects in general, and from a core of the academic to the
extracurricular. In other possible dimensions of specific/
diffuse orientation, inconsistent findings render it difficult to
interpret the significance of the research.

Control in girls' classroom interaction
The existence of girls' independent classroom interaction raises
the question of how control is exercised in girls' classroom
interaction. The topic of girls' classroom controls has received
even less attention than that of boys (Deem, 1978; Meyenn,
1980; Shaw, 1976). Researchers have described fights but not
pursued questions of control implicit in these fights. Girls'
verbal aggression against teachers tends to be dismissed by
teachers in terms of uncomplimentary animal metaphors: 'bitching'
and 'cattiness' (Davies, 1978; Thomas, 1981). None the less, it
is effective. If effective against teachers, verbal aggression is
likely to be effective in girls' classroom fights (Meyenn, 1980).
It thus needs to be asked whether verbal aggressiveness can
lead to development of a system of control in girls' classroom
interaction. It also needs to be asked whether any control
exercised through verbal aggression is compatible with girls'
particularistic values.

The suggested sexual specialisation of controls into girls'
use of verbal fighting and boys' use of physical fighting has
implications for a study of the relationship between domination
and values in the determination of classroom interaction. On the
one hand, dominant students determine, activate and interpret
the prevalent values. On the other hand, the values dominant
students use to signify their status are determined by interaction between the symbolic and social resources of the classroom,
intrusive sexual and other values, and the exigencies of control
facing dominant students. Moreover, the suggested sexual
specialisation of controls indicates that there may be overriding
values which determine the propriety and effectiveness of the
use of controls.

RESEARCH QUESTIONS

This discussion of how Parsons' models of schooling, peer groups and sex differences may be applied to an analysis of students' classroom interaction raises two sets of questions. One set asks what dimensions of classroom activity and existence are central for students. It has to be determined which are the significant performance dimensions, which are the qualitative statuses, which are the foci and extensions of the specific/diffuse continuum, which are the foci of particularism, and which are the dimensions of activity and status to which universalistic considerations apply. Answers to these questions are a prerequisite for answering the second set of questions. This is concerned with the autonomy of the classroom peer group in relation to teachers and the extent to which the dominant values realised in classrooms reflect the expected values of male and female students' classroom groups.

Particulars of previous theoretical expositions and the closed assumptions of some previous research each need testing. The most important of these is the assumption that teacher sponsored and controlled dimensions are central to students' classroom interaction. This assumption entails a belief that academic attainment as defined and evaluated by teachers forms students' primary performance dimensions.

The model advanced here throws doubt on these assumptions. It suggests that dependence on teachers implicit in acceptance of their definitions of academic success may ensure that such success is not seen by classmates as a performance dimension. This raises the concomitant questions of whether there exist within the classroom alternative performance dimensions and of how students interpret academic attainment.

Intrusive sex differences offer similar difficulties. It needs to be determined on whom girls' classroom particularistic values are focused: parents, teachers, same-sex peers, other-sex peers. It is also necessary to ask what behaviours are associated with each focus of students' particularistic loyalties.

Intrusive sex roles also cause problems of interpretation when associated with conventionally accepted differences. Whatever the actual motivation of action, activities usually associated with boys have often been unquestioningly interpreted as performance dimensions, and activities associated equally with each sex have been interpreted differently according to the sex concerned.

All these problems of interpretation are compounded by considerations of how control is exercised within the classroom peer group. The establishment of control within the peer group is a corollary of the peer group's autonomy. It offers students another status dimension which has wide ramifications for the operation of the normative order of the classroom. The exercise of control on any occasion may govern the selection, activation, and interpretation of definitions of success, failure, conformity and deviance.

The succeeding chapters try to answer these questions about the operation of controls, performances and norms in the classroom. Chapter 2 describes the research population. The sequence of the later chapters takes into account the establishment of control in peer interaction and the relevance of students' performances and classroom norms to the establishment of that control.

Chapter 2 describes the social context of the research population. It describes aspects of the host community and school which form the macrocontext of the school class and which are likely to have influenced the operation of classroom controls, performances and norms. A major finding of the present study is that the microcontext of the classroom or where students sit is strongly related to different types of interaction in the classroom. Chapter 2 describes a code which allows the identification of individual students by seating position within their school class. This code facilitates the description of microcontextual effects. The code also identifies the sex of the student concerned. It thus aids the description of sociosexual differences in classroom interaction.

Chapter 3 applies a Parsonian model of control to a study of control in students' classroom interaction. Special attention is given to the sex-specialisation of controls. Boys are shown generally to exert control through the use of power, with a base of physical force. Girls are shown generally to exert control through the use of influence and the activation of commitments.

Chapters 4 and 5 describe the dimensions of classroom interaction most closely related to the construction of boys' power and girls' influence. Chapter 4 shows that a specific performance dimension, competitive mucking around, celebrates boys' relative power. Chapter 5 shows that a diffuse intrusive dimension with a particularistic focus shapes girls' ability to exercise influence over classmates.

Chapters 6, 7 and 8 describe how dominant students control, in their own interest, students' interaction with teachers. Chapter 6 describes 'stirring' and 'clowning' as activities which challenge teachers' authority. Dominant students are shown to control definitions of acceptable and successful stirring. Some sex differences in the definitions of these activities are apparent: boys tend to emphasise performance aspects of the roles, and girls emphasise qualitative definitions with a particularistic focus. Chapter 7 shows how dominant students extend the scope of their classroom control through definitions of the proper use of invoked and delegated teacher authority. Chapter 8 similarly shows how dominant students, by controlling definitions of the significance of students' helping and talking to teachers, monopolise the advantages of doing so.

Chapters 9 and 10 demonstrate how dominant students' management and redefinition of teachers' evaluation of students enable these dominant students to determine important aspects of the realisation of universalistic and performance values in the class-

room. Dominant students are shown thereby to monopolise effective high academic status and legitimate teacher favour.
Teachers' definitions of low academic status are shown to form
an ineluctable reality with wide implications for students'
interaction with classmates. Real or alleged victimisation by
teachers is shown to offer dominant students a chance to draw
classmates' attention to themselves as champions of justice.

Chapter 11, the last empirical chapter, shows how students'
perceptions of advantage and disadvantage associated with
seating in various classroom localities are structured in terms
of students' constructions of reality described in earlier chapters.
It details how students are pressed to choose between certain
control and value considerations. It thus explains the grouping
and location of certain values and their incompatibility with,
and physical separation from, others.

Chapter 12, the concluding chapter, discusses implications of
the findings for Parsonian theory in general, and the models of
schooling, peer groups and sex differences in particular. It
finishes with a statement of questions opened or left unanswered
by the present research.

Research methods are described in Appendix A. It shows how
open questions supplemented by probes to expand initial responses elicited accounts of classroom interaction. It also shows
how, parallel to theoretical considerations, the significance of
students' culture was indicated by its relation to students'
classroom social structure distinguished by sociometric techniques. This combination of criteria of significance allows for
openness to what students consider important in their culture,
tests the importance of these aspects of culture against the social
structure of the peer group, and permits interpretation of
these significant aspects of culture and social structure in terms
of a general theory.

Chapter 2

The research population

Grade Nine students of a Queensland state high school, called here Goldtown High School, were the research population. This chapter discusses how the context and structure of Goldtown High School may have modified realisation of universalistic, specific and performance values in this research population. The chapter begins by describing the demography and economy of the City of Goldtown and the surrounding Shire of Kimberley. Next, an account is given of the educational setting of the research population. The code used in the text to identify individual students by school class and seating position is then explained. This precedes, awkwardly but necessarily, discussion of how the system of assessment of academic attainment may have affected student interaction.

THE HOST COMMUNITY

The populations of Goldtown and Kimberley are stable or declining and, compared with the population of Queensland, show a strong relative decline. Between 1961 and 1971 the population of Queensland rose by over 20 per cent, the population of Goldtown rose insignificantly, and the population of Kimberley declined by over 12 per cent.

Relatively low rates of immigration, a factor in the comparative decline of the population, contribute to the cultural homogeneity of Goldtown and Kimberley. More than 95 per cent of the population originates in Australasia. Less than 2 per cent of the population has immigrated from countries other than the British Isles.

Emigration also contributed to the relative decline. Statistics given in Table 2.1 show that every cohort between the ages of 10 and 60 declined in excess of mortality rates between 1961 and 1971. There were specially high rates of migration in the fifteen years after leaving school. The need to migrate to obtain work after leaving high school may influence Goldtown student perceptions of the relevance of academic knowledge and schooling compared with areas having higher employment opportunities (Montague, 1978: 237-278).

Table 2.1 Goldtown and Kimberley population cohorts in
1961 and 1971

	GOLDTOWN					
Age	Males			Females		
	1961	1971	% change[a]	1961	1971	% change[a]
0-9	1,160			1,184		
10-19	1,128	1,085	- 7.4	1,196	1,111	- 6.2
20-29	573	633	-44.9	673	707	-41.9
30-39	672	540	- 6.8	673	583	-13.4
40-49	599	647	- 4.7	654	634	- 5.8
50-59	517	555	- 8.3	540	597	- 9.1
60-69		455	-12.0		532	- 1.5
	KIMBERLEY					
0-9	1,051			957		
10-19	868	761	-17.6	742	626	-34.6
20-29	486	536	-38.3	426	386	-48.0
30-39	539	410	-16.6	489	389	- 8.7
40-49	546	477	-11.5	461	404	-17.4
50-59	433	423	-32.5	271	334	-17.5
60-69		262	-39.5		186	-31.3

[a] The percentage change is that of each ten year cohort of 1971
compared with the same cohorts in 1961.
Data from Australian Bureau of Statistics 1971 Census,
'Characteristics of Population in Local Government Areas
(Queensland)'.

Occupational status of the Goldtown work force, shown in
Table 2.2, is typical of the wider Queensland work force.
In Kimberley there are high proportions of employers, self-
employed and unpaid helpers, and fewer employees. The kind of
family farm associated with self-employment and unpaid help has
been attributed special virtues as 'the classical family of
Western nostalgia' (Goode, 1963: 6). For example:

> In the family farm situation children learn to make independent
> decisions, important to the farm operation; concerted group
> action and cooperation among families in such activities as
> marketing is common; and the independence that Jefferson
> extolled as the bulwark of democracy is compatible with the
> life in family farm areas (Loomis and Beegle, 1957: 149).

Family farms are alleged to lead to a low degree of social stratification, broad development of personality, and, improbably,
higher average intelligence (Smith and Zopf, 1970: 170-196).

More important than these hypothetical advantages are factors which affect students' perceptions of the value of academic qualifications and the utility of school knowledge. Self-employment makes school qualifications irrelevant. Farm children, compared with their urban classmates, were concerned with knowledge rather than qualifications (cf. Collins, 1979). Farm children's access to their father's skills (Smith and Zopf, 1970: 323) also transformed teachers' authority. The students saw the agriculture and animal husbandry courses as vehicles for communicating knowledge between peers rather than for rendering advice by an accredited expert.

Table 2.2   Occupational status of Queensland, Goldtown and Kimberley work forces in 1971

POPULATION		OCCUPATIONAL STATUS			
		Total work force	Employer	Self-employed	employee	Unpaid helper
Queensland	% of pop.	100.0	6.9	8.7	83.7	0.8
	number [a]	3997	333	265	3369	30
Goldtown	% of pop.	100.0	8.2	6.5	83.1	0.7
	number [a]	2803	363	802	1526	112
Kimberley	% of pop.	100.0	13.0	28.6	54.4	4.0

[a] Numbers and percentages in this table refer to only those parts of the work force in employment.
Data from Australian Bureau of Statistics 1971 Census.
'Characteristics of Population in Local Government Areas (Queensland)'

EDUCATIONAL CONTEXT

Cultural parameters of Queensland education
Rigidity, conservatism and authoritarianism are characteristic of Queensland education. In a comparative study:

> Australian teachers in general, and Queensland teachers in particular, emerged as more traditional and authoritarian than their counterparts in the United States, Great Britain and New Zealand. (Adams, 1970: 50)

Queensland student-teachers compared with those in other Australian states are dogmatic, pragmatic and socially, economically and politically illiberal (Anderson and Western, 1970; Anderson, Western and Boreham, 1976).
  Political, social and ethical aspects of the curriculum are monitored by fundamentalist Christian and authoritarian pressure groups with access to the State Premier (Freeland, 1979; Smith, 1978; Smith and Knight, 1978). Following such pressures,

Cabinet has modified the curriculum (Henry and MacLennon, 1978) and quashed reforms by the State Education Department which were designed to reduce cultural absolutism (Smith and Knight, 1978).

Goldtown and Kimberley primary schools
Queensland students commonly spend seven years in primary school. The model of schooling which was presented in Chapter 1 assumes that children of about the same age are given similar tasks in the classroom. These criteria are minimally met in the case of small primary schools, such as many in Goldtown and Kimberley, where students of different ages are grouped in the same classroom.

Most of the Kimberley students came from very small schools. Of the Kimberley students, 82.5 per cent came from schools with less than 75 students. In these schools two to seven age-grades were grouped in each classroom. Even within Goldtown there were two one-teacher schools where all seven age-grades were grouped in one classroom.

Studies of schools without age-grades indicate that performance values are unimportant. Briody (1960: 28-38), Grant (1979: 111), Griffiths (1971) and Martin and Harrison (1972) show that little peer competition exists in primary schools without age-grading. Performance status is replaced by ascribed status of age and associated size and older students have a diffuse responsibility for their younger classmates (cf. Dreeben, 1968; Kohl, 1976: 63; Young and Whitty, 1977). Subversive student behaviour tends to be absent in age-heterogeneous classrooms (Elder, 1967; Griffiths, 1971).

Goldtown High School
High school students resident in Goldtown and Kimberley either attend Goldtown High School, Catholic boys' and girls' schools in Goldtown or boarding schools outside Goldtown and Kimberley. In the year of the study less than one quarter of Goldtown and Kimberley students attended the Catholic schools. These schools had higher student-teacher ratios and less facilities than the state school and were seen as superior only in offering a religious education. The number of students attending boarding schools away from the district is unknown but small. With this exception and that of the Catholic students, all high school students from the Goldtown and Kimberley district attended Goldtown High School.

Grade Eight at Goldtown High School comprised ten classes in the year before the study. Seven classes had academic parity and offered similar courses. Three classes had varied, but lower, academic status. For the following year, Grade Nine, students were redivided according to ability and choice of course.

Grade Nine and consequent Grade Ten course structure comprised three course levels and five course specialisations.

Each course level incorporates different expectations for students' school careers. Level I presumes that students will continue through to Grade Twelve, with the possibility of tertiary education. Level II courses terminate at Grade Ten. Level III courses are for students who have learning difficulties or who pose special discipline problems. The five course specialisations are 'a', the academic at Level I, 'b', the industrial course at Levels I, II and III, 'c', the commercial course at Levels I and II, 'd', the home economics course at Levels I and II and 'e', the agricultural course taken at Levels I and II.

The membership and designation of Goldtown Grade Nine classes departed from the structure just described because recruitment into some courses was too low to form a single class and for others sufficient for as many as four classes. Where recruitment for a course level was low, students in that course level combined for most school subjects with students in another course at the same level. Students were taught their specialist subjects apart, or grouped with students having the same course speciality at another level. Where there were enough students to form several classes in a course level, the school administration varied courses in ways that reflected perceptions of the relative status of school subjects and the corresponding status of the students studying them. Thus, these students were streamed by ability and subjects taken within a course level with a sequence continuing from Level I through to Level III. The resulting composition and designation of Grade Nine classes in the year of the study is given in Table 2.3.

Table 2.3   Composition[a] of Grade Nine classes by level and course

Class	Level		Boys	Girls
9ad1	I	Academic, home economics	13	22
9b1e1	I	Industrial, agricultural	29	
9b2	II	Industrial	37	
9b3e2	II	Industrial, agricultural	29	2
9b4	II	Industrial	33	
9b5	II	Industrial	30	
9b6	III	Industrial	24	
9c1	I	Commercial	2	38
9c2	II	Commercial	1	32
9c3d2	II	Commercial, home economics	2	37
9c4	II	Commercial	2	33

[a] Composition of classes varied through the year as students came and left. Figures are correct for the time I began interviewing each class.

A small minority of students chose course levels incompatible with their previous academic achievement. They as often chose lower as higher course levels. Their presence did not alter the perceived status of their classes.

Student choice of courses was usually guided by perceptions of sex propriety. As a result although there were one or two boys in each commercial class and two girls in one industrial and agricultural class, all classes except the top academic and domestic class, 9ad1, were dominantly of one sex.

The research showed that the fully co-educational class, 9ad1, had distinctive patterns of interaction and that sexual minorities in other classes were not integrated with the members of the other sex. Accordingly, 9ad1 and the sexual minorities have been excluded from the research population. Only the classroom interaction of males and females in classrooms that are dominantly male or female respectively are considered.

Classrooms and pedagogy The school class of the present research has a membership of from twenty-four to forty pupils. Their form rooms had generic features. These are illustrated in Figure 2.1. All held rows of double desks facing the blackboard. Between the front row of desks and the blackboard was a space of from nine to six feet, within which was contained the teacher's desk. There were eight columns of desks, grouped in pairs, across each room. Outside the door of each room was a verandah down which school traffic passed.

There were some variations in classrooms. Lockers occupied the space of the extreme right back row of desks in 9b1e1, 9b4, 9b5, and 9c4. 9b3e2 and 9c2 had four rows of desks. All other classes had five rows.

Patterns of schooling in these classrooms correspond with Parsons' model of schooling and Bernstein's description of 'closed education' (Bernstein, 1973, 1977). The teaching groups are homogeneous by age and ability. The pedagogy stresses solution giving, and the curriculum is streamed and strong-framed and classified. Success is prescribed according to formal criteria limited to the high ability range. Teacher-pupil relations are positional rather than interpersonal.

Classroom actors and physical objects in closed classrooms form patterns easily distinguished from those outside the boundary. A synmorphic relationship exists between the physical layout of the classroom and the behaviour of class members (Adams and Biddle, 1970; Dale, 1972: 51, Farber, 1972; Lundgren, 1972; Sommer and Becker, 1974: 60). Unity of the classroom is not due to simplicity of parts but to inter-action of parts. Events in different parts of the classroom influence each other more than equivalent events beyond its boundary.

Interaction in this kind of classroom in Queensland is like classroom interaction elsewhere. Power (1972) compared Queensland high school teacher-student interaction with a study

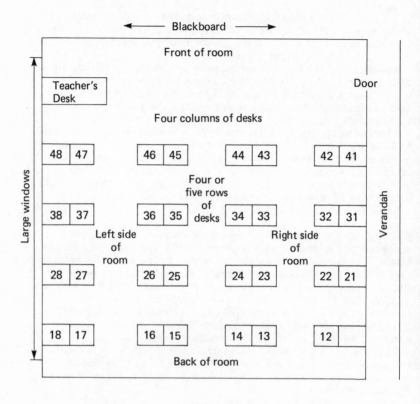

Figure 2.1 Physical features of Goldtown form rooms

(Bellack, 1966) of New York high schools, and found only minor differences consistent with the distinctive values of Queensland teachers. He concluded that:

> In both settings, the teacher dominated the classroom game by making most moves and doing most of the talking. It would appear that teachers are teachers and students are students regardless of nation, grade level or subject. If anything, the rules in Queensland appear to be more rigid than those in New York. Queensland Grade 8 students rarely usurp such teacher roles as structuring, soliciting or reacting; their role is to respond to teacher solicitations. (Power, 1972: 231)

The style of classroom and pedagogy at Goldtown thus conforms to requirements of the Parsonian model and allows generalisation of the findings of the study to a considerable population.

Implications of the choice of a streamed Grade Nine class for analysis

Limited resources forced a choice between researching a cross-section of students in all grades or researching a single grade. The research was confined to a single grade because of the advantages of studying a complete cohort (van Zeyl, 1978: 81) and of preserving the school class as a unit of analysis. Grade Eight was not considered because at that point students are not yet fully integrated into the school (Hargreaves, 1967; Lacey, 1970). All cohorts after Grade Nine are incomplete because some students leave school when they turn fifteen years of age. Grade Nine was therefore chosen for study.

Academic streaming of school classes has been shown to influence classroom culture. It has been commonly argued that the dominant culture of high academic stream classes is pro-academic, and the dominant culture of low academic stream classes is anti-academic (Barker Lunn, 1970; Hargreaves, 1967; Lacey, 1970; Polk and Pink, 1971; Schwartz, 1981; Stinchcombe, 1964; Sugarman, 1973). Grade Nine streamed classes may offer maximum cultural polarisation. Polarisation in streamed schools is most marked in the penultimate year of compulsory schooling, the year before pupils reach the minimum experience of schooling (Hargreaves, 1967; Lacey, 1970).

Other studies emphasise continuities between high and low stream classes. McKennel (1969) found low stream students would have liked academic success and high stream pupils admired the toughness, solidarity and independence they perceived among high informal status low stream boys. Sugarman (1968) shows that high academic attainment and student challenges to teacher authority are resources for leadership in cliques, whether these cliques were mostly distinguished by good or poor school conduct, high or low academic attainment. Indeed, poor conduct was a greater resource for leadership status in groups with high levels of student conformity to teachers than in groups with low levels of conformity to teachers, a finding consistent with an hypothesis that student challenges to teacher authority became important insofar as they were rare resources. Similarly, popularity was more closely related to high academic attainment in groups with low levels of academic attainment.

The research on streamed schools so far discussed describes boys' rather than girls' classes. The few studies of girls' streamed classes show academic streaming does not affect interaction. King (1973: 120) found that a tendency to involvement in school activities among high stream boys compared with low stream boys disappeared among girls. Lambart (1976) found that deviant groups of girls did reasonable amounts of work, while Hargreaves (1967) found similar groups of boys had low academic commitment. Brown (1972), replicating in a girls' school

Hargreaves' study, found lower streams more committed than higher streams to official school values.

Some polarisation existed in Goldtown Grade Nine classes. Statements were elicited from students which associated academic stream with academic commitment. Correspondingly, students who did not conform to the academic stream moral stereotypes were said not to belong properly to that class.

However, Goldtown High School was less polarised into pro- and anti-academic cultures than male streamed schools described elsewhere. One reason may be that diffuse relations between Goldtown students reduced the importance of academic status. Goldtown boys, in contrast to boys in other streamed schools (Barker Lunn, 1970), frequently associated with students from other ends of the academic continuum and often did not know what class the associate was in.

Goldtown students more often attributed individual classes' academic commitment and classroom behaviour to location and quality of the form room than to stream levels. Distance from administration offices explained levels of misbehaviour. Students in the lowest stream boys' class explained their failure to work and teachers' failure to control them by alluding to excessive noise from a woodwork shop next door. 9b6 were sufficiently committed to school that they collectively, but unsuccessfully, asked for another room more conducive to work.

The present research describes continuity across academic streams. This complements a tendency in earlier research to report differences between academic streams.

REFERENCES TO THE STUDENT POPULATION

Each student in the research population has an alphanumeric identification. This discriminates between male and female students and thus aids discussion of socio-sexual differences. The alphanumeric identifies the student's class and so helps in understanding the class as a unit. It also locates the student's desk in the classroom and so identifies his class neighbours and something of the student strategy of seating. The alphanumeric identifies the student's academic stream and thus allows an assessment of continuities and differences across academic streams.

The coding also allows illustration of how analytically distinct aspects of classroom interactions cohere in single students. Where possible the same students have been used to illustrate these distinct types of interaction. These students where mentioned have had an asterisk placed by their alphanumeric identification, and are indexed at the back of the book. This index offers a picture of the variety of experience and concerns of different students in the same classroom.

The first part of each alphanumeric identifies the student's class membership. A student identified as a/n_1n_2 is a member of

the class 9ad1. A student identified as b1 . . . b6/n_1n_2 is a
member of 9b1e1, 9b2, 9b3e2, 9b4, 9b5, or 9b6, respectively.
A student identified as c1 . . . c4/n_1n_2 is a member of 9c1, 9c2,
9c3d2, or 9c4, respectively.

The second part of the alphanumeric identifies the seating
position of students in all classes except 9b6.[1] n_1 gives the row
of the desk measured from the back to the front of the room
(see Figure 2.1). n_2 gives the column of the student's desk
measured from the right to the left of the classroom (see Figure
2.1). In this code, for example, c4/31 is the girl in 9c4 who
sits three rows from the back of the room and three columns
from the extreme right. b3/43 is the boy in 9b3e2 who sits four
rows from the back of the room and three columns from the
extreme right.

A suffix is used with the alphanumeric identifications of some
students. Members of class sexual minorities are indicated by
suffixing 'm' to their alphanumerics.

INTERNAL ASSESSMENT, WORK NORMS AND COMPETITION

The system, used in Queensland, of internal assessment with a
rigid distribution of grades often results in strong competition
in less cohesive classes (Coleman, 1959; Deutsch, 1949; Hughes
et al., 1962) and work norms limiting academic effort in more
cohesive classes (Bidwell, 1973; Blau and Meyer, 1971: 48-80;
Coleman, 1959; Staines, 1963). Both these outcomes are common
in Queensland (Campbell et al., 1976; Fairbairn, McBryde and
Rigby, 1976).

Internal assessment has reportedly led to students working
harder and co-operating less (Pascoe, 1973). Intense academic
competition often becomes unscrupulous (Covington and Beery,
1976: 35). Queensland secondary students often resort to malice,
deception, and sabotage of other students' work, monopolise
library materials and conceal information to increase relative
academic attainment (Campbell et al., 1976). However, Goldtown
students seem exceptional. They reported little unscrupulous
behaviour. Goldtown teachers and the school librarian reported
no such behaviour.

Metropolitan students, interviewed for the pilot study, were
strongly aware of work norms and related them directly to
internal assessment. These students monitored the amount of
work done by classmates. Those who worked too hard were
rejected on sociometric work criteria for this reason alone.
Metropolitan students also spoke of a type of student, the 'conch',
who worked assiduously to obtain high marks.

Goldtown students, by contrast, had no single term to impute
a reified status to students who worked consistently and con-

---

[1] 9b6 students had been reallocated seats just prior to interviewing. They are therefore identified by a nominal code.

scientiously. Students did extra work in free time, without being
isolated or distinguished as a group within their class. The
common response to this work was incredulity rather than
intolerance. For example:

> c3/34   c3/14* just stays in the room all the time doing her
> homework. . . . I just don't understand that. I
> couldn't stand being cooped up like that.

When, as a result of these efforts long projects were rewarded
with higher marks, the hardworking students were not met with
jealousy or anger. Instead, as in the following examples, they
were admired and their possession of higher marks or their
demonstration of academic achievement legitimated:

> I c3/45   c3/14* would do a fairly long project because she
> wants to get higher marks. . . . I think if she has
> got the energy to do a great big long project and she
> wants to get good marks then she should put more
> effort into it and get good marks.

> II Q   Do people ever remark on other people handing in
> longer assignments?
> b4/27   With b4/31* no one says very much because they
> can expect a thump on the head or something like
> that but they really don't say much to anyone who
> hands in extra length work. If it is a really good
> story or something like that they will say how good
> they thought it was.

Work norms were not totally absent. There were examples,
as below, of their activation against low status classmates:

> Q   Would people stir c3/51* if she brings in a long project?
> c3/32   Yeah. Cos she once brought in three foolscap pages
> when we only had to do one foolscap, 'What are you
> trying to do, c3/51*? Trying to get more marks?'

Students also objected to classmates who did extra work when
levels of academic attainment were unusually important:

> Q   Any pressure against people who do longer projects?
> c1/44   I don't think so.
> c1/43   One of them for German went to extremes and the
> girls didn't like it much. It was c1/17*. She did pages
> and pages of writing – there was a prize for it.

These, however, were rare exceptions.

CONCLUSIONS

The Goldtown High School host community has a declining
rural and static urban economy. Many young people leave the
district to find employment, immigrants are few, and local
culture is relatively uniform. Diffuse, particularistic roles of
family farms and small primary schools create values antithetic
to those inculcated by schooling as described in Chapter I.
Thus, distinctive student subcultures may be weaker in
Goldtown than in urban centres with large primary schools.

Features of Goldtown pedagogy correspond with Parsons'
model of schooling. The style of classroom conforms with a
pattern common in many countries. Research shows that patterns
of teacher-student interaction resemble those found elsewhere,
although Queensland teachers tend more to dominate the formal
aspects of the lesson.

Grade Nine, the grade studied, is streamed by vocational
interest and ability into largely sex-segregated classes. The
definitive streaming of students occurs at the beginning of
Grade Nine. Thus students' culture may not express a group
reaction to streamed status.

Goldtown students do not have the strong work norms or
academic competitive behaviour found in other Queensland high
schools. This may be a consequence of the intrusion of community
values.

Chapter 3

Students' control systems

Questions of control were central to Goldtown students' classroom interaction. In this chapter a model of control is applied to a description of how dominant students establish their control or potential control over classmates. Later chapters show how dominant students legitimate and extend their control by determining the selection and activation of the symbolic resources originating in schooling, peer interaction, and intrusive values.

The chapter begins with a consideration of inducement and deterrence as controls. These controls and their use among boys, where they predominate and are legitimated, are discussed concurrently. The chapter continues with a discussion of influence and activation of commitments as controls and their use among girls, where they predominate and are legitimated.

MODEL OF CONTROLS

By cross-tabulating negative and positive sanctions with situational and intentional channels of control, Parsons developed a fourfold model of control, illustrated in Figure 3.1. For each control is specified the mode of control, the symbolic medium and the base to which the symbolic medium is, in principle, convertible (Parsons, 1967: 264-382; Parsons and Smelser, 1956). It can be seen from Table 3.1 that each control is linked with the variables used in Chapter 1 to construct models of schooling, the peer group and socio-sexual roles (Parsons, 1967, 1969; Parsons and Smelser, 1956). Thus, the centrality of inducement as a control indicates the importance of universalistic, specific and performance values; the centrality of deterrence as a control indicates the importance of particularistic, performance and specific values; the centrality of influence as a control indicates the importance of particularistic, diffuse and qualitative values; and the centrality of the activation of commitments as a control indicates the importance of universalistic, diffuse, and qualitative values.

It was seen in Chapter 1 that Parsons associates male roles with specific performance and universalistic values. Female roles are associated with diffuse, qualitative, and particularistic values. The experience of schooling is associated with acquisition of specific performance and universalistic values. The model of socio-sexual roles suggests that male interaction is marked by the use of inducement, and female interaction by the use of persuasion.

Table 3.1 Model of controls

CONTROL	inducement	deterrence
CHANNEL	situational	situational
SANCTION	positive	negative
MEDIUM	money	power
CONVERTIBLE TO	utility	force
ORIENTATIONS	universalism	particularism
	specificity	specificity
	performance	performance

CONTROL	activation of commitments	persuasion
CHANNEL	intentional	intentional
SANCTION	negative	positive
MEDIUM	generalisation of commitments	influence
CONVERTIBLE TO	integrity	veridity
ORIENTATIONS	universalism	particularism
	diffuseness	diffuseness
	quality	quality

(Adapted from Parsons, 1967: 364)

The model of schooling, however, suggests that classroom interaction will be marked by inducement as the prevalent control. These formulations are tested and modified in the examination of peer classroom controls below.

The discussion below modifies Parsons' discussion of symbolic media. Luke (1974) misunderstood Parsons' use of the concept of 'power'. He has extended Parsons' concept beyond one kind of control to include all controls. None the less, his criticism that Parsons' concept of 'power' fails to take account of conflicts of interest and relations of control between individuals is justified and accepted here. These and other modifications of Parsons' models are not discussed at length in this book.

Inducement
Inducement occurs when a person is inclined to change behaviour by offer of a positive change in his or her situation, contingent on compliance. The archetype of inducement is economic exchange. Money serves as a reward convertible to what the person to be controlled perceives as utility (Parsons and Smelser, 1956).

The present research found inducement unimportant in student interaction. Teachers induced classroom behaviour by the award of marks roughly commensurate with academic attainment. Marks, unlike money among adults, are not transferable between students. In place of marks as a medium of exchange, the intrusive medium, money, unrelated to classroom performance, is

used. However, opportunities for the use of money in the classroom are rare.

Occasionally students bought homework from classmates. When
they did, the students receiving money gained status through
recognition of academic status.

More often money induced low status students to ritually
degrade themselves. For example, token payments induced
students to engage in the degraded behaviour of a 'scunge'
or 'Jew':

b2/28*   b2/46 and b2/23 are always after bottles.
Q   What word do you use for someone who goes after
         bottles?
b2/51   'Jew'. You have probably seen them out there.
         (Other people) throw one cent pieces out to them and
         they run after them.
         Very stupid looking!
b2/28*   Everyone looks out and calls 'Jew, Jew'.

Similarly in the classroom token payments induced low status or
deviant acts which confirmed the low status of those, such as
b3/24*, who performed them:

b3/24*   Most of my stirring comes from him. I just take up
         bets. I suppose it is silly really.
Q   What sort of bets do you collect?
b3/24*   'I bet you can't stir that teacher', 'I bet you can't
         stir this period', something like that.
Q   Does he pay up?
b3/23   Yes, I do. It's not that I get him to do my dirty work
         because if he didn't do it I wouldn't do it I can assure
         you of that. And so you might think that by me saying
         he can't stir for five minutes . . . that I am trying
         to get him to do my dirty work but him doing it for
         me saying that, 'I bet you can't do it' proves him a
         nut. Fair dinkum it proves him a nut because if some-
         one said to me, 'You can't stir so-and-so', I'd say
         'I bet you can't either'. I probably could but I would
         never indulge. I'm not the same nature as b3/24*.

These uses of inducements were rare and confined to male
students. Although the degradation ritual celebrated relative
student status, the use of token rather than real payments
suggests that it has small independent significance. Chapter 9
shows that status accrued to students who practise largesse
with money earned in outside jobs. However, largesse without
consideration of specific advantage does not constitute inducement. Overall, inducement was not important.

Deterrence

Deterrence occurs when a threat of a negative change in a parson's situation prevents that person doing something he or she would have otherwise done. Power exists when subordinates believe that failure to comply with a dominant person's wishes will lead to the dominant person exercising effective negative situational sanctions. When power works smoothly as a control, the negative situational sanctions on which it ultimately depends are:

> not highly visible because compliance is the rule rather than the exception. Negative sanctions therefore often remain, not only unimplemented, but also only implicitly threatened. (Parsons, 1967: 281)

This invisibility of effective power presents problems to students in establishing power and to researchers in discovering its use. Students wishing to exercise power need to establish a normative order to be obeyed and must convince subordinates that contraventions of this order will be punished.

Power-in-being is characterised by subordinate students' belief that power will be used on nonconforming students. So long as this belief is maintained, the powerful student, like b2/21* in the example below, need not punish subordinate classmates to obtain obedience:

> b3/46* b2/21* always forced me to dob. He knows a bit of judo and that and he told me if I didn't dob on everybody that he would punch me down.

Typical of the creation of power is a fight after an offence and then a decision in terms of the power thus established that the offence will either continue or discontinue:

> b3/26* The kids started calling me poofter and I've been called poofter since I came to the school. I finally got round to stopping it. I threatened to fight one kid and the rest stopped.

Where power is uncontested, physical sanctions are exercised only when instructions are not obeyed. If instructions are obeyed then, as in the following example, no physical sanction is used:

> b5/57* b5/42* bosses everyone around. He acts as if he is just it. Everything has got to be done his way. Say you are down in woodwork and you are halfway through a sawcut and he tells you that [the teacher] tells you to pack up and b5/42* goes around and thumps everyone that doesn't. Say you are halfway through a sawcut you can't start it the next period to do it. You

try to finish it off that period and b5/42* goes around
and he smashes you if you don't pack up straight away.

Boys' use of controls
The most important male control was deterrence. The two
principal sets of negative situational sanctions were physical
punishment by classmates and classmates' invocation of teachers'
punishment. The former is by far the more important. The
latter is shown in Chapter 7 to be ineffective against power
based on physical force. Its use against physical power does not
make the 'dobber' or student who invoked teacher aid powerful
but is taken as tacit admission of lower power.

Boys merged perceptions of control and use of physical
sanctions. Questions in interviews about 'toughness' and
control elicited similar responses. Students' descriptions of an
aspirant to high control status, b2/22*, illustrate this identification of physical dominance and control:

b2/35*   b2/22* reckons he's topdog.
Q   How does this show?
b2/35*   He picks on b2/38 and people like that, tells people
         to shut up, might try to take a swing at you, stuff
         like that.

Power tends to be exercised over actors less able to use physical
sanctions and only rarely over actors more able to use physical
sanctions. b2/22*'s control, for instance, was largely limited to
physically weaker students:

b2/32   b2/22* goes around bossing everyone. If they don't
         co-operate he'll thump them.
Q   Would he thump you, for instance?
b2/32   If he did I would hit him back. He tries to act too
         tough.
Q   Anyone else who would stand up to b2/22*?
b2/32   b2/44 would, but if b2/44 started shaping up to
         b2/22*, b2/22* would just walk off. b2/22* can dish
         it out but he can't take it. I think I can stand up to
         him pretty well. If he hit me I'd hit him back.
Q   Who does what b2/22* tells them to?
b2/32   b2/38 and all those people who are pretty small,
         those who get scared, people like b2/41 and b2/36.
         I suppose b2/22* might tell b2/46 and b2/36 to do
         something and b2/36 would say, 'no', but b2/22* would
         say, 'Do it!' and I suppose they would do it then.

In so far as power is a symbolic medium, failure to ground
attempts at control in force speedily reversed perceptions of
relative power:

b2/33   b2/22*'s one of those sorts who like to show you up,

	pick on you, things like that.
Q	How would he pick on you?
b2/33	Makes some smart comments and I'd say, 'That was sick', and he came over and whack! Last time he did that I smashed him in the face.
Q	What did b2/22* do then?
b2/33	Went back to his seat, red in the face. I don't think b2/22* is as tough as he's cracked up to be.
b2/35*	Nor do I.
b2/33	He just puts it on.

Ability to fight is not the same as power Two conditions for translating fighting ability into power were that the student exercise his fighting ability and that the fighting ability be used discriminately as a sanction system. Students with great fighting ability who failed to do these things were powerless.

b2/35* is an example of a boy with fighting ability but no power. He was known by classmates to be proficient in martial arts. He was nonetheless the butt of constant jokes. All classmates attributed him with low power:

b2/34	b2/35* gets pushed around for no reason. He's a bit of a weak bloke and people just take advantage and push him around.

He, believing that power was largely meaningless, refused to react when provoked:

b2/35*	b2/22* calls me names, 'Poofy Pete', and things like that, just to stir me up. And he thinks he is big and tough because he tries to pick fights on you.
Q	What do you do then?
b2/35*	Walk away most of the time. I don't think you can prove anything by flattening anybody.

b2/35* status, however, rose, when he gave a lecture on the subject of judo. This ended in an impromptu demonstration of his skills in which he indeed 'flattened' two of his tormentors:

b2/41	[b2/22* and friends] were shouting at him while he was doing his lecturette. They reckoned people who do judo are just queers and that. And then afterwards b2/31 and b2/22* were walking round the back of b2/35* and they tried to get hold of b2/35* and he dropped them.

This single demonstration translated fighting ability into a short-lived consensus which attributed power to b2/35*. Classmates made comments such as:

b2/17	b2/22* had better watch out or b2/35* will 'origami' him.

b3/34, too, was exceptionally strong. He had proved his fighting ability by winning a silver medal in a national wrestling competition and gold medals in state competion. Unlike b2/35*, he used and advertised his fighting skills. His wrestling and participation in physically demanding activities such as calf riding in rodeos were widely known to classmates. For example:

b3/47   b3/34 is pretty strong. He is a good wrestler.
b3/48   He is a champion wrestler. He has got gold medals.
b3/47   He would probably beat everybody in our class. I went up to see if I could beat him and he just threw me flat in five seconds with a hold on me.

He, however, did not use fighting ability to establish a normative order or to enforce his wishes on classmates. Thus he had no power. His classmates, uncomfortable in such boisterous company, shunned him:

Q   Why didn't you want to be interviewed with b3/34?
b3/45*   Grabs him round the neck all the time.
b3/46*   Yes, that is one reason.
b3/45*   He is a wrestler and every time he goes up to b3/46* he grabs him like this and chokes him and chokes him and chucks him round the room.

Because he did not enforce his definitions of the situation, and because he abstained from certain activities which signified 'toughness', b3/34 despite his strength was seen by some class-mates as:

b3/33   A fairy bloke, don't get into trouble, a little goody goody all the time.

How is power made visible? It was shown earlier in the chapter that visible aspects of the construction of power, such as fighting and negative situational sanctions, were used when power was not working as a control. Besides recollections of fighting and of the use of negative situational sanctions, students referred to four indices of effective power. These were demands by powerful students for respect and privilege, the relative size of students, constant physical abuse of less powerful students, and a competitive 'mucking around' which celebrated toughness in delivery and tolerance of physical punishment. The first three indices of power are considered in this chapter. Competitive mucking around has an independent interest as a performance dimension and is discussed in Chapter 4.

Sporting and athletic prowess were conspicuous by their absence from students' discussions of classmates' power. They are discussed in Chapters 5 and 10. Chapter 5 briefly describes the account students take of classmates' sporting and athletics prowess and participation. Chapter 10 discusses the extent to which students accept teachers' acknowledgement of classmates' athletic or sporting prowess. The findings reported in those chapters show that the classroom significance of athletics and sporting prowess depends on control relations established within the classroom.

Privilege and respect Powerful students demanded respect and privilege. Such privilege in both demand and possession signalled domination. For example, b2/22* claimed exclusive use of the most comfortable chair in his class:

> b2/47 There's a nice vinyl chair in the room and b2/22* thinks it's his so if anybody else sits in it he goes up and says for them to give the chair. They let him take it because they're a bit scared of him.

Another powerful student regularly insulted teachers. He resented and punished students who similarly insulted him:

> b5/31* Like I have told the teacher, 'Drop dead' and b5/55* says, 'I wish you would b5/31*' - the little dickhead - or something like this. Anything you do or say, he will call you names or something. It gets on your nerves.

Thumping and pushing around Powerful boys frequently thumped and pushed around less powerful classmates. These actions were neither ill-tempered nor intended to enforce a wish to norm. They were for 'fun':

> b2/43 b2/22* goes around telling people to piss off or, 'Do you want a smack in the head?', or if you do something he can't take it and he'll belt you over the head. In fun it is. It's just the way they go on.

Powerless students could not reciprocate and disliked 'the fun'. It became a species of ritual degradation (Garfinkel, 1956). In the following extract two such powerless students detail what 'pushing around' meant for them:

> b4/45 b4/31* and b4/32 reckon that they can push us around. . . .
> Q When you say 'push around' what do they do?
> b4/46* Sometimes when you're walking he will stick his foot out and you trip over it. I don't like it much when . . . I walk down by where . . . b4/31* and his mates are standing. . . . I am a little bit scared of getting between them because one of them is going to stick their foot out or they will hit me or something like that.
> b4/45 . . . They will just trip you for fun.

Powerless students who did not resist pushing around were seen by classmates as physical cowards and labelled 'sooks' or 'sissies'.

Relative size Size and power were largely coterminous in students' speech. Small size, without reference to power or fighting ability, explained inability to control events and definitions of situations. For example:

> I b5/55* Someone tries to make you look silly and that and when you are small you can't really get up and go back at them and make them look silly.

> II b5/41* b5/55* gets put in the rubbish bin all the time he is that small.

Large size similarly became synonymous with power:

> b5/32*   b5/25 sometimes thinks he's a bit bigger than all the others and he thumps into you a bit. . . .
> Q   Don't you thump him back?
> b5/32*   No, I'm not game to.

Influence
Influence rests on communications assumed to be verifiable, just as money is assumed by the person controlled thereby to be convertible to utility, and power by the person controlled thereby to force. A person makes comments which if believed change another's behaviour. Despite the principle of verifiability, belief follows not from potential verification but from the ability of the person uttering the statement to establish himself as an authority:

> The user of influence is under pressure to justify his statements which are intended to have an effect on alter's action. . . . The function of justification is not actually to verify the the items but to provide the basis for the communicator's *right* to state them without alter's needing to verify them. (Parsons, 1967: 369)

Control by influence operates according to the credibility of the speaker. The definition of credibility and of control by influence used here relates to the extent to which an individual's assertions are accepted publicly by his audience. Control by influence, like control by power, was often imposed on individuals who privately dissented. In such cases, students are defined as influential when, like c1/16* in the following quotation, they are reported controlling the overt definitions and outcomes of situations:

> c1/51*   We had a beauty contest and c1/16* was the one that

was going to win and she had to be the one that was
going to win and sure that she was going to do
beauty and things like this.

Q   How did she get the part [in the play]?
c1/51*   She just said that I am going to be the person who
wins and that was that. So we got no choice. I
reckon that we should have had a vote on it.

Three criteria were used in the research to define students'
lack of influence. Lack of influence is shown when, as with
c1/51* in the example above, a student's definition of a situation
is ignored. Lack of influence is also shown by classmates verify-
ing by reference to logical arguments or other sources of
information any statements made by the uninfluential classmate.
For instance, in the following interview extract, c3/42 is shown
to have low influence because the information she gave was
subject to verification:

c3/45   c3/42 reckons
c3/32*   that c3/23* was a lesbian or something.
c3/45   that c3/23* wanted to go with c3/42. c3/42 told everyone that c3/23* was a lesbian and she is not. She
couldn't be. She is too dumb.

Whether or not the information proved correct is irrelevant to
the fact that classmates felt it necessary to verify the assertion
and thus doubted the credibility of the informant.
Extremely uninfluential students consciously depend for their
knowledge on the assertions of influential classmates. In the
example below, such a student faced with conflicting assertions
from two influential classmates and lacking confidence in her own
judgement, claims to have no knowledge:

c2/32*   c2/41* reckons that I am fat and other people reckon
that I am not. I don't know who to believe.

Activation of commitments
Activation of commitments differs from persuasion in appealing
to the integrity of the person to be controlled. Where influence
depends on trust, the co-ordination standard of commitments is
pattern consistency, and where influence deals with questions
of empirical reality or value interpretations of that reality,
activation of commitments deals with the response of the individual to that reality. Sanctions attached to non-implementation
of values or commitments are negative and consist for the
individual in guilt or shame (Parsons, 1964: 448).
The extent to which individuals feel shame or guilt depends
on the degree to which they have the values and commitments to
which the person activating commitments is referring. The
activator does not have to have these values and commitments.
It was therefore possible, and indeed not uncommon, for

dominant students to tease low status students by activating unpopular commitments held by low status students. The following extracts show how a dominant girl, c1/52*, controls a subordinate girl, c1/53*, by a combination of persuasion and activation of commitments. She first imposes a definition on an otherwise neutral activity. She then activates c1/53*'s commitment against that activity as defined:

> c1/44   c1/53* doesn't swear or anything and she said something like, 'Oh pig!' and c1/52* was over her all the time and c1/53* is getting very frustrated and saying, 'I don't swear' and c1/52* is saying, 'Don't you, c1/53*?'

c1/52* herself swore. She accepted neither c1/53*'s commitment against swearing nor the definition that she imposed on c1/53* of 'oh pig!' as swearing:

> c1/52*   c1/53* goes 'oh pig!' . . . We act as if we thought it was a swear word and she gets real mad.

c1/53* took the whole matter seriously. She accepted the imposed definition that she was swearing. She had the commitment against swearing activated by c1/52*. She was thus controlled by c1/52*:

> c1/53*   It is really on religious matters that c1/52* stirs me on. I am a Christian, you see. And she always goes off about this. I swear most of the time but I cannot help it.

Girls' use of controls
The important female controls were influence and activation of commitments. This section illustrates the importance of these controls by examining girls' vocabulary of control and showing that indices of power are irrelevant in girls' classroom interaction. It then describes the use of influence and activation of commitments under conditions of consensus and conflict.

The term 'fight' among girls referred to verbal rather than physical fights. For example:

> Q   When you talk about having a fight what do you mean?
>
> c2/32*   We will say things to each other but we don't hit each other or anything.

The occasional physical fights usually lacked significance. Girls derogated classmates' attempts to convert physical fighting ability into power. For example:

> c1/46   c1/23* goes real stupid sometimes. Like you will tell her not to be a twit or something like that and then

she will thump you or something like that.

c1/23* with low influence could not convert her physical fighting ability into power as did boys with a similar ability. A few influential girls, such as c4/56*, who boasted of their physical fighting ability refrained from its use in a way confined to the most resolute male pacifists:

c4/56*   c4/21 makes me sick. I would like to thump her head in. I just get like that.
Q   Why don't you do that?
c4/56*   I know I can fight better. I know that I can beat most of the girls in our class. I was always taught how to fight. Like my brother, he was a bikey in Sydney, he always taught me to fight so I reckon that I could beat most of the girls. True, I think I could – but what's the use?

The indices of power used by boys had altered or reduced significance among girls. 'Picking on' referred not to physical bullying but to efforts by influential girls to make subordinates feel inadequate by drawing attention to alleged failings. Interaction between an influential student, c1/16*, and her subordinate classmates illustrates the female use of 'picking on'. The extract also shows that inability to withstand verbal abuse marked the subordinate girl a 'baby', in the same way as inability to withstand physical abuse marked boys 'sooks' and 'sissies':

c1/52*   If c1/16* feels like picking on anybody she will go up and pick on them if it suits her. If you have got a funny last name she will try and make something out of it – like she will change it to 'horseshit' or something like that and she will tease you like that – or what else? – if you have got a big nose or something like that she will call you things like that.
c1/21   And c1/23* – she is not from a very wealthy family and she doesn't comb her hair very often and she is not very well dressed and all that – c1/16* really rubs it in. She says, 'There's a nit' or something like this, 'You had better not touch her.' She is horrible. She says, 'Do you ever have a bath, c1/23*?' and she is going on like this. Sometimes c1/23* gets really furious and starts calling her names and then c1/16* starts to tease her about getting mad and that and, 'Ooh, I am really scared' and . . . c1/23* starts crying and c1/16* says, 'Now she is crying, the little baby.'

Under conditions of conflict, classmates perceived the construction of influence between dominant and subordinate students in terms of ability to impose labels. Subordinate students could not resist this imposition:

Q   When c1/16* stirs c1/23* what do you think of that?
c1/17* I reckon she is pretty mean because c1/23* mightn't
        be real clever but c1/16* seems to think that she is
        a lot better than her. And c1/23* doesn't have the
        power to just argue against that and call her things.

Influential students who were concerned to impose a consensus
displayed a great virtuosity in running down subordinate classmates and rivals. Even dominant girls, such as c3/14* below,
commented on the discomfort evoked by rivals:

c3/14* c3/11* says to me, 'Look at her legs rubbing
        together at the top' and picks you to bits and that.
        It really gets under your skin.

Often in interviews girls delighted in running down even
immediate associates:

c3/33* c3/23* 'stick chick'. She is all right but if you called
        her that she would kill you.
c3/32* She is real skinny.
c3/33* And she hasn't got any figure. If she turns on her
        side she disappears. If you turned her on her side
        and poked out her tongue she would look like a zip.

Girls recalled admiringly, as in the following example, the
competent and amusing signification of deficiencies:

c4/24   Sometimes in sewing c4/23* gets teased.
c4/36   By c4/47* and c4/48*.
c4/24   She brought this pattern in.
c4/36   The pattern was nice but it was the material.
c4/24   The material had flowers like this. Ugh! It was awful.
c4/36   c4/48* said, 'Ugh, I wouldn't wear anything like
        that' and then after awhile she goes over, 'c4/23*,
        I must have some of that material, I really must'
        [Giggles from c4/24 and c4/36].

Consensual use of influence and activation of commitments was
rarer than the conflictual use. In three of the four girls' classes,
however, small groups of highly respected and liked girls had
control which rested on a use of influence to assert and not to
derogate the worth of classmates. c1/14* and c1/13* were such
respected and liked girls:

Q   How do you get on with c1/14*?
c1/21   I reckon that she is nice.
c1/22   Ah yes. She is nice. c1/14* and c1/13* they make a
        good pair.

	They are real nice.
Q	In what way are they real nice?
c1/21	They don't fight. They don't swear or anything.
c1/22	They don't go around calling people names and things like that.
c1/21	And they make up good jokes. Whenever you see them you are naturally in a good mood when you are talking to them.

c1/14*, typically, was careful to assert the value of the interests of her generally disliked and teased classmates, c1/23* and c1/53*:

Q	Do you find yourself taking to c1/53*?
c1/14*	I like horses, just like them, don't go overboard for horses, but c1/53* does. Everything she talks about is horses. I just create an interest and talk to her about that. Like I talk to c1/23* about her pigs and that and I talk to c1/22 about the motor bikes and then they thaw out and they can talk to you.

CASE STUDIES OF DOMINANT STUDENTS

Two exceptionally dominant students, one male and one female, are used as case studies in later chapters to show how control is exercised and legitimated. These students are introduced in the remainder of the present chapter.

No theoretical advantage is claimed for choosing dominant students to illustrate the operation of controls. Aspirants to domination equally show the operation of controls in the success and failure of attempts to control others. Subordinate students illustrate the use of controls in the manner and area of their subordination. A methodological advantage is that dominant students are well known by classmates and teachers.

c2/18* - an influential girl

c2/18* is used as the exemplum of female controls because she, more than other dominant girls, displays both consensual and conflictual control. She also goes beyond most dominant girls in the range of classroom activities with which she was concerned.

Classmates consistently named c2/18* as leader. Her control was based on capable use of influence and activation of commitments. A perceptive teacher commented:

'The kids in that class are at the stage where they don't dare to go against her because she has a sharp tongue. It's a game in that little gang that they rubbish the rest of the kids. The rest of the kids are so colourless compared to c2/18* and they are shy and they would just be scared that she would rubbish them because of it.'

Classmates adopted her imposed definitions, so that imposition became, so far as the majority were concerned, consensual:

> c2/36   Everybody kind of follows c2/18*. She starts picking on somebody and they pick on her as well.

She supplemented the use of influence with physical force. There were reports like:

> c2/22   c2/18* went pushing c2/41* down the steps and acting tough.

Even these physical fights were conducted in ways that classmates considered correct:

> c2/16*   c2/18* might hit c2/41* but not hard or anything. We don't have any scratch fights.

Despite abusing classmates and initiating physical fights, c2/18* was not seen by classmates as pushing too hard for control. Her leadership was legitimated and her use of sanctions justified by particularistic values. For example, I asked if c2/18* was ever too pushy in her exercise of control and was told:

> c2/35   No. . . . She is just a good friend. She's nice to practically everyone. I reckon if she does fight with anyone she has a good reason.

b5/42 - A powerful boy*
b5/42* exemplifies control among boys. He represents a concentration of power found in four of the six male classes. He resembled other dominant males in the scope of control exercised and the coercive base of the control. He differed from one or more of the other dominant male students in sometimes failing to legitimate the order imposed on classmates.

b5/42* was physically stronger than classmates. Thus, fights, which presume some parity of strength, were rare. When they occurred, he summarily dismissed the opposition. For example:

> b5/57*   b5/32* tried to boss b5/42* around this morning and b5/42* stood him up.
> b5/58   Yeah.
> b5/57*   Down in metalwork b5/32* started throwing stuff at b5/42* and b5/42* turned around and got him by the scruff of the neck. He picked him up and looked him in the face. That was it just about.

More common than fighting was 'thumping'. This was sometimes legitimated by smaller students, such as b5/55*:

b5/55*   If you do something wrong like giving cheek [to b5/42* and his friends] they will hit you.

These physical rebukes were good natured but substantial:

b5/13   b5/42* thumps into you if you say something wrong.

Thumps hurt enough that their memory prevented repetition of any offence:

b5/54   b5/42* half killed me one day when I called him 'Artie'.
Q   You wouldn't call him 'Arthur' too often?
b5/54   Once he thumps you is enough. You know what to expect.

b5/42* physically and verbally abused other students copiously and effectively. He overwhelmed any return abuse by employing his power:

b5/26*   b5/42* will say jokes but if you say something back to him then he will just thump you and he will say, 'Oh, stuff it!'
b5/25   He will make fun of you and think that his are real funny jokes but if you say something –
b5/26*   'Ah, that is a heap of bullshit!'
b5/25   He reckons that it is real junk.

When smaller students rebelled against these imposed definitions, b5/42* meted out solid punishment:

b5/32*   b5/47* mostly gets a bit stirred up when we call him 'Grub'. b5/42* started that. b5/47* gets so stirred up that he hit b5/42* one day.
Q   b5/47* is a small fellow, isn't he?
b5/32*   Yeah.
Q   What happened? Did b5/42* hit him back?
b5/32*   Yeah. He always hits them back. He never thinks whether he is wrong.

b5/42* evaluated classmates by their ability to exercise power. Each evaluation was to his advantage. Rivals' exercise of power and subordinate students' failure to resist greater power were each normatively condemned. Smaller students were thought unmanly if they did not stand still and accept physical punishment from him. b5/47*, for example, was blamed for using physical controls on smaller students in the same way as b5/42* did and was condemned for returning verbal abuse in kind rather than using physical retribution:

b5/42*   If you call b5/47* 'Grub' and you are real small he

> will come up and lash out at you but I'm pretty big
> and if I call him these names he will just say, 'You
> bloody dickhead, you.' He doesn't like picking on a
> person that is bigger than him. He likes picking on
> someone that is smaller.

However, when b5/47* reacted physically in the only practical
manner he was also condemned:

b5/42*   Christ! b5/47*'s a dickhead cos I just don't like him
cos he will come up to you and hit you and then he
will run away so you can't lash out at him.

Those students who responded neither physically nor verbally
received special condemnation:

b5/42*   If you go and hit him he will go, 'Don't do that'
like a girl.

CONCLUSIONS

In this chapter a model of control in students' classroom interaction which complements a normative model of that interaction
has been advanced and applied. Normative elements were shown
to be important at two levels in the mode of control. Socio-
sexual values determine the mechanisms of control used legitimately and effectively by members of each sex. The use of
controls takes account of the symbolic resources available in the
classroom.
   The model of sexual roles combined with the model of mechanisms of control suggests that male student interaction is distinguished by the use of inducement, and female student interaction
by the use of persuasion. Lack of the necessary symbolic media
ensured that inducement was not important in male student interaction. Power, instead, became central. Among girls, persuasion
and activation of commitments were important.
   The following chapters show how dominant students, using
symbolic resources afforded by the classroom and by intrusive
roles, determine the realisation of salient values. They show
that dominant students by exploiting ambiguities in the objec-
tivation of reality (Hargreaves et al., 1975: 63-193) appropriate
norms to control classmates (Turner, 1975). The chapters demonstrate that norms and values stated absolutely by students are
selectively activated and interpreted by dominant students.
They show that students' explanations of classmates' high or
low status by reference to conformity to overt normative and
value systems are, in part at least, constructions of reality by
dominant students which justify pre-existent differentiated
control statuses.

Chapter 4

Mucking around

This chapter and Chapter 6 examine two sets of classroom activities which teachers see as misbehaviour. These are 'mucking around' and 'stirring'. 'Mucking around', largely discussed in the present chapter, includes most activities which define student sociability and prevent devotion to work. It excludes 'stirring', the systematic annoyance of teachers, which is discussed in Chapter 6.

This chapter begins by outlining the distinction between 'mucking around' and 'stirring' and examines in detail the concept of 'mucking around'. Then, boys' competitive mucking around is shown to be a performance dimension which celebrates and refines the construction of power. Next, the throwing, flicking or blowing of objects across the room, and the passing of classroom notes are shown to be two types of mucking around which unite the spatially dispersed classroom collectivities. Finally, the significance of the identification of UFOs with boys and the passing of notes with girls is explored.

Some types and conditions of classroom mucking around are discussed in other chapters. Chapter 3 showed that one type, physical pushing around and picking on, is an index of boys' power. Chapter 6 looks at 'clowns' who have a specialised role based on mucking around. Chapter 9 shows that students excluded extremely low academic status students from the sociability defined by mucking around. Chapter 11 looks at the spatial distribution of classroom mucking around.

STUDENTS' CONCEPTS OF 'MUCKING AROUND' AND 'STIRRING'

Students, when asked to distinguish between 'stirring' and 'mucking around', gave responses like the following:

I c1/24   'Stirring' is when you deliberately try to get the teacher mad and 'mucking around' is just acting stupid in class - that would probably get the teacher mad too.

II c2/16* 'Stirring' - you know when you are stirring the teachers. 'Mucking around' - you might just be mucking around, writing a letter to someone. It's not as bad, I think.

III b2/56*   'Stirring' is when you are trying to get the teacher
to hit you more or less, get the teacher mad. Like
the day b2/21* and me put the tack on Mr Riemann's
desk, that was stirring. But you could say 'mucking
around' was like putting a tack on somebody else's
chair.

IV Q   Is there a difference between 'stirring' and 'mucking
around'?

b3/24*   Yes, there is. There's a great difference. Mucking
around is mucking around, two people just mucking
around and not including anyone else but when you
stir up you stir up people and the teacher.

b3/23   When I said b3/24* doesn't know when to stop, it's
stirring the teacher, but b3/24* and I, we draw on
each other's books and everything. We are always
doing that.

Analysis of these and other responses shows three differences
between 'stirring' and 'mucking around'. 'Stirring' does not
directly involve interaction between students, and is intended
to enrage the teacher and entertain the whole class. 'Mucking
around' is between two or three students, is not directed to the
class as audience, and is not intended to enrage the teacher.

Students used the term 'muck around' to denote classroom
activities, other than stirring or girls' expressions of mature
sexual interests, which preclude academic work. The concepts
of 'work' and 'muck around' were often used antithetically. For
example, students who wanted to work rejected as workmates
students who mucked around:

b2/35*   b2/31 and b2/21* would muck around too much.
You wouldn't get anything done.

Mucking around became a form of sociability which obviated
boredom with classwork, and prevented classroom isolation.
Students were reported to enjoy mucking around for its own
sake:

b4/26   b4/17* likes school pretty good. He likes school if
he can muck around a bit. He likes to stir and
muck up.

b4/25   Him and b4/18*, they would get lonely if they
weren't next to each other. I think they just like
having fun at school. They get bored just doing
work.

The term 'mucking around' connoted friendly interaction. So,
for instance, a student was rejected as interview partner with
the following comment:

b1/16   Not b1/17* because he thinks he is pretty good and
         that and I don't like mucking around with people
         that think themselves good.

Students' identification of sociability with mucking around and
their perception that mucking around was antithetical to work
were such that the acceptability of b2/28*, shown in Chapter 9
to be popular as a result of high academic performance, was
challenged. High academic commitment was seen as incompatible
with sociability. Some students saw him, despite his customary
diligence, as sometimes mucking around and therefore sociable.

b2/14   b2/28* mucks around sometimes. Not very much
         though. Just enough to keep him in with the rest
         of the class.

Others found him sociable despite not mucking around:

b2/26   b2/28* gets stuck into his work, doesn't seem to
         muck around.
b2/31   Or talk to anyone.
b2/26   Not that he's not sociable. He's a good kid, not sour
         or anything.

These definitions were manipulated by hostile classmates. For
example, b2/22*, jealous after being supplanted by b2/28*
as star in the class play, linked b2/28*'s academic attainment
with an allegation that b2/28* had no friends:

b2/22*   b2/28* is the brainy type. All he does is study,
         study, study and he gets real good marks, knows
         everything, has got no friends in the class either.

The polarity between academic commitment and mucking
around and sociability was complicated in girls' classes. Girls'
sexual interests, discussed in Chapter 6, also competed with
academic commitment. Only what were seen as immature
expressions of sexual interest were labelled 'mucking around'.
Girls with more mature sexual interests engaged in intense discussion of boyfriends. Their behaviour, less flamboyant than
that of less mature girls, militated against academic commitment
but was not seen as mucking around.

Mucking around includes a number of functionally and
phenomenally distinct sets of activities. In the sections below,
three of these types of mucking around are analysed to show
how they help define sociability and status within the classroom.

COMPETITIVE MUCKING AROUND

Competitive mucking around celebrates and refines students' power. Chapter 3 showed that power was important among boys but not among girls. Competitive mucking around therefore is important among boys and has a reduced and transformed significance among girls. This section begins by describing the normative structure of boys' competitive mucking around and its significance among control peers. It then examines how powerful boys selectively activate and apply the norms governing competitive mucking around. Finally, it looks at competitive mucking around among girls.

Competitive mucking around as an activity celebrating boys' power differs in four ways from 'picking on' and 'pushing around' seen in Chapter 3 to indicate the power of one student over another. It has a normative base with reciprocity of action expected. It is between students of approximately equal power who each define the action as 'fun' or 'just mucking around', and is a performance dimension requiring skill and effectiveness.

Competitive mucking around assumes multiple forms while preserving its identity. Among boys, these forms included 'horsebiting', a method of slapping legs, 'slagging' and 'dropping a greenie', two ways of discomfiting classmates by spitting, 'thumping' when between equals, some exchanges of verbal abuse, giving each other small electric shocks, rubbing sandpaper on legs, and putting chilli on classmates' pens.

The identity of the various forms of competitive mucking around is phenomenal as well as analytic. Students, although without a single term for the underlying reality, take for granted the equivalence of its manifestations. In the following quotation, for example, the student understood what I wanted to know when I nominated the wrong form of competitive mucking around:

Q   Has anyone given you horsebites?
b2/11   No one has given me any horsebites. There's a few pins, no thumbtacks stuck upside down in the seats for a while; and there was a chilli thing, you know where you rub chilli over somebody's face. That's over now. Nothing going on now.
Q   Did you join in any of these?
b2/11   The chilli part. It didn't last long. Only one day, I think, and then they got caught and got the cane – and the thumbtacks, yeah, I put a couple around the place.

The normative and control aspects of competitive mucking around are schematised in Figure 4.1. It shows that compliance with the norms of competitive mucking around delimits the bounds of classroom association and that success and failure within these norms determine small differences in the power of

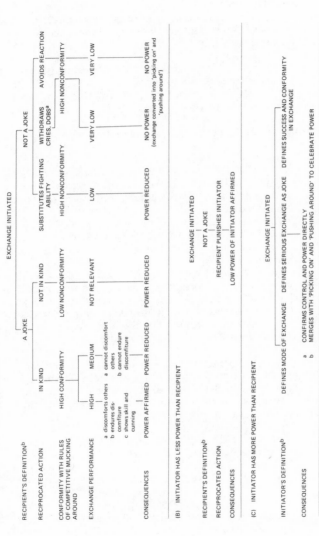

a 'Dobbing' or 'informing' teachers of students' misbehaviour' is discussed in Chapter 7.
b The asymmetry of significance of initiator and recipient definition follows from differential control status.

Figure 4.1 The control and normative structure of competitive mucking around

students. It also shows that very powerful students' ability to manipulate the definition and norms of competitive mucking around allows them to extend their control over classmates.

Norms of competitive mucking around
The proper response to initiation of competitive mucking around is strict reciprocity. A student who sits on a tack should place a tack on the suspected culprit's chair:

b5/22   b5/17 and b5/26* usually put a drawing pin or a tack
             or something on to somebody's chair. You don't
             worry about it. You just put something on their
             chair when they sit down.

Horsebites are similarly returned as horsebites and tripping as tripping:

b4/38   Horsebites. They come up and whack your knees
             if you are standing straight and then they punch
             you on the back of the knees and then you just fall
             backwards.
Q   What would you do?
b4/38   I would do it back to them when I had a chance.
             They did it to me on Monday and I got them on
             Tuesday.
b4/57   There is another one. You lift your foot up and when
             you walk they come right up behind you and they
             kick your foot right in the middle there and your
             leg goes forward and it jars your leg. If someone
             did it to me, I would wait for a chance to get them
             back, do it first if I had a chance.

Whatever the anger or distress caused by the initiation of competitive mucking around, the recipient needs to remember that it is only a 'joke' and that he should carry on the joke. Students stressed the importance of hiding annoyance and taking the exchange as fun. For example:

b1/36   If b1/38 stuck a pin into me I'd laugh because
             everyone else would be watching you and say you
             lost your temper then you would be classed as a
             bad sport so I would just have to laugh.

At its most vigorous, competitive mucking around promotes violence to a degree where participants find it difficult to distinguish between joke and serious intent. Students stated the need even under such conditions to recognise the joke:

Q   Any fights in your class?
b3/42   A few but not now. They only muck around now.
Q   Tell me about this mucking around.

b3/42   We were walking back from the library. . . .b3/18
sort of tried to rip my boot off and I got mad with
him and by the time I got back in the classroom, I
sort of cooled off. So me and b3/41 grabbed him
hard . . . and we hit him in the chest a few times,
not hard. We pushed his head into the wall, the
door, and he sat down looking at it and then I
walked out to the front and b3/32 picked me up
and dumped me around the shoulder and picked me
up again. So I picked him up and put him on the
desk and hit him in the belly a few times. It never
goes past ragging around - yeah - you never get
serious about it.

Students who rejected the definition of the initiation of competitive mucking around as a joke did so in one of three ways.
They could take the mucking around seriously by precipitating
a fight or showing distress, or they could discontinue the joke
by refusing to react. When initiator and recipient of competitive
mucking around began with equal power, each way of refusing
the joke caused the recipient specific problems.

Equals in power who reacted to an initial joke by starting a
fight were accused of being unable to 'take a joke' and of being
unable to accept the physical pain inherent in most competitive
mucking around. For example:

b2/21*   b2/26 can get rough when he wants to. He can't
take a joke.
b2/31   He can give it but he can't take it. He often
punches you.

Such students could also be accused of 'thinking themselves
tough'. This was an accusation that the student concerned had
unrealised pretensions to power based on fighting ability. This
is illustrated in the following example of a student whose claim
to indulge in the one-sided thumping typical of very powerful
students was rejected by his classmates. His classmates instead
saw him as properly obliged to act in the reciprocal mucking
around of equals:

b4/36   b4/48 doesn't get on well with people cos no one
seems to like him. He really thinks he is tough.
He comes up and says, 'How are you going?'
[demonstrates giving a thump] but if you hit him
back he will start to have a good fight with you.

When the ill-tempered student was weaker and his reactions,
however intended, did not need to be taken seriously, he became
an object of derision. The ineffective response, as in the
following example, demonstrated his low power:

b1/31	b1/35, oh boy! He can't take a joke!
Q	What does he do?
b1/31	Loses his temper! He goes mad, crazy.
b1/36	His face goes red and his hair starts going red.
b1/31	And he chases you and he tries to thump you.

Obvious distress as a reaction to the initiation of competitive mucking around is typical of 'sooks', powerless and cowardly students such as b1/17*:

b1/23*	b1/17* is a sook. He was giving horsebites to every-body but when we gave one to him he was bawling his eyes out.

Such students became targets for the physical teasing and pushing around seen in Chapter 3 to indicate boys' relative power.
Outright refusal to respond to initiation of competitive mucking around led to persecution by classmates even if the refusal was unaccompanied by bad temper, arrogance, or cowardice. Refusal to reciprocate negated what were otherwise virtues in competitive mucking around. b2/35*, whose unwillingness to use his fighting ability was described in Chapter 3, was such a student. He dismissed as 'stupid' the initiation of competitive mucking around:

b2/35*	b2/22 is all right but acts stupid sometimes. He thinks he is smart because he gets around with all the other tough boys in the class.
Q	When you say 'he acts stupid' what sorts of things does he do?
b2/35*	He will run up behind you and horsebite you and things like that and generally muck about and think that it is very funny.

b2/35* decided to ignore what was overtly intended by the initiator as a joke. Instead, he tried to invoke a counter defini-tion of the situation:

b2/21*	b2/22* kept punching him around. Like b2/22* 'Why don't you punch him back?' He said, 'Why waste my time on idiots?' He just ignores him.

Refusal to reciprocate converted the initiation of competitive mucking around into 'pushing around', an index of relative power. b2/35* was condemned as powerless:

b2/34	b2/35* gets pushed around for no reason. He's a bit of a weak bloke and people just take advantage of him and push him around.

b2/35* thus receives no credit for withstanding stoically the pain inflicted on him although this, as the next section shows, is normally a mark of success in competitive mucking around.

Success in competitive mucking around
Each act of competitive mucking around was evaluated according to the ability to give and receive pain as an index of 'toughness'. Effective performance was an acquired and considered skill. For example:

b5/57*   The other day I found out how to do horsebites really good. They did it to me really soft and I just turn around and go 'bang!' and they go, 'Ow!' and they yelp.

Ability to give and receive pain were sources of comparison and pride. Pride was evident in boasting about inflicting considerable discomfort:

b1/51   I gave b1/58* a good one. Only hit once and his leg was redder than b1/38's and b1/38's leg had been hit about ten times.

Conversely students boasted of enduring without signs of distress the punishment inflicted in competitive mucking around:

b5/22   My legs haven't got much nerves. They give us a real hard one and it doesn't sting that much and I turn around and go, 'Whump!'

The ability to accept a painful 'joke' in good humour was praised and sometimes used to justify choice of classroom associates:

b2/21*   A good bloke!
b2/31   My friend.
b2/21*   Mine too - b2/32 can take a joke too. You can hit him as hard as you like and he is still grinning.
Q   What will he do?
b2/31   He'll do it back again.

Thus the criteria of success and the norms of competitive mucking around constitute a compulsory male classroom performance dimension which celebrates students' power. Competitive mucking around generally has a physical base which corresponds with physical ability. The ability to give and receive pain is a constituent of success in both fighting and competitive mucking around. Students who refuse to compete with classmates are subject to pushing around and picking on as indices of their low power. Students who with an ill-tempered response refuse to admit reciprocity in competitive mucking around are either accused of falsely claiming power or subject to teasing which affirms their low power.

Competitive mucking around and differential power
The continuation and definition of acts of competitive mucking
around often depended on the relative power of the students
concerned. Physically weaker students could not reciprocate.
Powerful students could define the propriety of competitive
mucking around to their own advantage.

Weaker students found it too painful to continue competitive
mucking around with more powerful students. In discontinuing,
they, as in the example below, recognised the power of the
other student:

b4/23*   b4/24 comes up and thumps you like this and annoys
         you. He doesn't really hurt you. He just annoys you.
Q   Do you annoy him back?
b4/23*   Sometimes if we are having a game.
b4/24   Sometimes.
b4/23*   When you are thumping back he thumps you harder
         and you have to stop because he keeps on thumping
         you hard.

Other students, conscious of relative physical weakness, did
not begin to respond. Either responding or not responding
opened them to further punishment. For example:

b3/48   b3/42 . . . put all my books in a bin and I had to
         pick all the scraps off. . . .
Q   Would you do it back to them?
b3/48   No, because they are too big. I wouldn't do it back
         to them.
         I reckon it's stupid.
b3/47   No, but if you don't do it back to them they just do
         it again and again and again.

When the initiator and recipient of competitive mucking
around diverged widely in power, the exercise of power determined the propriety of behaviour in the mucking around. When
less powerful students attempted to initiate competitive mucking
around, their more powerful classmates determined whether it
was a joke or not. In doing so, the powerful students could
blatantly manipulate or ignore the norms governing competitive
mucking around. b5/42*, as one such powerful student, introduced a form of competitive mucking around in his class. He
preserved its definition as a joke while using it seriously to
punish an associate too weak to retaliate:

b5/42*   I started [horsebites] in the class. . . . I was sitting
         with b5/33. He sits around like this and . . . I get
         up him and give him a clout or thump him.
Q   Does he give it back?
b5/42*   No, he wouldn't be game. . . . I was hitting into
         b5/33 mainly because he used to give me the shits.

He was a real pain in the neck.

Even within his own group, b5/42* signalled his dominance by ignoring the norm of reciprocity in competitive mucking around:

b5/51*   Somebody would put a bottle of R.C. or something out in the middle of the grounds and Jews come to pick up the bottle and you try and hit them with a big spit.

b5/41*   I usually hit b5/51*.

b5/51*   b5/42* usually gets me. It is all right when he gets us. We can't punch him or anything but when we hit him we cop it.

Where the 'slagger' or spitter was not a member of his clique, b5/42*'s reaction was peremptory, hard and effective. In the following quotation, b5/42* describes how he exempted himself from reciprocal mucking around with such a student:

b5/42*   b5/26* was spitting water down and when I got up there they all said it was him so . . . I was thumping into him and he was nearly bawling and he said, 'It wasn't me, it wasn't me', like this. I gave him a few more and he shut up and they haven't done it since. . . . So long as it isn't me, so long as they don't slag at me.

b5/26*, unhappy at being thumped, asserted that b5/42* used fighting ability improperly. He could not, however, resist b5/42*'s use of power or counter the imposed definition of the situation:

b5/25   b5/42* is a bit of a bully.

b5/26*   He thinks he is just it because he is the biggest in the class.

Q   What way does he bully other people?

b5/26*   Up in G Block the other day the kid next to me threw some water and I was the nearest one so he just started thumping into me.

Notably b5/26* did not challenge b5/42*'s right to use force in what was structurally competitive mucking around. He was objecting instead to being wrongly identified as the offender. The operation of competitive mucking around thus confines sociability to power peers and signifies power differences. Weak students' physical inability to reciprocate powerful classmates' initiation of competitive mucking around signifies power differences. Very powerful boys' control of the definition of competitive mucking around allows them to punish less powerful classmates' attempted initiation of competitive mucking around.

Girls' competitive mucking around
Both sexes believed - correctly - that competitive mucking
around was a largely male activity. Boys who did not join in
competitive mucking around could be accused of 'acting like a
girl'. Influential girls did not join in competitive mucking
around. Girls' successful competitive mucking around did not
create influence.

Girls' competitive mucking around was confined to girls with
active but immature sexual interests, and usually focused on
these interests. It often involved interaction with boys. When
it involved only girls there were suggestions that boys would
have been welcome. For example:

> c3/38   c3/41 can't take a joke if it is on her. She can give a
> few jokes but she can't take them. c3/42 and c3/41
> were walking along and it had been raining and c3/41
> pushed her feet down and c3/42 got all wet and c/3/41
> was having a good laugh about it and when c3/42
> did it she got mad. When c3/41 does a joke to her she
> gets mad and if a boy does it to her she will just
> laugh it off.

Incipient courtship of low academic stream girls and their
school boyfriends often took the form of competitive mucking
around. So, for instance, b5/36 and c4/25 considered themselves
boyfriend and girlfriend. b5/36 in the following quotation
describes a playground activity:

> b5/36   c4/25 slagged on my leg and I got a big gully and
> slagged on her back and took off and she chased me.

Competitive mucking around among high academic stream girls
with immature sexual interests was also focused on boys but did
not directly include them in the interaction. A frequent and
acceptable way for these girls to bring themselves to the attention of a boy was, as in the example below, to have a girl act
as intermediary:

> c1/25   I liked this boy and c1/17* knew him and I said I
> liked him and c1/17* said, 'I'll go up and tell him that
> you like him.' I said, 'Oh, don't!' and she said, 'I'll
> just say you like him' and I said, 'Well, don't say
> anything stupid.'

Such messages became a form of competitive mucking around
when girls gave false messages regarding their class friends to
boys:

> Q   Anybody in the class that can't take a joke?
> c1/46   c1/34, sometimes. Like you tell her that you went and
> told a boy that she likes him and she gets all upset.

> She doesn't like it. . . . She just goes off and tells
> someone that you like them.

UFOs AND NOTES

Two kinds of mucking around span the classroom. These are
what one student termed 'UFOs', or unidentified flying objects,
and the sending of letters. The first prevailed among boys and
the second among girls. Neither had the importance of competitive
mucking around and they are therefore discussed more briefly.
The motivation of boys in sending UFOs and of girls in sending
letters is shown to manifest the distinctive values of each sex.

UFOs
Three motivations, each reflecting performance values, were
associated with boys' sending objects across the room. One was
appreciation of skill in constructing or sending UFOs. Another
was celebration of power. Another was annoying the teacher, a
motivation discussed in Chapter 6.

Paper planes and spitballs gave opportunities for craftsmanship
in construction and sending. Skill, especially of powerful
students like b1/24* in the example below, was admired by classmates:

b1/52   b1/24* is real good at it [sound of spitball landing].
        He could knock a fly off a teacher's ear if he wanted
        to and then the teacher wouldn't know.

At times, objects were being sent by large numbers of the
class. Students in one class boasted of the many spitballs on
their classroom ceiling. In another class a student commented,
'We've got an international airport, planes everywhere.' Students
named powerful classmates as initiating the throwing around of
objects. For example:

Q   Who started the throwing of aeroplanes in your class?
b4/23*   b4/31* and b4/21 and b4/22 and we joined in.

The general throwing around of paper planes made conspicuous
the few students who abstained. These were usually subordinate
goody goodies or one of the rare dominant goody goodies:

I Q   When a paper plane lands by you what do you do?
b5/55*   Usually I just pick them up and screw them up.

II b2/28*   I haven't made any [planes], don't throw them either.
           If they land by me I either stand on them or grab
           them with my hand and scrumple them up. [Throwing
           planes] is a bit childish really.

Thus UFOs, when undirected at classmates, offer an arena for

performance and play a small part in signifying students' classroom commitments and association.

More important in male student interaction was the use of
UFOs to hit and annoy classmates. These projectiles took different forms. Sometimes chalk was thrown. Paper pellets were
propelled by rubber bands and spitballs ejected through empty
ball point pen tubes.

Students who aimed these missiles at classmates tended to sit
in the back corners or the sides of the room. Their position
allowed such students to view the whole classroom and avoid
encirclement by hostile classmates. The usual targets were
students on opposite sides or corners of the room. The exchange
of missiles, commonly termed 'wars' or 'fighting' by the students,
celebrated the normative unity of powerful students. It was a
form of competitive mucking around which stretched across
classrooms:

> b1/17*   b1/18* is friends with b1/32* and usually there are
> fights going on between those two.

Special proficiency in these wars was admired. For example:

> b4/58   He had a war with us. He hit the desk [with a paper
> pellet] and hit us on the head, it was that powerful!

Occasionally, the targets were the less powerful students who
sat in the front and centre of the room. The students who sat
at the back and perimeter of the room defined these students as
inactive because they did not muck around but worked solidly.
The less powerful students were fair game:

> b4/13   Kids [down the front] just sit there doing nothing,
> just sit there watching the board and you think,
> 'Oh, I will have to liven this set of dodoes up' and
> you just chuck a pencil at someone.

These less powerful students found it difficult to retaliate.
Often they could not identify the culprits. When they did
identify culprits they were unable to return fire effectively.
To do so required that they turn around, an action awkward in
itself and readily visible to the teacher. Thus powerful students'
shooting pellets and other objects at less powerful classmates
were one-sided affairs. They reaffirmed the relative status of
the students concerned.

The use of UFOs was a male phenomenon. Girls less often
threw objects across the room. The objects that were thrown,
like lollies and books in the example below, indicated co-operation
rather than 'war':

> c4/48*   Sometimes we throw [lollies] across the room to c4/21.
> c4/47*   And sometimes we take them across.

Q   You just walk across the room?
c4/48*   No.
c4/47*   We get up and get a book out of our locker and take
          it over.
c4/48*   And sometimes we just throw them across.

Notes between students
Just as UFOs unite spatially dispersed male classmates, so notes
unite spatially dispersed female classmates. They allow girls with
similar interests, usually sexual, or girls who are fighting, to
communicate where distance or the teacher prevents talking.

Notes were supposedly private but students knew they were
often made public by teachers capturing them or classmates
opening them. Students who sent notes sometimes combined the
myth of confidentiality with the reality of disclosure to obtain a
public effect. Notes could be used to annoy the teacher who
captured them:

c1/25   c1/41* will write, 'Goodday' on a piece of paper and
          she will tell the whole class to pass it around in the
          hope that it will stir him.

Girls also manipulated classmates' interdiction of notes to
their own advantage. An example illustrates the extremes of
manipulation sometimes reached. c3/32* wanted to gain the
attention of a boy, b5/32*. Through modesty she could not
approach him directly, nor, since he was not friends with any
member of her group, could she use them as intermediaries. He
was, however, known to unsympathetic classmates. Accordingly, she used her knowledge that unsympathetic classmates
will use knowledge of her unrequited sexual interest, obtained
from interdicting notes, to tease the girl who had written the
note.

To carry out this scheme, c3/32* wrote with two friends a
long class letter which expressed her interest in the boy. This
letter is reproduced in Appendix C. She initially planned that
the letter come into the hands of c3/16m, one of the two boys
in her class. It was hoped that he would tease her by telling
the boy of her interest in him. c3/32* said at the time:

c3/32*   c3/16m has been getting a couple of notes that I have
          been writing and c3/16m hangs round with b5/32*
          and I liked b5/32* so I wrote this note and said how
          I liked b5/32* and we were going to put it on his desk
          so he would get it. It was all set up and c3/16m
          didn't get it so we told c3/33*, 'Look c3/33*, go out
          and give him the note', so we told her to say, 'Don't
          let c3/31 and c3/23* know that I have got this but I
          have got it and I don't want them to know about it.'
          So she goes out and gives it to them and c3/33* said,
          'Ah Hell! Sucked you in! Got one of your letters!'

and we said, 'How did you get that?' but really we
wanted c3/16m to get it all along but I don't know
whether he has given the note to b5/32* yet.

The plan changed. The letter was given to c3/12*, whose boyfriend it was. c3/12* as planned told the boy of c3/32*'s interest
in him. c3/12* reported that:

c3/12*   It was about my boyfriend, how they liked him and
         one of them had fallen in love with him or something
         and how she is going to get around him by dropping
         a rock on his toe or something like that.
c3/11*   This is all in my letter.
c3/12*   I showed it to my boyfriend yesterday and he laughed.

This happened in the last week of interviewing. I never learned
whether the whole scheme succeeded in c3/32* obtaining b5/32*
as a boyfriend.

CONCLUSIONS

This chapter has shown the value of the integrated model of
schooling and the peer group. Performance dimensions unrelated
to academic work are important within the classroom. Further,
these performances are in no sense secondary to academic work
but owe their significance to their part in the construction of
boys' power, which they celebrate and by which their definition
is determined.

Chapter 5

Intrusion of external statuses and associations

A wide range of statuses and associations intruded into Goldtown classrooms. To describe each would require devoting more space to the overall topic than its importance warrants. One intrusive dimension, sexual interests, was so much more important than the others, that it was chosen for intensive analysis. To balance this emphasis on one dimension, the overall significance of intrusive concerns is explicated in the final section of this chapter. This section describes the use two dominant students make of external statuses and associations.

The chapter argues that the overwhelming importance of girls' sexual interests is compatible with Parsons' model of sexual differences. Here among girls is a diffuse, particularistic dimension which frequently excludes consideration of classroom specific performance dimensions, and which is strongly related to the construction of influence.

SEXUAL INTERESTS

The terms under which permission to research was granted excluded discussion of external associations, statuses and activities. Information on these came from questions on other topics. Fights, for instance, were frequently over boyfriends, alleged promiscuity or homosexuality. Descriptions of classroom interaction and seating patterns included talking or passing notes about boyfriends. Expanded responses to the sociometrics referred to shared interests in a group of boys or shared acquaintance with a particular boy. Thus, the classroom manifestations of external activities, and not the external activities themselves, are discussed below.

Girls' sexual interests are discussed first. Boys' sexual interests are then discussed briefly to offer a basis for comparison.

Girls' sexual interests
The following section shows how sexual interests define girls' interaction with teachers and classmates. It shows how expression of sexual interests limits school authority and impedes academic commitment, while conversely absence of active expression of sexual interests is associated with acceptance of teachers' authority, but not always with increased academic commitment. Expression of sexual interests is shown to be related to students'

perceptions of maturity and propriety in classmates and to the construction of influence.

Five case studies are used below to illustrate how maturity and propriety of sexual interest determine classroom relationships. Each case study describes the interaction of a sociometric group or rejectee defined by classmates' use of these considerations. These case studies cover instances of a moral isolate, girls with high status sexual interests, girls with low status sexual interests, conformist students with nonintrusive sexual interests, and girls who are embarrassed by the presence of boys. The place of highly influential girls as arbiters, confidantes and advisers in sexual affairs is left to the next section.

Moral outcast c2/32* was a 'moll' whose classroom interaction was governed by reputed promiscuity. Most of her classmates shunned her. Even students who would otherwise have been her associates limited their contact with her because of this reputation. On all sociometrics she was rejected by her three neighbours, who, none the less, when they could avoid being stigmatised through association with her, kept her company. c2/41* associated with c2/32* in the playground until she began to share c2/32*'s reputation. Thereupon she decided to find new companions:

> c2/41*   The boys used to call c2/32* and I 'molls' or 'warts' or those sorts of things and one day c2/32* was away and the boys did not call me anything and the next day c2/32* was back and they were back calling us 'molls' and things like that and when I started going round with c2/42* I realised that it was c2/32* that made them say it to me because they didn't say anything like that anymore unless it was joking.

c2/41*'s decision to dissociate herself from c2/32* was made despite a personal liking:

> Q   It sounds as if you quite like c2/32*?
> c2/41*   Yeah. It's just you get a bad name. . . . She understands problems some of the time and you can talk to her about different things and she is nice to have as a friend.

c2/41* and c2/42* mixed, however, with c2/32* on other occasions, including activities which had led to c2/32* being labelled a moll. At the time of interviewing, for instance, c2/32* was planning to leave home with c2/41* to join some boyfriends, in a city north of Goldtown. In the classroom, classmates frequently observed c2/41* and c/42* turning around to gossip with c2/32*.

Other girls were generally hostile. Classmates alleged she stole boyfriends:

c2/16*   I took c2/32* out my place one weekend . . . and
          there was this boy there that I liked and she kind of
          got around to him, just started liking him a lot and
          she tried to get him to like her a lot. I think he did
          after a while.

This fight was carried on by notes across the room:

c2/42*   c2/16* sends notes to c2/32* especially fighting. She
          is always fighting her about Danny.
c2/41*   Boys.
c2/42*   Dan is not interested in c2/32* and every time c2/32*
          sends a note saying that she is not interested.
c2/41*   But c2/16* just keeps going.

This controversy resulted in loud name calling and attempts to
label the opponent:

c2/21m   The fight was up at the Hall. It was c2/41* and
          c2/32* about interfering with Dan. c2/16* was yelling
          out, 'molls', and things like that. I thought there was
          going to be a war or something. Then the teacher
          came and they cooled down a bit. Every time one
          sees the other they walk the other way. They talk
          around their friends and say, 'She has been around
          too much.'

Unlike other girls with high sexual interests, c2/32's sexual
interests did not compete with academic commitment. She was
rejected on all sociometrics by most classmates. However, only
a sexual rival, c2/16*, and a single academically committed
conformist believed sexual interests precluded attention to work.
Others rejected her because of her sexual reputation.

c2/32's relations with teachers were amicable. Her neighbours
believed she was a committed, if erratic, worker:

c2/41*   c2/32* tries. Some times she wants to work and
          others she doesn't. She does try because she wants
          to get ahead but she is not all that good at things.

This assessment was generally shared by teachers, such as
the following:

'She used to try very hard and she wasn't very smart but
she used to try and she used to just pass and she was very
pleased with this. . . . She does like to answer questions when
she knows the answers so in that respect she is quite co-
operative. Homework is very seldom done. When you get up
after her she will come up and do it for you and she doesn't
give you any backtalk. In fact, in some respects she is a

little submissive'.

None the less, the same teacher also believed that c2/32*'s interaction with her neighbours inhibited classwork and disturbed
classmates:

> 'I told them off because they were getting very, very noisy
> and annoying everyone else and I was quite nasty to them
> because I felt they needed it.'

Attempts to break up the group were ineffectual because teachers
did not enforce the seat change. The teacher commented:

> 'I separated c2/32* from c2/41*. . . . c2/32* worked well on
> her own and eventually by steps she moved back across the
> room, very gradual steps. She thought I would not notice and
> she is back in that little group.,

Other sex-related activities brought c3/32* into conflict with
teachers. The school administration attempted to stop her
wearing a very short school tunic, which classmates alleged was
intended to lure boys:

> c2/11   It is stupid having [the uniform] that short. She
> just wants to show her knickers off or something.
> Q   It mightn't be that she hasn't a hem?
> c2/11   She would prefer to have it up short anyway just for
> the boys to gawk at her.

c2/32* also smoked in the school grounds and truanted. Each
activity brought her into contact with boys, the smoking with a
group of Grade Nine boys, and the truancy with older boys who
had left school. Both smoking and truancy, the latter compounded by forging notes from parents, led to trouble with the
school authorities.

Boycrazy girls with mature sexual interests 'Boycrazy' girls
with mature sexual interests led involuted classroom lives. They
tried to sit at the back of the classroom to avoid teachers'
disrupting their talk about boys. 9c1 contained eight such girls,
composing four dyads of seatmates. c1/11* and c1/12*, one of
these dyads, sat in the corner mainly talking with each other
but sometimes with a similar pair of girls in front of them.
  Classmates attributed to c1/11* an active sexual life with
older boys in situations which required independence from
parental supervision. They alleged physical relationships with
boys:

> c1/25   c1/11* would have to be the biggest boy chaser this
> side of the Black Stump. . . . She would strip for a
> boy.

Their boyfriends were seen by classmates as having exceptional
sexually-related material resources, such as panel vans, and
to engage in 'wild' behaviour such as drinking and smoking.
   These girls' outside social activities reflected their sexual
maturity. Goldtown girls scaled dance venues according to
degrees of respectability, supervision, and maturity of associated
sexual interests. At one end of the scale were the chaperoned
school 'socials' with foxtrots and waltzes. At the other end were
rock dances and discos in city hotels with associated drinking
and fights. In between were country dances in small halls outside the city. These were family affairs with milder drinking
and occasional fights. c1/11* and c1/12* placed themselves in
between the country dance and rock dance points in the
continuum. They spoke scornfully of girls who attended the
socials:

c1/11* . . . like girls who go to socials - dead.

Their common level of sexual interests often promoted discord
among the eight girls in the class with active and mature sexual
interests. They competed for the limited number of eligible
boys. c1/11* in this way fought with c1/21, who was after
c/12*, her closest friend in the class:

c1/11*   Once [c1/21 and I had a fight] over boys. You see,
         I was just friends with this guy - it was true - just
         friends and she took it the wrong way and she got mad
         about it.

The proximity of girls with different opportunities to realise
similar sexual interests converted statements about sexual
activities into comparisons of status. For example:

c1/16*   I find c1/11* a bit smarty. If you say, 'I went out on
         a Saturday night' she says, 'I went out with my boy-
         friend' if I didn't go out with a boy.

Despite these sources of dissension, the cultural homogeneity
of girls with mature sexual interests led to their exchanging
choices on work sociometrics:

Q   [English sociometric.]
c1/16*   [Names of girls with mature sexual interests.] c1/12*
         is about the same as us, goes the same places, does
         the same thing. We would be able to work better and
         talk better together too, talk while we were working.

Within the group thus formed, the girls had a rough parity of
control status. However, not all the girls exercised the control
frequently. c1/11* and c1/12* were able, for instance, to return
the verbal attacks of c1/16*, shown in Chapter 3 to label class-

mates aggressively and effectively:

> c1/51*   c1/11* and c1/12* stick up for themselves really good.
> If c1/16* says something to them they'll have some-
> thing else to say back.
>
> c1/52*   Even worse.

c1/11* and c1/12* generally exercised their influence when
provoked by associates. They did not often use it otherwise.
c1/11* and c1/12* asserted that freedom to talk about sexual
interests helped them work better. Classmates such as c1/27, a
'brain' assigned to a work group with them, and c1/15, a classroom neighbour, asserted that c1/11* and c1/12* did not work
and that their talk prevented workmates or neighbours working:

> I c1/27   Our group doesn't do very much work, c1/11* and
> c1/12* - they are always talking about boys . . . and
> we just hardly ever get anything done.
>
> II c1/15 c1/11* and c1/12* talk nearly all day and they get
> rather annoying after a while with their continual
> buzzing.

Girls with lower levels of sexual interest tended to avoid c1/11*
and c1/12*. They rejected c1/11* and c1/12* on work sociometrics and if sat near them in class sometimes moved away.
One commented:

> c1/51   I moved to the front because c1/11* and c1/12* would
> not stop talking or anything and they were getting on
> my nerves.

Reciprocally, c1/11* and c1/12* did not choose less sexually
interested girls as work partners. They labelled them as
'goody goodies'. As they used it, this term referred to the
phenomenally merged dimension of 'not mucking around' and
'not going out with boys':

> Q   When you talk of someone as a 'goody goody'?
> c1/11*   They don't muck around and generally most of the
> time they don't go out much either.

c1/11* added an explanation that:

> c1/11*   A social is going out but - it is not really.

They did not consider themselves stirrers. Classmates attributed to them only the gentle forms of stirring, described in
Chapter 8, of referring to the private life of teachers. Nonetheless, continual talk about boys annoyed teachers. A classmate
commented:

c1/58m Some people [stir] unconsciously. That is c1/11* and
c1/12* talking all the time.

Like the moll, girls with mature sexual interests wore uniforms
which advertised their sexual interests. Instead of the unsubtly
short tunic, they wore perfume and obvious make-up. This too
brought them into conflict with the teacher:

c1/13* c1/11* and c1/12* got copped the other day for
wearing eye shadow and they were sent to wash it off.

Unlike the moll, they were not interested in schoolboys and
therefore did not meet them in the playground. Instead they
talked with two girls with similar sexual interests from another
class.

Boycrazy girls with immature sexual interests Boycrazy girls
with immature sexual interests formed large though ill-defined
groups. 9c3d2, from which the present values are taken,
included sixteen girls who expressed active sexual interests
and were seen as immature by maturer girls and boycrazy by
girls without active classroom expression of sexual interests.
A subgroup comprised of six girls, c3/23*, c3/24, c3/31, c3/32*,
c3/33* and c3/34, is used below to illustrate the activities of
such girls.
The girls' contacts with boys outside school were closely monitored by parents. Only one had been allowed into town with
her boyfriend, a Grade Nine boy known to her parents. This
privilege ended when her father saw love bites on her neck.
Telephone calls and home visits from boyfriends were similarly
limited, with fathers often reported not letting their daughters
take calls. When the girls did meet boys it tended to be by
subterfuge although classroom accounts, as perhaps in the
following example, were liable to exaggeration:

c3/31 [talking of spare time activities] I go to judo every
Thursday night. About all. The rest of it is taken up
by boys anyway.
Q I thought you did not get much freedom from your
parents.
c3/31 Behind their backs. . . . Some of the ones I like
. . . come round the side and I say, 'I am going down
to c3/14*'s place. Goodbye!' and then you go off
before they can say anything and go round the side,
'Good day' and then Mum and Dad, 'c3/31'. 'I'm
coming. Boy! Is it a long way to run from c3/14*'s
place to here' and they don't suspect anything but I
think they are getting suspicious now.

The girls were allowed to go to school socials. These socials were
sexless affairs dominated by adults and the girls did not enjoy them:

c3/33*   [Socials] are too slack for me. If you sit next to a
         guy he has got his arm around you like that. Along
         comes [a teacher named], 'It is too hot for that. You
         have to get up and dance', and the boys have got to
         wear a tie.

c3/32*   I don't like it because it is supposed to be the kids'
         night and yet the teacher tells you what to do.

The focus of the girls' sexual interests, perforce, was within
the school. They met Grade Nine boys in the playground. These
boys were not highly regarded by the girls' classmates with
mature sexual interests. These classmates alluded to the boys
in terms such as 'some drag she goes around with'. The style
of the girls' approaches was also criticised by more mature
classmates. For example:

Q   If c3/32* or c3/31 wanted to get the attention of a
         boy how do you think they would go about it?

c3/11*   They just act stupid. That's the way they usually
         do.

c3/12*   They just go up to them and start putting their
         arms around them and it makes you sick.

c3/11*   They are standing around and act real smart and
         follow the boys around. It doesn't really attract (the
         boys') attention. I think it more or less turns them
         off.

c3/31 saw herself as subtle in her approach to boys compared
with her friend c3/33* who was condemned as too obvious:

c3/31   c3/33* would crawl up to guys and all that so I
         decided I did not want to go round with her. . . .

Q   What is the difference between your and c3/33's
         approach to guys?

c3/31   I just get other guys to drop hints here and there
         that I like him and I try to get my friend to get a
         time-table of his so that I can see which lessons he
         goes to. Say I have got his time-table and he is
         going to be in [Room] D9, that is our homeroom,
         and we have got to go to [Room] H11, I usually take
         my time and wait till he comes to D9 and then [smiles]
         and walk off.

Q   What is the difference between what you do and what
         c3/33* does?

c3/31   She makes guys know straightaway [gives details].

The girls' relationships with individual boys were evanescent.
Much classroom time was spent discussing the latest permutations
in relations between the limited groups of Grade Nine boys and
girls:

Q   What do you talk about in class?
c3/33* Boys.
c3/32* Boys, boys, boys.
c3/33* What you did on Friday night and making me real
        jealous because I am not allowed out.
c3/32* We went [out with sister and boyfriends]. I went with
        b2/41.
c3/33* He doesn't like you anymore.
c3/32* He goes with another girl. We went down to the back
        of his friend's car and we had fun and everything
        and the next time two weeks after me and b4/23* went
        down by the river and I got into trouble over this.
        . . . Dad thinks you meet guys all the time. I admit
        it is true but still –
c3/33* How would he know?

When the distance was too great for talking or the teacher
prevented students' talking, the students communicated by
notes:

c3/31   When the teacher tells us not to (talk), I just keep on
        writing notes about guys – which one she likes and
        that.

The subject matter of the notes was the same as in the conversations. Through them girls learned more about their and their
classmates' boyfriends:

c3/22   I passed a note to c3/32* about her new boyfriend
        and I said I knew someone who liked her new boy-
        friend – we were supposed to be doing S.R.A. – and
        she wrote a note about [the girl who liked her new
        boyfriend] [details] and I wrote back asking whether
        her mother knew she had broken up with her last
        boyfriend because her mother liked b4/23* and she
        didn't like b2/41 and she wrote something back about
        her mother really liking him because she thought he
        was cute and he had a babyface and all that and her
        mother didn't know she was going out with b2/41.

Teachers' interception of notes led to the girls' sexual interests,
which often seemed designed for public consumption among
classmates, losing the semblance of privacy. The girls, although
they might not admit it on any particular occasion, felt they
could control teachers' publicisation of girls' sexual interests:

c3/33* Sometimes when we really want to get into trouble we
        pass notes for the teacher to look at but when we do
        not want to get caught we do it when the teacher is
        not looking.
c3/32* I was writing to c3/22. We were writing backwards

and forwards one time about a boy [b4/23*] and anyway Mrs Shelley got hold of it and she pinned it up on the notice board.

c3/33* She read it out in the class and pinned it up on the board.

c3/32* I was embarrassed.

Girls with mature sexual interests despised this use of notes. They, with their introverted discussion of sexual interests, professed not to understand the girls' purpose in having notes intercepted:

c3/14* [The case study girls] do it stupidly, they always get caught. They will pass it when [the teacher] is looking or something. They think she is stupid and she will be out there and she will grab the note.

Nor were maturer girls, with their intense concern with individual boys, sympathetic to the jocularity of many notes:

c3/14* I don't get on well with c3/33* because she is real childish. We found this note [from c3/33*] on c3/21's desk and it said 'Sugar Daddy does John or somebody want to go with you? If so, I suppose he was drunk when he asked you and if he was I would ask him again when he was sober. Don't trust him when he's drunk.'

Classmates believed that girls with immature sexual interests let these interests interfere with work. c3/33* and c3/31 were frequently rejected on sociometric work criteria for this reason. For example:

c3/22 If we are doing something we explain something to them and tell them to write something down they have these books and they are writing all over it and they are writing to their boyfriends and hearts and all that.

However, some girls in the group were seen by classmates and teachers to work well. c3/34 was described by a teacher as:

'A nice kid. Not very bright but she tries very hard. When I tell her to go and read something in science she is the one that actually does it. Some of them don't bother doing anything but she is a very, very hard worker even in maths.'

c3/33*, her seatmate, is described in Chapter 9 as a student who successfully manipulated low academic status in order to avoid doing any schoolwork. c3/32* was described as 'really quiet' and her seatmate c3/31 as noisy. I asked why these seemingly disparate seatmates sat together and was told:

c3/22   Their boyfriends.
c3/21   All their boyfriends are in the same group.

These girls' relations with teachers were largely independent of their expression of sexual interests in the classroom and school. The passing of notes brought them into a sympathetic relation with certain teachers. Smoking was associated strongly with the meeting of groups of girls with groups of boys and was confined to immature boycrazy girls and molls. Their omission of belts from the uniform and wearing of make-up caused some conflict but more with the school administration than with teachers. Most teachers permitted some conversation. Thus, talking about boys did not lead to conflict unless supplemented by continual mucking around and abstention from work.

Goody goodies with weak or no public sexual interests Groups with weak or no sexual interests were well defined in all girls' classes except 9c1. Four such girls in 9c4, c4/31*, c4/32*, c4/57* and c4/58*, are used as a case study here. They chose each other on all three sociometrics. They made very few choices outside the group and were chosen only by a conformist low academic status student.

The four girls were aware of the cohesion of their group. Two of them, explaining the choice of friends on a work sociometric, described their friendship and activities in the following terms:

c4/31*   They are real true friends and they would not do as
         most people do when you can't get proper friends,
         and they are going with you for one day and the next
         day they are going with one of the real cheeky kids.
         Most people do this sort of thing and they are telling
         all about you and picking fault with you but . . . we
         always stick together and we are real true to each
         other.
c4/32*   We tell each other what happens at home [while we
         are working] and we try to discuss what we have
         seen on t.v. and what we think of school and what
         we think of our teacher . . .
c4/31*   Not very often do we talk about boys. We leave them
         out.

Despite not talking about boys, three of the four had or had had boyfriends. One of the two current boyfriends, b1/52, used to meet with c4/31* in the playground. Her classmates did not respect b1/52. She was teased when she defended him:

c4/44*   c4/31* keeps on saying b1/52 is real nice underneath
         and we take it the wrong way and she got teased for
         the rest of the week.

c4/58* had a boyfriend but her associates reported that the relationship was not physically passionate:

> c4/31*   c4/58* is allowed to go out with her boyfriend so long as the family is with them, but she has never kissed him, just had her arm around him.

She did not let her sexual interests intrude into the classroom. She refused invitations from classmates with maturer sexual interests to talk about her boyfriend:

> c4/48*   c4/58* has a boyfriend but if you ask her where he lives or how old he is she will just go quiet and won't say nothing and then she'll just say, 'That's for me to know and for you to find out.' You know if she asked us we would probably tell her.

These girls illustrate the empirical identity of girls' dependence on teachers and the absence of sexual interests asserted by the girls with mature sexual interests examined earlier in the chapter. One pair of these goody goody girls sat at the front. The other pair, c4/32* and c4/31*, wished to sit at the front 'because it is closer to the blackboard and it is closer to the teacher'. The front, as Chapter 11 shows, is the position in the classroom associated with acceptance of dependence on teachers. The girls described themselves as diligent in classwork and never mucking around, a perception shared by classmates:

> c4/17   They are always listening. . . .
> c4/18   These are the only persons who never muck around.

This absence of mucking around was given by their classmates as the reason for rejecting the four girls in the sociometrics. Classmates also saw the goody goodies' abstention from mucking around as a cause of their social isolation:

> c4/26   They are all quiet. They don't talk with any of us really. Cos most of the rest of the class are all rowdy and talk and everything in school.

The girls were said to be willing to give teachers disinterested help. Even here they were ineffective as more influential classmates pre-empted their offers to help. The girls reported enjoying talking to teachers. The teachers found the girls' conversation welcome. One commented:

> 'Very, very nice personalities, friendly without being over-friendly. They can talk to you as students without being familiar if they come across anything interesting or noteworthy in their reading.'

More mature and influential classmates, however, deemed this willingness to talk with teachers 'crawling'.

Other aspects of the girls' activities and self-presentation confirmed their isolation. Their games in the playground were seen as indices of immaturity:

c4/43* We saw them playing a real childish game we used to play in Grade Three - Statues. They all stand up in a big row and we all stood there watching them and they asked us if we would like to join them and we all took off.

Their uniforms conformed very strictly to the school administration's veto on short tunics. Their conformity in this was a matter of comment even among teachers:

c4/18 They all wear their tunics down to their knees and when we had our uniform inspection [the senior mistress] said, 'Gee! They wouldn't have to take theirs down at all.'

The uniform identified them as pejoratively goody goody even among non-stirrers such as c4/42:

c4/42 c4/31*'s goody goody. No, she's not but she wears long skirts.

Classmates derided the girls' uniforms:

c4/55 They tell c4/32* that her dress is too long. They say her dress is so short when it is really so long.

c4/56* They say it to c4/31* all the time. We always say to her that we wish our uniforms were the same as hers because hers look awful.

The style of uniform was by itself sufficient cause for classmates' refusal to associate with them. A hardworking classmate commented:

c4/56* Not c4/58*. I would work sitting next to c4/58*. It is just that I couldn't stand sitting next to her - the way she dresses.

Overall, the muted sexual interests and associated characteristics led to imputations of immaturity and stupidity. This in turn led to isolation in classroom interaction, and classmates picking on the girls as an index of their subordination. Their class neighbours commented:

Q What about talking with c4/57* and c4/58* in class?

c4/56* Ugh! Yuk! We don't mix with them at all. The only

	thing we say to them is 'turn around'.
c4/55	They are too –
Q	Too what?
c4/56*	Daggy![1]
c4/55	They are too old fashioned.
c4/56*	They are old fashioned, snobbish.
c4/55	Some of them are a bit babyish, too.
c4/56*	Yeah.
c4/55	Yeah and act a bit stupid.
c4/56*	I like more mature people than what they are.

Goody goodies against expression of sexual interests   A few
girls opposed expression of sexual interests. Three girls
exemplify here these goody goodies. They are a pair of girls
in 9c3, c3/52* and c3/51*, and c3/51*'s twin in 9c1, c1/53*.
c3/52* and c3/51* had no mutual choices with other students on
any sociometric and were very frequently rejected. c1/53* was
mutually chosen by the subordinate class brain on the interview
sociometric. She had a succession of seatmates of whom the
latest at the time of interviewing was allocated the seat by the
form teacher.

The girls were uneasy when with boys. Each more than once
during the interviews asserted this with comments like:

c1/53*   I don't like boys. I am scared stiff of them.

Any interest in boyfriends or marriage was passive. When asked,
for instance, the date of expected marriage, replies were
indefinite as to time, and the date was to be determined by an
outside agency:

c1/53*   c3/51* and I have already started our glory box and
we never think of what time we will be married. I
leave that up to God.

The attitude to relations with boys became a joking matter
among classmates with more active sexual interests. These
stigmatised the girls as 'old maids':

c3/41   c3/51* would not dream of having a boyfriend. She
is going to wait until she is twenty.
c3/42   Maybe thirty.

Half serious accusations of lesbianism were laid against these
goody goodies:

c3/32*   [Giving a reason for not being interviewed with
c3/52*.] She hangs round with c4/57*.

---

[1]Etymologically: like the dag or soiled wool around a sheep's
crutch.

c3/33*   She is a lesbian with c4/57* because I saw them
together. I wouldn't doubt a word of it.

The effects of disliking boys intruded strongly into the classroom. The phenomenological division of girls' classroom activities
into academic work, and into discussion and activities focused on
sexual interests, applied strongly to them:

c3/38   Workwise they all do their work except that c3/52*
is a bit docile in the head. But c3/52* and c3/51*
don't seem to get around and talk like we talk. They
don't ever talk about guys or anything like that. They
just talk about schoolwork.

Different levels of sexual interest led to conflict between deskmates and workmates. c1/17*, a boycrazy girl with mature
sexual interests, was shifted by the teacher away from the
back corner to sit with c1/53* in the front. She lamented her
exile:

c1/17*   It's like sitting next to a brick wall. No offence on
her, but with c1/18 if you say something she will
talk to you and you can talk about boys or anything
to her and other kids you sit next to but c1/53* is not
interested and it is kind of - you have nothing to say,
to talk about. You just sit there and feel silly.

c1/53* maintained her status as a brick wall by ordering c1/17*
to be quiet and enforcing the command:

Q   How are you getting on with c1/17* next to you?
c1/53*   She's alright to sit next to. She's a bit of a chatter-
box. She talks too much.
Q   Does this disturb you?
c1/53*   No, not really. I just tell her to shut up.
Q   Does she shut up?
c1/53*   Yes.
Q   Does she get offended?
c1/53*   No. You see if she doesn't shut up I have a habit of
kicking. I kick and so she shuts up.

Similarly, these girls when in workgroups were reported by
workmates to urge the group to do more work. These urgings
were largely ignored by the other girls who continued to talk
about boys:

c1/11*   c1/53* gets a bit snooty because if we mention a boy
- she hates boys, she is dead against them but she
just sits there and acts superior.

These girls, explaining why they preferred not to mix with
boycrazy classmates, emphasised their feelings of unease when
boys were discussed:

> c3/52*   I can't mix with the other kids much. Most of them are
> teenage. Everybody is teenage in our class. Mostly
> they talk about boys and going out and that. It just
> doesn't get me.

Their dress, like that of girls with weak sexual interests,
conformed to school administration requirements. It included a
long tunic connoting lack of interest in attracting boys and
excluded the make-up and jewellery associated with sexual
maturity. Other girls commented:

> c1/52*   [The twins] both look as if they are going to grow up
> old maids. They wear their skirts half-way between
> mini and knee lengths.

These girls' self-presentation was further derided because they
did not shave their legs or pluck their eyebrows. Their classmates associated this failure with lack of interest in boyfriends:

> Q   Anybody who would be strict on boyfriends?
> c3/17   c3/51*.
> c3/18   'Naturalist'. She doesn't shave her legs or pluck her
> eyebrows, she doesn't use make-up.

Boys' sexual interests
Boys' sexual interests intruded more weakly than those of girls
into classroom interaction. They were unrelated to seating
patterns and sociometric choices and rejections. The association
between sexual maturity and students' control status found in
girls' classes was not found in boys' classes.
    It was shown earlier that high status Grade Nine girls had
older boyfriends. As a result Grade Nine boys either had
Grade Nine low status girlfriends, younger girlfriends, or no
girlfriends. Boys were aware of this. They made comments
like:

> b3/47   Most of the good looking girls would go for the older
> blokes, like the blokes that have got a bike and a
> big machine. We can't afford it. We are left with the
> ugly girls.

Boys granted their girlfriends little respect. One boy, who
mixed with the group of goody good 9c4 girls, expanded a
comment that he 'always got chucked off at', by saying:

> b1/52   About my girlfriend. b1/51's girlfriend is my girl-
> friend's sister and she is uglier than my girlfriend

> and my girlfriend is pretty ugly.

Classmates did not openly envy boys with girlfriends. b3/15 was a boy mentioned favourably by Grade Nine girls. He received, typically, the following evaluation from a classmate:

> b3/44   b3/15's a twit really. . . . He goes around with those ugly girls in Grade Eight, gets them at the Drive-In and hangs round with them outside. Any girls that come along really.

Boys without girlfriends suffered none of the anxiety that girls without boyfriends suffered. They were not embarrassed by lack of interest or success. The following are typical comments:

> b2/28*   I was never really interested in girls when I was a kid and I'm not really interested in them now either. Think maybe I'm a bit young yet.
> b2/44   Yeah, I'm going to get one when I'm a bit older.

Boys' sexual interests were muted in the playground. Some mention was made of repartee from low stream male stirrers:

> b6/3   They call b6/18's sister, 'Cavern Cunt'.
> b6/18   And b6/5's sister, 'Grand Canyon'.

Threats of being beaten by the administration discouraged some boys from mixing with girls in the playground. Teasing from classmates discouraged others:

> Q   Do you talk to your girlfriend during lunch?
> b1/45*   I would like to talk to her quite often but it is just the comments they throw up at me.
> Q   'They'?
> b1/58*   Me.
> b1/45*   Just about everybody.

Among girls such teasing was only done to and by the sexually immature. Among boys it had very limited status connotations, although there were a few comments deprecating such teasing:

> b1/31   They are babyish. They think just because you are going around with some girls.
> b1/36   Just because you are talking to some girls, 'Ah Gee! b1/36 likes. . . .'

A very few boys distinguished sexual interests in terms of maturity. Even they generally disclaimed respect for the objects of their interest:

b3/12   You go and grab an ugly looking slut. You don't
         think so at the time and you hang round with her all
         the time and she gets boring and that.
Q   Anyone stir you about playing around with sheilas?
b3/15   Oh yes. All those coons in that class. You see they
         are all boys. The don't go in for girls much.
b3/12   Yeah. They play tiggy and all this and run round
         chasing each other. Poofs!

However, b3/12 chose mates for lunchtime activities who shared
his other interests, 'fags and boozing', rather than his interest
in girls.
    Boys did talk about girls in class but their conversation often
merged sexual interests inconsequentially with other interests.
Statements would begin with a comment on sexuality and, without developing the theme, turn to another topic:

b4/34   Girls like b4/23* and he likes the girls. He's a pretty
         good golf player.

Even boys with established sexual interests did not talk about
girls, or they kept the discussion private, so that other boys
were not aware of the conversation:

Q   Do any boys talk about girlfriends?
b1/56   A lot of them keep it quiet between themselves if they
         have got a girlfriend cos I have hardly ever heard
         of anyone talking about girlfriends.

Notwithstanding boys' general lack of sexual interests, on
rare occasions these interests influenced status and association.
Some praise accrued:

b4/31*   b4/23* is pretty good really. He gets on pretty well
         with all the girls, knows nearly every girl in high
         school so it is good to get around with him.

However, sex-focused associations tended to be shortlived and
specific:

b4/41   You get the odd one or two who want to date with a
         bird or something like that. They will suddenly become
         his mate but most of the time it is just considered
         that they are his friends and that and he just talks
         to them.

Overall, intrusion of sexual interests into boys' classes was
weak. It neither defined group membership nor became a prerequisite for power. Powerful students were often, so far as
classmates were concerned, without girlfriends. Less powerful
classmates professed little interest. A student known to be able

to 'get a win on with the sheilas' would sit with a student who
was uninterested.

DOMINANT STUDENTS AND INTRUSIVE ROLES

An influential girl and intrusive roles
c2/18* was seen by classmates to excel in outside activities and
interests. She was named as the best in the class at sports and
athletics. She was seen as the girl who could go to the drive-in
cinema when other girls were prevented by their parents.
Lunchtime was spent with Grade Eleven and Grade Twelve girls
of whom other 9c2 girls commonly shared c2/18*'s evaluation:

> c2/18* I like to get on with older friends because they have
>   more idea of what to do and more sense than us.

Only she in her class earned a significant income. This enabled
her to practise general largesse:

> c2/25   c2/18* is always giving things away. She has a packet
>   of chips and she holds it out to everyone in the class.
> Q   Is that because she has more pocket money than other
>   girls?
> c2/36   . . . She works downtown and gets money there.
>   She has got two jobs.

This largesse was a sign of successful performance. Classmates
condemned, as improper boasting about family, equivalent
largesse from students who received generous pocket money.
c2/18*'s performance in outside activities was such that classmates generally took her as an index of status on scales of
control, success and popularity in these activities:

> I c2/43 We don't really talk to c2/41* much because she is
>   real bossy. Just yesterday we were playing volleyball
>   and she doesn't and she was bossing us around and
>   she tries to act like c2/18*.
> c2/12   c2/32* tries to do better than c2/17 and c2/18*.
>   c2/17 and c2/18* never go down to the bus shed or
>   anywhere to smoke so c2/32* decides to be big and
>   she does.

> II c2/42* c2/28 hangs round with c2/18* and c2/17. Because
>   they are so popular round the school she thinks
>   everyone else likes her too.

c2/18*'s reputation and competence in relations with the
opposite sex were more important than her other outside activities
in determining her status in the class. Boys in the school,
commonly believed that c2/18* was promiscuous. Far from

condemning c2/18* as a moll, the boys considered themselves
fortunate if allowed to associate with her:

>b1/52   If you find c2/18* you're pretty lucky. . . . She is
>supposed to have been to bed with nearly all the
>boys in Grade Eleven and Grade Twelve.

The boys believed that other girls envied c2/18* her relations
with boys:

>b1/58*   Every night c2/18* has a different boy about eighteen.
>b1/28   And she is only about fourteen herself.
>b1/58*   c2/17 is the same. They hang round together.
>Q   How do other girls regard this?
>b1/58*   They are probably jealous.

As a result of the stratification of dating locations, only
classmates with mature sexual interests mixed with c2/18*
outside school. Among such girls, she gained respect and
gratitude for her championing of them when attacked by others:

>c2/46*   When they were at a dance, c2/18* had this argument
>with a girl in Grade Ten. It was just because the
>night before at another dance they were pushing
>c2/27* around and c2/18* did not like that much so
>she got them back for it.

c2/18* discussed these outside activities with her associates in
the classroom. Other girls listened and these activities became
general knowledge:

>c2/45   In the morning c2/18* and c2/17 get together with
>their friends and sometimes other people like me.
>We just listen and she is always talking about how they
>have got a party she goes to at [a hotel known for
>disco and rock dancing, fights and teenage drinking].

The core of c2/18*'s control over the class rested on the
authority due to an acknowledged expert in handling relations
with boys. In exercising this control she displayed a strong
concern for harmonious and caring relations within the class.
Classmates used her as confidante and comforter. Almost any
girls who had any overt degree of sexual interest mentioned
consulting her or having seen her give advice and comfort.
For example:

>c2/25   A boy went away that c2/35 liked and . . . c2/18*
>was prepared to listen and to be kind to her.
>c2/36   If c2/35 is crying she won't talk to anyone but she
>will talk to c2/18*. c2/18* always makes her laugh
>or something.

This concern extended to the class moll. She testified:

> c2/32*   c2/18* is really nice. . . . She just talks to people about their problems and she is just nice to talk to.

c2/18*'s comments on her relations with c2/32* indicate an active care for the sexual outcast:

> c2/18*   c2/32* is nice.
>
> c2/17   She has a lot of problems with boys.
>
> c2/18*   I don't like the way some of the kids in the class act. They are always calling her names, I just don't like that.
>
> c2/17   They don't really mean it. They don't know how much they really hurt because the way they act is pretty childish. . . .
>
> Q   Do you ever try to get the other girls mixing with c2/32*?
>
> c2/18*   I tried to because c2/32* wanted to come around with us for a while and we had her around with us for a couple of days.

c2/18*'s qualifications to give pastoral care were undisputed. However, leadership aspects of affording such care were perceived and resented by the rival aspirant class leader, c2/41*. c2/42*, distressed at the loss of a boyfriend, was, as usual in her class, consoled by c2/18*. c2/41* objected but lost the ensuing fight with c2/18*:

> c2/42*   I was a bit upset about my boyfriend and c2/18* asked me what was wrong and everybody was asking me and I was sick of telling them because every time I got upset about it and c2/41* just told her to leave me alone.
>
> c2/41*   Just in a friendly way.
>
> c2/42*   She did not try to offend her or anything and c2/18* got upset about it and she went off at c2/41* then.
>
> c2/41*   She bashed me one.
>
> c2/42*   She pushed her down the steps . . . and c2/18* was trying to be helpful to me but I did not want anyone . . . but c2/18* is the one that always helps me.

Two spectators attributed the fight specifically to c2/18* wanting control and demanding respect:

> c2/11   c2/42* was upset about her boyfriend and c2/18* saw that she was crying and c2/18* asked what was wrong and c2/42* said to leave her alone and c2/18* said, 'I will do what I like', and they started punching into each other.

Q   Why did c2/41* get so mad?
c2/12   Because c2/41* is real good mates with c2/42* and
         c2/18* just doesn't take talk like that.
Q   Could c2/18* have been trying to help?
c2/11   Yes, she was. She helps them when they are crying.
         She asks them what is wrong with them and tells
         them they can go around with her at lunch time.

Although c2/18* initiated fights herself, she was quick to
prevent fights between other students. When girls began to
label each other sexually she arbitrated in the disputes. For
example:

Q   What sort of names does c2/32* call you?
c2/16*   'Moll' and things like that. She just comes out with it
         and boy! do I feel like fighting her then!
Q   So what happens?
c2/16*   c2/18* and c2/17 tried to get us back together again.
         They don't like fighting and after the lesson we
         made up.

Similarly when another girl derogated a classmate's boyfriend,
c2/18* intervened. Her intervention was hastened by knowing
that it was against a leadership rival:

c2/41*   c2/18* thinks that I am going to take a bit of her
         leadership off her but I wouldn't. For example, if one
         time I said that I did not like somebody's fellow – I
         made that mistake once and she went really against
         me and a big fight. She would thump me a few times
         and I never hit her back. They think that I am
         afraid to fight but I am not.

Other students believed c2/41* had lost the fight:

c2/36   c2/41* came out the worse end of the stick. c2/18*
         went pushing c2/41* down the steps and acting tough.

c2/18*'s sexual sophistication was discreetly displayed through
an armatorium of make-up and jewellery. This included a
friendship ring, perfume, and tunic short enough to denote
sexual awareness and yet not so short as to be condemned for
excessive immodesty.

A powerful boy and intrusive roles
b5/42*'s outside activities paralleled those of c2/18*. Like
c2/18*, he was named the best in the class at sports and
athletics, was said to attend adult parties, and mix with friends
from higher grades during lunch. Like her, only he in his
class had a regular job, but, unlike her, he confined his
generosity to his associates.

These outside interests and statuses were, however, largely
irrelevant to association with classmates. Typically, b5/52*'s
discussion of his sexual interests was of little significance to
classmates:

Q   Does anybody in 9b5 talk about girlfriends?
b5/13   Oh yeah. b5/42* does a bit and so does b5/27.
           Most of the time people keep it to themselves.

Much of b5/42*'s talk about outside activities was dismissed as
'skiting', that is boasting. Classmates did not take it as a
legitimate claim for status:

Q   Anything else people skite about?
b5/31*   b5/42* about parties on the weekend. About shooting.
b5/32*   Wild pigs or something like that.
b5/31*   Or he might be at a hotel or he might be at a party.
           He thinks he's just it.

b5/42* was the outstanding sportsman not only of 9b5 but of
all Grade Nine. He was in the First Football and Cricket sides.
Achievements there would have been exceptional even for a
Grade Twelve student. For example, for the school's First
Cricket Eleven:

b5/42* hit out for 112 Not Out. This [was] the only century
for the school in at least four years. (*School Magazine* 1975: 38)

b5/42*'s associates saw b5/42* as popular. They occasionally
attributed this popularity to sporting achievement. They made
comments like:

I   b5/41*b5/42* is good at footy and that is why everybody
           likes him.

II Q   How much respect do athletes and sportsmen get in
           your class?
    b5/31*I reckon it is more mates. For instance, b5/42* is
           good at cricket and everyone hangs around him.
    Q   Who is everyone?
    b5/31* [Names the sports enthusiasts in b5/42*'s group.]

In fact, even in b5/42*'s group sporting prowess was rarely
mentioned as a reason for association or discussion between
classmates. b5/42* himself placed little emphasis on sporting
ability. He was asked to describe each of his classmates. In
these descriptions of classmates, he uniformly employed
criteria of 'toughness'. He used the indices of power and fighting ability discussed in Chapter 3, and smoking in the school
grounds, truanting and stirring. He did not use sporting
ability.

b5/42*'s sporting prowess was not respected outside his group. It was irrelevant to other classmates who, in any case, disliked his gamesmanship. His leadership in sport was thus granted little legitimacy:

> b5/55*   b5/42* tries to get the ball every time . . . and no one else can get it and when we lose the game because we are kicking the ball to him and the others are getting it and at the end of the game he goes on about how dumb we are doing the things that we done during the game and actually he gets us to do them.

b5/42*'s control of the significance of other activities was also limited to his group. Although not joining in such activities himself, he praised classmates' dangerous and criminal activities. Students outside his group rejected his definition of the situation. For example:

> I Q   What did you think about b5/17 throwing the dart at the kid? [The dart went through the boy's ear.]
> b5/47* It was stupid. . . . b5/42* makes a bit of a hero out of b5/17. He would be the only one. The others just stick by b5/42* but b5/42* would be the one that starts it.

> II Q   Would anyone think that b5/17 was a bit of a hero because he had trouble with the law? [Burglary. His accomplice was gaoled.]
> b5/33 Yeah. b5/42* and some of the kids that don't do it would think that it was smart.

Other boys' classes produced similar findings. In only one other boys' class, 9b1e1, was sporting prowess associated with the dominant clique. It was not important there in signifying or legitimating power. Instead, outside association in sports lent cohesion to the clique.

In all classes, including girls' classes, a few students were derided for cowardliness or awkwardness in sports. To some extent, a minimum level of sporting achievement thus became a condition of power or influence in the classroom. However, in most classes there were students who because of their grossness preferred not to participate in sports but were respected because of fighting ability or 'toughness' shown in other activities.

OMISSIONS AND CONCLUSIONS

The choice of one dimension, however central, and the use of case studies, however illuminating, bias a presentation of the significance of intrusive statuses and associations. The relative strength of intrusive factors in girls' classes has been overstated because such elements as proximity of residence, and primary school of origin, which equally influenced both girls and boys have been ignored.

The significance of sporting activities has been simplified. Boys' perceptions of 'toughness', beside the factors associated with signification of power discussed in Chapters 3 and 4 and participation in sports discussed briefly in this chapter, included a continuum of playground games from impromptu soccer to a violent student-organised game called 'Red Rover'. However, although these games did to a slight extent help to signify power, the correlation between performance in them and the official games with power in the classroom was spurious. Physical strength was a requisite for each. Sporting and athletics participation and prowess in fact has its greatest significance in a girls' class, 9c1, where strongly expressed admiration for swimming and track competitors did not carry over into a wish to associate with them. Instead, commitments to training in lunch time led to sporting stars being isolated from classmates for the same reason as truants tended to be isolated. Students wanted as associates classmates who were available for company.

Even the discussion of manifestations of sexual interest, though extensive, has been simplified. Conspicuous display of evangelical Christian convictions was strongly associated with girls' goody goody status and refusal to join in classroom expressions of sexual interests. The emphasis on sexual interests in explaining the isolation of these students has led to an underemphasis on the part played by other manifestations of evangelical fervour.

Another omission, social class, is theoretically significant. Although important in sociological and educational literature, social class was unimportant in student phenomenology. The rare pretensions to informal status on the basis of social class were strongly rejected by classmates, thus supporting Parsons' (1959) assertion that specific performance values of schooling reduce the importance of ascribed status. Possession of certain skills and material resources was related to parents' prosperity and became a minor source of classroom association and respect. Students sometimes explained a student's behaviour by alluding to a 'poor home'. Classmates attributed the alleged unkempt appearance of conformist low academic status girls to parents' incompetent management of a small income. Male clowns and small but powerful boys were often said to have 'poor homes' with alcoholic fathers.

Far more important than these variables in aggregate is the single dimension of sexual interests. Later chapters will show that female sexual interests are a focus of association and status which transcends such classroom based variables as academic status, commitment, and stirring. Sexual interests are one pole of a particularistic continuum of which the other pole is loyalty to teachers and classroom associates.

Sexually inactive girls tended to form highly cohesive groups which conform closely to teachers' authority. They often tried to establish diffuse and dependent relations with particular teachers. Although making independent assertions of their ideology of behaviour, these girls tended to be defensive in their relations with their sexually active classmates.

Sexually active girls divided according to the maturity of their sexual interests. The mature girls tended to sit at the back of the room, where they formed closed dyads devoted largely to the discussion of their boyfriends. They were potentially influential over other classmates. Sexually active but immature girls formed loose and large groups devoted to the public discussion of their sexual interests. These girls in prestige and influence fell between the sexually mature and the sexually inactive girls.

This chapter has shown that Parsons' account of female value orientations may require revision. Girls have strong particularistic classroom values which shift with increasing maturity from classroom associates and teachers to boys. These particularistic loyalties have diffuse implications for all girls. However, although lack of sexual activity is associated with acceptance of an ascribed inferiority in their relations with teachers, sexual activity and associated statuses are a performance and not an ascriptive dimension. Influential girls, therefore, have a performance rather than a quality value orientation.

Chapter 6

Stirrers and clowns

'Stirring' was defined in Chapter 4 as students' behaviour which annoyed the teacher and entertained the class. This chapter examines stirring under four major headings. The first, discussing boys' perceptions of success and propriety in stirring, argues that it is an important but not central performance dimension. Second, the complex role of clowns is considered. Important themes are that clowns are stirrers who disrespect the position rather than the person of teachers who often share the joke and that clowns' dramatic presentation is a performance dimension. Third, the relationship between male controls and stirring is discussed. Powerful boys are shown to control definitions of proper and successful stirring and to initiate stirring. This last is seen as leadership by classmates. Male clowns are shown to influence the form of stirring used by classmates. However, because control is exercised through influence and not power, classmates do not recognise it as leadership.

Lastly, girls' stirring is examined. It is shown to be less of a performance dimension than boys' stirring, and because girls respect stirring which does not upset the teacher, the roles of good stirrer and clown merge. As a result of girls' association of leadership with influence, classmates regard clowns' influence over stirring as leadership.

MALE STIRRING

Effective stirring
Boys frequently delighted in, and admired effective stirring. They stressed teachers' indignation and classmates' laughter as indices of the success of stirring. For example:

b4/17* b4/38 is a real big stirrer.
b4/18* He gives a lot of cheek to the teacher.
b4/17* They go mad at him and he'll give cheek straight back - just go 'uuuh' [imitation of chimpanzee].
b4/18* We really laugh at him and then the teacher goes mad at him.
        'Right, b4/38. See me at lunch.' [Chimpanzee noise again.] And he pulls a funny face at the teacher. The teacher really hates that.

Within the aura of success attached to stirrers, classmates ranked
the performance of each:

> b4/27   b4/17* stirs real good but he doesn't seem to have
> the quality. In stirring there is a quality you have
> to have. He is just behind b4/31*.
> Q   Tell me more about this quality.
> b4/27   Most people think for a stir you just have to do some-
> thing – that is what you have to do – but b4/31* can
> think it out better than that – what the teacher is
> going to do.

Success in stirring was measured by the strength of teachers'
reactions against the stirrer. Sometimes in the low academic
stream classes, specific types of teachers reaction were tallied.
Harsh teachers' punishments demonstrated the success and the
'toughness' of the stirrer. As a result there was some boasting
about, and competition in, the punishments received:

> b6/13*   b6/10's got one more cut than me so far but I'll catch
> him up. We have a competition to see who can get the
> most cuts.

Success is part of the male definition of 'stirrer'. Boys who
failed in attempts to stir were not defined by classmates as
unsuccessful stirrers. Instead, they were defined as would-be
stirrers. Their failure to achieve the status of stirrer led, as
in the following example, to their being despised by classmates:

> b5/51*   He tries to be a stirrer but he is not. He thinks he
> is.
> b5/41*   He tries to be – put it that way.
> b5/51*   The other day down at the library there was a balloon
> down there and he just blew it up and let it go and
> then he tried to get himself into trouble but nobody
> took any notice of him.

A time and place for stirring
A decision to stir affects the whole class. Each act of stirring
distracts the teacher from presentation of the lesson, diverts
students from work, and risks the class receiving group
punishment. Not all students' priorities are the same. Some wish
to work when others want to stir. Some resent the detentions
and loss of privileges sometimes caused by classmates' stirring.
Thus, the decision to stir is a matter of control or negotiation
among classmates.
    Some students rejected all stirring and all stirrers. These
goody goodies emphasised the absolute strongness of stirring.
They formed well demarcated groups and, whatever the individual goody goody's status in his or her own group, could not
control other classmates' definitions of the proper occasion for

stirring. The goody goodies, like b4/56* in the example below, passively acquiesced in, or intervened impotently against, classmates' decisions to stir:

Q	How do you feel about b4/56* when he turns around and tells people to shut up?
b4/13	He is a nut. I wish he would shut up himself.
b4/37	He thinks he is good. He acts like a teacher, thinks he can tell everyone what to do.

Beyond the goody goody subculture, a working consensus (Hargreaves, 1975: 132-144) defined the propriety of stirring on any occasion. Justification for the decision to stir depended formally on rules relating to losing valued lessons and incurring class punishments. The intending stirrer needed to know if the lesson was valued by associates and dominant classmates. Often associates helped to define the occasion:

c4/56*	You just tell c4/48*, 'Gee - this is boring!' and she will see what she can do to make it unboring.

When stirring was deemed inappropriate it was discouraged:

b2/43	If it gets too noisy I say, 'Aw! Come on, b2/22*', or 'Cut it out, will you? I want to listen.'
b2/44	It all depends how interesting the topic is.

Stirrers who persisted in stirring when others wanted to work were threatened by classmates:

b3/23	Everyone will be trying to do an essay and b3/24* burst out into song or something like this. . . . This is the one thing that really stirs the kids. Really stirs them. In fact he has a threat that . . . they are going to flush him.

Good stirrers as well as knowing when to begin had to know when to stop. Too much stirring led to teachers' punishing classes. Therefore:

b4/27	There is a limit to how much you can stir in the class and once you reach the limit you should not go over it. . . . They will keep going over it and get the whole class into trouble.

Stirrers who knew when to stop were praised:

b2/35*	Not a bad bloke. Pretty good. b2/21*'ll have a joke and that but he doesn't carry things too far. Sometimes they keep stirring and get the rest into trouble but when they say, 'Keep quiet or we'll be

kept in', he just keeps quiet.

Student differentiation and stirring
It was shown above that there was no consensus either on the
general propriety of stirring, or on the proper occasion for it.
At any one time, some students may be stirring and others
watching approvingly or disapprovingly. The distinction between
stirrers and nonstirrers then becomes conspicuous as in the
example below:

b2/22*   Nearly everybody stood up and got on our hands
          and knees and said, 'Hail Mary!' down on our knees.
          The goodies like b2/27 just stood up but we did that.

Class identities and associations tended to follow these general-
ised dichotomies. Students became known by classmates as
stirrers or nonstirrers, and sociometrically distinguished groups
were defined by this variable. Students frequently made comments
like:

Q   b2/56* doesn't seem to get on too well with b2/31?
b2/15   No, because he wants to be a goody goody and they
          want to be a baddy baddy.

Ascription of the epithet 'stirrer' was taken as praise or condemnation according to the values of the student using the term:

b1/17*   If you say he is a stirrer when all his friends are
          around him then it is for him. For people who like to
          stir it is for him but if they are people who don't
          like to stir it is against him.

However, an element of status in the term 'stirrer' was absent
from most descriptions of the nonstirrer:

Q   When people call you a 'stirrer', how do you feel?
b1/47   It says there is a bit of life to the fellow.

Nonstirrers attributed stirrers high though illegitimate control
status. For example:

b4/46*   b4/31* acts as if he owns the place.
Q   Why do you say 'he acts as if he owns the place'?
b4/46*   He gives the teachers disrespect. He answers the
          teachers back.

Conversely stirrers like b4/13 in the example below tended
to speak of nonstirrers as nonentities:

b4/13   The class is divided into two groups really: the
          active kids - all the kids jumping around the place -

and the ones especially down the front, the dull ones,
they just sit there not asleep. They work hard.
They probably work harder than any of us up the
back.

The image of goody goodies as subordinate is compounded by
other students merging the categories of goody goody and would-
be stirrer:

Q	How does a goody goody behave?
b3/42	They are real good in every period bar English and then they are sort of the big top stirrers and they really stir Mr Swinburne but when we have Mr Euclid for maths they sit up and talk to each other.
b3/41	Mr Euclid is real strict and they are not game to do anything with him.

CLASS CLOWNS

Prevalence and theoretical considerations
In the high stream classes, 9b131, 9b2, 9b3e2, 9c1 and 9c2 were
found 'clowns'. These were students whose joking was enjoyed
by both students and teachers. The clown has an 'asymmetrical
joking relationship' with teachers (Woods, 1976). The asymmetry
of the relationship is shown in the clown's joking at the teacher's
expense and the teacher's acceptance of 'the teasing good
humouredly but without retaliating'. Although there were only
one or two clowns in each class their presence was reported
enthusiastically and frequently by classmates.
    The next section describes students' perception of the clowns'
relations with the teacher, and the clowns' relations with classmates. Clowning is shown to be a performance dimension which
extends into clowns' relations with their peers. Likenesses and
differences between male and female clowns, which include the
differential attribution of control status to clowns by classmates, are elaborated later in the chapter under the topic of
'stirring and control'.

Male clowns
Boys did not rigorously define the activities of clowns as
either stirring or mucking around. They included clowns in
their lists of stirrers. However, when elaborating reasons for
nominating students as stirrers, boys distinguished between
core stirrers and class clowns. Clowns, such as b3/46* and
b2/21* in the discussion below, were called 'stirrers', but
their activity was termed 'mucking around'. The disrespect
shown to teachers was, like stirring, public and intended as
a joke. Unlike stirring, clowns' disrespect was not intended to
annoy the teacher, but to entertain him as well as the class.
The clowns' interaction with affable teachers allowed them to

translate academic work into joke. This joking extended to licence in their presentation of stories and poems:

I b3/12   We have to make up a poem but what b3/46* does do, he makes up all these dirty jokes and he reads them out in class.

II Q   Who are the most amusing of the stirrers?
  b2/31   b2/21*. He's really funny when he does a poem or something like that, swearing and mucking around, nothing like what the other kids do.

The clowns' self-presentation was consciously dramatic. Their joking carried over into what was acknowledged by teachers and students to be considerable acting ability. This ability earned them respect both for 'gameness', willingness to perform under conditions that daunted classmates, and for their humour:

I b2/35*   b2/21* is willing to make a fool of himself.
  b2/36   And he will go, 'I can act' and he will get up and act and do all these stupid things and you can't help laughing at him.

II b3/31   b3/46* and b3/45* are not chicken. They will get out and do it. When I put that play on they were acting two dogs in front of a whole hall of people.

The clowns took drama seriously. In choosing the cast they went outside their circle of friends to select the classmates they considered best for the parts. This was a rare instance of students departing from the mateship consideration usually evoked by sociometric work criteria. For example:

Q   b3/41 is not one of your normal mates, is he?
b3/46*   No.
Q   How came he to be doctor in your play?
b3/46*   He is just that type of person. Like you try out different people to see who is best and then you pick the best out.

Other students respected the care taken in choosing the cast and the authority used in directing the play:

I b3/22   b3/46* usually picks the ones he wants in his play. He knows their character and he picks out the one that will do best.

II b3/41   b3/46* wants to take over all the time. . . . He wants to make it up and everything and you have to do what he says or else he gets real cranky.

Classmates tended to discuss and encourage the clowns' comic dramatic presentations. However, the clowns' genuine concern with drama is shown by their equal attention to serious roles:

I   b3/23   b3/46* isn't all laughs. He can do a serious play if he wants to.

II Q   Who would you have in your play?
    b2/35* b2/21* is good because he carries on and exaggerates like there's no one else around, pretty good actually, get a good laugh out of him.
    b2/31   He can do a good job and not muck around when it's serious.

Clowns also have a joking relation with classmates. This allowed clowns to exploit classmates in ways that would be strongly resented in other students. Tricks were excused by classmates and even by the victims, such as b3/47 and b3/48 in the example below, on the grounds that the clowns were 'mad' and so not responsible for their actions:

b3/48   I lent b3/46* a rubber which I had just bought for 10¢ and he gave it back to me in about ten thousand pieces. He just cut it up into pieces.

b3/47   A little bit ago I lent b3/46* a protractor and he broke it and I told him to repay it and he said, 'Next day'.

b3/48   Every day b3/46* and b3/45* muck around and they will say, 'Ah, broke it', and you go up to him and he will say the other bloke broke it. It's endless.

b3/47   They need to get their heads smacked in.

Q   Do they get their heads smacked in?

b3/47   Not really – for a joke like. The other blokes will.

b3/48   A couple of times they have had a serious little punchup.

b3/47   But they go around cheeking everybody. They call you, 'Punkarse'.

b3/48   'Punkarse' and 'dickhead' and all this.

b3/47   And then you smack their head.

Q   Who has given them a really solid smack in the head?

b3/48   Not a really good smack in the head, but they get irritating after a while.

b3/47   But they cannot help it because they are mad.

b3/48   They go too far actually. But they are good blokes.

An unpleasant part of the clowns' life is the reciprocal of the licence given them. All that happens to them is defined as a joke. Clowns complained during the interviews of receiving physical and verbal abuse:

b3/45*   I don't like being called 'Ears' and that sort of thing.

> . . . They all say it. Whenever they see me they say,
> 'Elephant Ears' and all that. Whenever they hear the
> word 'Ears' in a play or anything they always say,
> 'b3/45*', all the time, 'b3/45*, b3/45*, b3/45*.'

All the clowns were relatively powerless. They could do little
to resist this bullying:

b2/21*   b2/38's a big bully. He pushes b2/31 and me around,
         thinks he can flatten us.
Q   Can he?
b2/21*   No!
Q   Why haven't you taken him on?
b2/21*   Cos I'm scared.

Clowns' lack of power does not entail low control status. The
next section of this chapter shows that clowns strongly influence
classmates.

STIRRING AND CONTROL

Acknowledged ability as stirrer and control status were closely
related. Only dominant students were very successful as
stirrers. Moderately powerful boys and moderately influential
girls tended to become moderately successful stirrers, with
the humour, effect or timing of their stirring occasionally
challenged by classmates. However, a few dominant students
did not stir, although they controlled the course of stirring.
This section argues that a correlation of control and stirring
status is largely determined by dominant students' definition
of the situation and selective activation of norms governing
stirring.
   The relationship between clowning, control and stirring is
then examined. It is shown that clowns' techniques are copied
by other stirrers and that the position of clowns depends on
sponsorship by powerful classmates.

Power and stirrers
Powerful students largely controlled stirring. They did this by
evaluating classmates' stirring and defining the proper time to
stir. Powerful students' evaluation of stirring allowed them to
shape the stirring of classmates. For example, powerful students
such as b4/31* coached associates' stirring:

b4/31*   b4/22 likes to think he is in all the stirring but he
         is a bit of a chicken really. . . . You say, 'Here,
         b4/22, you can throw this plane' and he says, 'No'.
         And then you hoick it and then he will go around
         telling everyone that we hoicked planes, you know.
Q   He lets you do all the hard work?

b4/31*   Yes, but lately he has been joining in. Like the other
          day I said to him, 'You are a bit of a chicken' and
          he doesn't like you thinking he is a bit of a chicken
          so he picks one up and he hoicks it.

Classmates accepted powerful students' definition of the proper
time to stir. The powerful stirrers' inception of stirring indicated that the time was right:

b4/24   b4/31* is the ringleader. Like if he does something
          everybody else will join in. Oh yeah, b4/31*'s in it -
          but if b4/21 or b4/33 or them want to do something
          and they do it then b4/31* won't join in and so some
          of the others won't join in.

When the proper time for stirring was disputed, powerful
students imposed a definition on weaker students. For example:

Q   Does anyone annoy you when they stir?
b5/42*   Down at woodwork when it is time to tidy up and
          they don't tidy up. You want to get out for dinner
          pretty quickly so you get around and you might
          give them a chop on the neck and tell them to get
          a move on.

Powerful students had well-developed ideologies of stirring to
reinforce their control. In the case of b5/42* the ideology related
to the utility of the lesson:

b5/42*   Me a stirrer? Put it this way you are neither
          interested in a subject or you are not interested in a
          subject and I am not particularly interested in science
          and cit. ed. because I reckon that when you go up
          for an apprenticeship, you don't need them.

In subjects they valued b5/42* and his seatmate did what they
considered sufficient work and then began to stir:

b5/41*   We get a fair amount of work done. We go flat out
          half the period and when we get ahead we stop and
          then we just muck around.
Q   What sort of mucking around do you do?
b5/41*   Mostly we stir the teachers.

Powerful stirrers' ideologies occasionally justified stirring
independently of less powerful students' initial definitions of
the situation. For example:

Q   How has b4/31* improved on acqaintance?
b4/27   I started to hang round with the group that b4/31*
          is in and we just started to know each other better.

> Like if you don't know a person very well, if they
> stir a lot you think they must be a real bad person
> but if you know them really well you know that they
> only stir for a certain reason.

When the stirrer, as with b2/22*, only aspires to high power,
he may enforce the proper time for stirring and escape enforcement against himself of an alternative definition. b2/22*'s efforts
in the following example lent a spurious legitimacy to his stirring
although his classmates were more vocal against him than against
truly dominant stirrers:

b2/56*   b2/22*'s queer that way. Like we'd be playing sport
         and if anybody gets us kept in he goes through them,
         bashes into them, but he's got us kept in more times
         than anybody else.

Subordinate students' objections to being kept in for dominant
classmates' stirring were discounted whatever the individual loss.
For example, b4/51 who 'laughs queer like a girl' and 'doesn't
like to get detentions' had his complaints disregarded when the
imposed consensus was that the stirring was enjoyable and the
class not losing overall by the detention:

b4/18*   If we get kept in for four or five minutes at lunch
         and everybody makes noise in the four or five minutes
         b4/51 turns around real angry like he really scares
         you, 'Shut up!' So we make a really loud noise and
         he's like this, nearly bursting into tears.

The influence of male clowns on stirring
Not all teachers enjoyed clowns' jokes. When the teacher made
evident his displeasure, the clowning turned into stirring. One
teacher who did not like a clown's jokes commented:

> 'b2/21*'s the real attention seeker in the class. The real
> funny man out the front. I'll give him a funny joke sooner
> or later.'

Typically, b2/21* reciprocated the teachers' rejection of him by
translating his good humoured clowning into serious stirring.
His techniques were generally imitated by classmates. He thus
controlled stirring through influence. This influence was
acknowledged by classmates. Nonetheless, as the following
quotation illustrates, because b2/21* used influence rather than
the sex-proper control mechanism, power, he was not named as
leader. Instead, his more powerful seatmate, b2/22*, who
emulated his techniques of stirring, was said to be the leader:

b2/56*   Mr Watts was hitting b2/21* one day and he got
         up and put his hands over his head and he said, 'Get

away, you big black dog.' That's a saying now in
our class. It seems as soon as b2/21* says something,
everyone copies him. b2/21* was the first to stand
up to Mr Watts and it got to be the thing to do.
[b2/56* gives another example of a technique of
stirring initiated by b2/21*.] As soon as b2/21*
does something most of the kids copy him. They can't
think up their own ideas. . . . Everyone copies
b2/21* but you couldn't say he was the real leader.
. . .

Q   Why not a leader if the others copy him?
b2/45   He doesn't actually lead. b2/22* seems to be the big
           bossy type. b2/21* just follows along. He's the ideas
           man.

Power and male would-be clowns

Failure to achieve status as a clown causes the would-be clown
severe problems. Assertion of a claim to be clown involves an
attempt to suspend norms governing respect for classmates and
relations with teachers. Failure to have this claim acknowledged
led to the activation of these norms against the would-be clown.
The following section describes two cases where would-be clowns
failed because they lacked sponsorship by powerful classmates.

b1/45* was typical of students who achieved limited recognition
as a clown. He belonged to a cohesive but relatively powerless
group. His associates named him the class clown:

b1/56   b1/45*'s the class clown, a real good actor. He always
           takes what the teachers say in a different way.
Q   Do the teachers get uptight?
b1/56   No. They know he's pretty good at work. They
           usually say to be quiet and laugh.

The English subject teacher shared the definition of b1/45* as
a clown:

'An extreme extrovert, always happy, always jovial, always
has something funny to say which could never be interpreted
as being objectionable although he is outspoken all the time.'

b1/45*'s subordinate status interacting with the teacher granting
him privilege as a clown led to b1/45* being condemned by
dominant classmates, in a manner described in Chapter 8, for
currying teachers' favour:

b1/35   b1/17* and b1/45* are the crawlers of the class.
b1/21   Every time we get a teacher they try to act good and
           they try to get pets and that annoys everyone in the
           class.

A similar relationship existed in 9b5 where b5/58 had established a joking relationship with some teachers. For example:

b5/55*   Like b5/58 says about Mr Plato's car, 'That old scrap
          heap! Why don't you take it off to the dump yard
          and leave it there?' things like that. . . . Mr Plato
          doesn't mind b5/58 going on like this.

Dominant classmates gave this incipient clowning relationship
between student and teacher an alternate definition. They saw
b5/58 as a 'teacher's pet', or unjustified teacher's favourite, a
status discussed at length in Chapter 10:

b5/17   b5/58 is the teacher's pet. . . . He will take things
         and then the teacher is looking for them and he will
         go out and get them and chat up the teacher. He
         does it on purpose. He will just walk in the room,
         grab the duster or the chalk and hide them and the
         teacher will come in and look around for them and
         b5/58 will start laughing and then will go out and
         get them and give them back.

b5/58 was judged not as a clown but by the standards of core
stirring. He was thus seen as a failure, a would-be stirrer:

I b5/31* b5/58 thinks he is a real big stirrer but he is a bit
           of a dickhead.

II b5/42* He tries to. He thinks that he can stir but he can't.

GIRLS' STIRRING

Girls' definitions of stirring resembled boys' definitions. Stirring,
however, was less of a performance dimension. The criterion of
effectiveness was irrelevant to girls' categorisation of stirrers.
Thus girls interpreted the questions, 'Who are the stirrers in
your class?' and 'Who tries to stir in your class?' as equivalent.
No phenomenologically based category of would-be or failed
stirrer emerged.

Girls' and boys' stirring also differed in that girls were often
concerned for the feelings of teachers. The stirrer who avoided
hurting teachers received greater respect than the stirrer who
hurt teachers. The highly influential student, c2/18*, for
example, was distinguished by this criterion from another stirrer
in her class:

Q   What's the difference between c2/18*'s and c2/28's
         kind of stirring?
c2/36   c2/18* is funny.
c2/25   c2/18* is kind, careful not to hurt people. c2/28 is
         always hurting people.

Concern for the feelings of teachers led to a merger in girls'
classes of the roles of clown and respected stirrer. Classmates
named c2/18* both as clown and stirrer. Her most admired acts
of stirring resembled the jokes of a male clown rather than the
acts of a male stirrer. For example:

c2/36   c2/18* is a pretty big stirrer. . . . Another day
         c2/18* was lying on the ground over the side where
         the desks are there and she was lying down with the
         ports [students' suitcases] around her so that Mrs
         Wolfe couldn't see and she says, 'Where's c2/18*?' and
         they said, 'She's up in the sickroom'; and half the
         lesson was over before she came out and she was
         just hiding there and then she got up.
Q   What did Mrs Wolfe say?
c2/36   Usually Mrs Wolfe just laughs.

As with other clowns, c2/18*'s stirring changed quickly when
she disliked a teacher. An example of her stirring to annoy
teachers is discussed in Chapter 10 under the topic of students'
definitions of teachers' victimisation of students.

c2/18* influenced classmates' stirring and definitions of
stirring. It is evidence of the sex-propriety and effectiveness
of influence as a control in girls' classes that this influence was
seen by classmates as constituting leadership and control. Her
techniques of stirring were imitated with varying success:

c2/14   You know how c2/18* stands up and cheeks back.
         Some kids use exactly the same words that c2/18*
         uses trying to be like c2/18*. c2/18* gets a lot of
         attention when she speaks and everyone looks at
         her as if they are paying attention to her and
         everybody else thinks that they are going to get
         attention if they try to.

c2/18* imposed a consensus of the value of her stirring even on
her rivals for class leadership whose private perceptions
differed:

c2/41*   It's funny.
c2/42*   It's silly really. 'If people stopped laughing at her
         she would stop,' Mrs Wolfe and other teachers often
         say to us.
         It's just that she likes to have attention.
c2/41*   And we agree. But I don't want to get on the bad
         side of c2/18*.

Stirring was less important among girls than among boys.
Where the importance of stirring among boys was shown by the
definition of groups according to commitment to and success in

stirring, the unimportance of stirring among girls is shown by the lack of groups formed around this criterion. c2/18*, for example, received support for her stirring and clowning from her seatmate. However, the other three girls associating frequently with her were conspicuous in that class for their opposition or indifference to her stirring and clowning. They only conditionally supported her stirring and were often critical:

c2/27*   If it is stupid what they are saying then we [tell them to shut up] but if it is not then we play around too.

Classmates were aware of the five friends' heterogeneous class-room behaviour. Their cohesion was explained by the outside activities they shared. For example:

c2/41*   c2/27* is shy, doesn't talk much in class. The shy one in that group, that is c2/18*, c2/17, c2/28 and her.

Q   How does she fit into that group if she is shy?

c2/41*   Because they all go out together.

c2/42*   They are not spoilt but they are allowed out. Their parents are fairly outgoing so the whole four of them when they go out, they are all together. . . .

c2/41*   c2/27* is always on the good side of the teacher. She does all her work.

c2/42*   Even with her mates who are not in good with the teacher, she is always on the teacher's side and she will try and tell her friends to keep quiet.

CONCLUSIONS

This chapter has examined two performance dimensions which challenge the dependence of students on teachers, and provide arenas for control and signification of high status by dominant students. Stirrers and would-be stirrers with varying success and humour assault teachers' pretensions to control over students. Clowns assert the common humanity of students and teachers by providing jokes at which both can laugh. These jokes free students from the prescriptions which normally mark their relations with teachers.

Stirring and clowning have, beside their focus on the teacher, important functions within the peer group. Successful stirring draws the favourable attention of their classmates to the stirrers. Powerful boys govern the occasion and significance of stirring, and use this control to monopolise proper and successful stirring. Definitions of clowning are less directly related to boys' power. None the less, acceptance of a student as clown requires sponsorship by powerful classmates.

The sex propriety of power as a male control is demonstrated
in the role of clown. The male clown's use of influence, which
includes promulgation of techniques of stirring and the suspen-
sion of power in their relations with classmates, is not recognised
by their male classmates as leadership.

Distinctive patterns of girls' stirring and clowning reflect
distinctive female values. Stirring, which boys define unambigu-
ously as a performance dimension, is less important among
girls, less likely to be defined as a performance dimension, and,
when present, more likely to take on the particularistic, diffuse
and influence creating aspects of clowning. Because of the sex
propriety of using influence as a control, clowns' exercise of
control through influence is recognised by their female classmates as leadership.

Chapter 7

Teacher authority and student control

This chapter examines ways in which students invoke or are delegated teacher authority. It first describes how students invoke and use teacher authority by informing on classmates. It then shows how students use authority which teachers delegate to them under two sets of circumstances: to the class captain in the absence of teachers, and to class officers elected in class elections. Each is examined to show how subordinate students try to use teacher authority to curb dominant classmates and dominant students use teacher authority to augment their control. It is shown that dominant students' control of norms and definitions of situations legitimates their use of teacher authority but stigmatises subordinate students' attempts to use this authority.

INVOKED TEACHER AUTHORITY

'Dobbing' is a Goldtown student term which means 'informing teachers of an offence committed by a classmate', 'telling the teacher if somebody has done something wrong'. Sociological analyses of dobbing in schools and related concepts in similar institutions suggest that categorical norms forbid the practice (Sykes, 1958; Tempest, 1950: 14; Waller, 1965: 110; Willis, 1977). The most recent analysis of dobbing describes almost reverently:

> . . . a universal taboo among informal groups on the yielding of incriminating information about others to those with formal power. Informing contravenes the essence of the informal group. . . . It is only by getting someone to 'grass' - forcing them to break the solemnest taboo - that the primacy of the formal organisation can be maintained. . . . But whoever has done the 'grassing' becomes special, weak and marked. There is a massive retrospective and ongoing reappraisal amongst 'the lads' of the fatal flaw in his personality which had always been immanent but not fully disclosed till now. (Willis, 1977: 24-25)

Goldtown students abstractly condemned dobbing. It was considered disloyal to classmates: 'Why should I dob them in? They're my mates, aren't they?' was a common response. A wide range of sanctions was said to be used against dobbers. Students feared being beaten up, ostracism and other punishments. They commented that 'she would fight with me', 'he could have killed me', and, 'you get gangbanged if you do usually'. Students often proceeded to condemn a specific dobber or act of dobbing. Mitigating circumstances were considered irrelevant:

c4/56*   [The deputy principal] said that she had to tell him. Well, she told him and I wouldn't have. I would just have kept my mouth shut. You know he can't force you. He can't kill you or anything like they used to in wars and things like that so I just wouldn't have said anything.

None the less, it was clear that on some occasions dobbing was generally practised and approved:

b3/32   When there is a kid they know is there and they wag [truant] the whole class dobs in and they yell out.

The following section explores the contradictions between the categorical imperative against dobbing and the practice. It shows how students use a set of.rules, outlined in Figure 7.1, to determine the acceptability of acts of dobbing. The discussion below first examines students' arguments that specific acts of informing are not dobbing, then the arguments used to justify what is admittedly dobbing, and lastly looks at the consequences of unjustified dobbing.

'Dobbing as a joke'
Students often claimed that an act of informing was just 'dobbing as a joke' and therefore 'not really dobbing'. Dobbing as a joke, unlike real dobbing, gave credit to the student responsible. The student who dobbed in as a joke was often mucking around. The dobbing was then part of a friendly interaction between peers.
   There was almost always some tension in the claim to be dobbing as a joke. Although dobbing as a joke might stir the teacher, it also involved giving teachers information which extended their control. Although dobbing as a joke was an act of mucking around, of association between friends, it could also involve unpleasant consequences for the friend dobbed in. These tensions in the definition of particular acts of dobbing were met in three ways: one lay in the normative pattern of relations between associates, another lay in the structure of control in peer interaction which allowed certain students to define when dobbing was real or a joke, and a third lay in the privileged position of clowns.
   The last chapter showed that clowns were free from many normative restraints. Abuse of peer norms governing relations with their classmates and teachers were defined by classmates as 'a joke', which enhanced rather than detracted from their standing in the class. This privilege extended to a freedom to

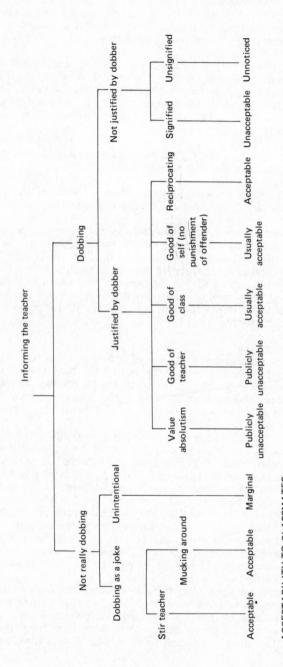

Figure 7.1 Normative structure of dobbing

dob arbitrarily, and still to be seen as dobbing as a joke. One student complained bitterly of the use of this privilege by b2/21* and another clown:

b3/33   If someone did something wrong he would be off to tell the teacher straightaway him and b2/21*. They would go right down and tell [the principal] and yet they would be doing things which were wrong at the time. No one dobbed them in and they get out of everything and if someone did something wrong – even if you just pushed them off the chair. I had a shanghai [small catapult] in my case one day and they dobbed. Down to [the principal] I went. They just thought it was funny. They can dob on everyone else and no one dobs them in.

A more general pattern of definition of dobbing as a joke was to be seen to be stirring the teacher. Dobbing as a joke was an effective way of stirring teachers. The teacher was often unaware of the offence or had been pragmatically ignoring it (cf. Hargreaves et al., 1975: 217-251). The teacher now had to choose between condoning a signified offence or intervening moralistically at the behest of a stirrer and thereby interrupting the lesson. For example:

b1/46   b1/51 is always dobbing people in for chewing gum or anything he notices. . . . He is always looking around the class and all of a sudden he will burst out, 'So and so is chewing gum, sir!' and if the teacher pretends he doesn't hear he will keep on saying and saying it.

The stirrer as dobber remained almost immune from teachers' wrath because of formal compliance with teachers' rules.

Dobbing was also used as a joke between friends. This dobbing, like the example described below, caused the friend some inconvenience. However, it did not lead to the teacher punishing the student dobbed in:

b1/24*   b1/31 often has a cake or something like this and you will yell out at the top of your voice, 'What are you eating, b1/31?' or something like this. You never do it seriously. You just do it for mucking around, getting into trouble. It is never done with me, other than with a friend. You are just joking at them.

Even between students of equal control status there was some doubt as to when dobbing was a joke and when it was serious because of overuse or too unpleasant consequences. The possibility of dobbing as a joke depended on sharing or imposing a definition of a joke. Successful imposition of the definition of dobbing as a joke 'all depends if they're big fellows and you can beat 'em or not'. Dominant students defined as serious any dobbing against them, whether the dobber intended it as a joke or not. For example, the dominant group in 9b5, b5/42* and his friends, imposed dobbing, which was defined as a joke, on their subordinate classmates. When one such subordinate classmate, b5/26*, attempted to reciprocate in a manner routinely taken as a joke, b5/42* denied the joke. He then punished the subordinate student with reciprocal dobbing which was intended and defined as having serious consequences:

b5/52   b5/26* had dobbed in b5/51* for eating peanuts in school, just to stir up – he says, 'Give us a peanut, b5/51*.'

b5/42*   He yelled out topnote across the classroom, 'b5/51*, put those peanuts away'. So he's a dickhead and so I had to see [the deputy principal] so I told him that b5/26* had [cigarettes] and I knew I was dobbing but I did not mind dobbing because I don't like him. You don't like dobbing on a person – if he was just caught passing peanuts across to him I wouldn't mind – but he makes you sick.

Unintended and indirect informing

Students sometimes claimed that they were not dobbing if they did not give both full and direct information to the teacher. They might tell the teacher of an offence without naming the offender, or, as in the example below, they might without telling the teacher directly name both the offence and the offender:

b2/57   b2/22* doesn't really dob people in but behind their backs. He says real loud, 'oh, so-and-so, what d'you do that for?'. Like he doesn't put his hand up and dob them in.

The permissibility of indirect dobbing did not extend to failure to conceal or deny the significance of incriminating evidence. Students like b5/51*, who without telling the teacher betrayed evidence of an offence, were condemned:

b5/47*   When I hit b5/51* he cried . . . and I got into trouble about him. He went blubbing. He put blood all over his face so the teacher could see.

Classmates usually rejected claims that the dobber was not responsible for information reaching the teacher. Dominant students dobbed openly and straightforwardly 'as a joke', and did not plead indirectness. Indirect dobbing also occurred frequently with failure to hide the evidence of a fight. Again it was always subordinate students who were guilty. Thus, the plea of no responsibility for dobbing was always associated with subordinate status. Such pleas were therefore frequently ineffective and taken as a sign of subordinate status.

Justified dobbing

Moralistic dobbing Under this topic is discussed dobbing intended to maintain either an absolute value, the good of the teacher, or the good of the class. Usually it was performed by subordinate students on dominant classmates. Dominant students who held moralistic principles enforced them directly and did not summon teacher aid. As a result although the dobbing could be justified among a minority, it, with the exception of dobbing for the good of the class, was never backed by a general student consensus.

In the case of value absolutism, the student wished to impose his sense of what was right, independently of what was accept-able to classmates. However, discretion ensured that these goody goodies either kept their dobbing secret or refrained from it. In the following example, the dobbers privately justified the dobbing. None the less, they were concerned that they would be condemned if it became generally known that they were the dobbers:

> c4/44* It was too awful!
> c4/43* And we told [the deputy principal] . . .
> Q   Who told?
> c4/44* I did and c4/53 and c4/54. I was a bit scared and I really didn't want to and I've never done it before but c4/53 said, 'It's gone too far!' So we came down after class. But that's our secret and [the deputy principal] just took down their names and said he would see them [c4/47* and c4/48*] afterwards.

The second example is of a subordinate goody goody who, although wanting to, felt unable to dob:

> b5/55* I have caught b5/41* and b5/42* a couple of times smoking. When I have gone home and you know when you are waiting to go to sleep you wish that you could have dobbed them in and tell [the deputy principal] about them and say to him not to tell who it was.
> Q   Why do you wish that you could dob them in?
> b5/55* Because it is wrong. They shouldn't be doing it.

Students also dobbed to avoid collective punishment of their class. As Chapter 6 showed, students whose behaviour resulted in classmates' loss of privileges or punishment became unpopular. Classes were commonly punished when a teacher thought a serious offence had been committed and did not know the identity of the culprit. In these circumstances, classmates blamed the offender for not owning up to the teacher:

b5/42*　He thinks he can stir but he is the person that starts
off and he doesn't know how to finish. He gets the
class into trouble and he doesn't own up.

Failure to own up often provoked dobbing which, though covert,
was generally supported by classmates. For example:

Q　　　　Have you ever dobbed anyone?
b2/13　　Yes, once [details] . . . . I thought why should we all
suffer when there was only one person involved with
the stupid idea. It was b1/38 who did it.

The outcome of this kind of justified dobbing changed when a
dominant student failed to own up. In the following example,
the influential student c2/18* did not own up to an offence
which led to group punishment. This initially justified her subordinate classmates dobbing her in:

c2/25　　There was some food thrown out of the window.
c2/18* and c2/17 are always eating apples and [the
deputy principal] came in and said to c2/18*, 'Have
you been eating apples and throwing them out of the
window?' and c2/18* said, 'No.' Anyway these three
other girls in our class went out and told on them
because they did throw the stuff out and our class
was going to get detention the next lunch hour.

The deputy principal's punishment of her class placed c2/18*
in a quandary:

c2/18*　I felt pretty terrible when [the deputy principal] came
up and asked me who it was but I wasn't going to say
it was me.
Q　　　　Why did you feel terrible?
c2/18*　Because he threatened to keep the whole class in for
the rest of the week or something and I felt real
guilty.

Being dobbed in extricated c2/18* from pressure to own up.
Usually hostile rivals for leadership helped her discover the
informers:

Q　　　　How did you hear about c2/24* and her friends dobbing
you?
c2/18*　. . . We didn't ask anyone. They just told us. c2/41*.
c2/17　　Yeah and c2/42*.

Armed with this information, c2/18* activated commitments
against dobbing:

I c2/25　c2/18* and c2/17 kept making faces in class and

muttering 'dobber', 'pimp'. . . .

II c2/14 When c2/18* and c2/17 were asked by Mrs Tennyson why they were late, 'We were kept in' and they looked at the girls who did it and said, 'c2/24* knows. You ask her why we were kept in.'

Students, following activation of commitments against dobbing and deactivation of commitments against incurring class punishments, joined in blaming the dobbers:

Q   How did you feel when you heard that they had dobbed c2/17 and c2/18* in?
c2/15   A bit upset because you know, we don't usually dob in our class. We like to keep it to ourselves if we do something.

Apart from the dobbers, the most consistent opposition to c2/18*'s selective activation of commitments came from her associates. Three out of four of these associates critically evaluated both factions:

c2/38   It was bad because c2/24* dobbed in c2/18* but actually I don't think c2/18* should have thrown the rubbish out of the window in the first place.

This opposition illustrates how girls' groups can withstand dissensus on apparently key classroom based issues. The finding lends itself to an interpretation of the female group as cohering because members share diffuse outside interests and associated loyalties whose importance overrides classroom specific disputes.

Justification for self-interested dobbing Two sets of circumstances legitimated dobbing by students in their own interest. They could dob to obtain the return of equipment necessary for schoolwork or to reciprocate earlier acts of real dobbing.
A cause of student conflict was borrowing and not returning classmates' possessions when needed. Between equals dobbing to obtain return of such belongings was justified and teachers were not seen to punish the offenders significantly:

b4/57   A lot of us would dob if someone took a book or something like that. We might just tell the teacher but he doesn't get into strife. He just gets a talking from the teacher and you get the book back.

However, attempts of subordinate students, like b5/55*, to regain their property were condemned as dobbing:

Q   Can you think of a time when b5/55* has dobbed someone in?
b5/31* In technical drawing mainly. Like we would be getting

the lend of his rubber or something and he will sing
out to the teacher, 'Sir! Sir! He has annoyed me' . . .
when all we do is keep his rubber.

Dobbing was also permissible when reciprocating a previous
act of dobbing. This was seen earlier in the chapter to occur
when subordinate students dobbed in dominant classmates as a
joke and the definition of a joke was not accepted by the dominant
students. However, the right to reciprocate dobbing was, as in
the case below, generally recognised:

b3/26*   b3/12 might wag a class, or he used to once or twice,
          and b3/24* said, 'b3/12 is away, sir', and b3/12
          got into trouble. It works both ways too. b3/24*
          wagged and we told. b3/24* didn't like that.

The dobbers
This section examines the signification of students as dobbers.
It does so by analysing the circumstances in which dobbers were
signified and the students who labelled them. At the same time,
for contrast, the unjustified and unsignified dobbing by dominant students is also examined. It is shown that in boys' classes,
where these kinds of dobbing most frequently occur, boys who
dob because they are otherwise powerless are most likely to be
signified as dobbers, but that powerful boys can dob with
impunity.

Students generally preferred to settle arguments personally
rather than by invoking teacher intervention. Students with
moderate levels of power or influence, like b6/15 in the following
example, used that power or influence and did not risk stigmatisation as dobbers:

b6/9   When they call b6/15, 'boong' and 'coon', he doesn't
         like that.
b6/5   Like he thumps them and they wonder why they got
         hit when they say that sort of thing.
b6/9   I suppose he would rather hit them than pimp [dob]
         because then he would be in real trouble with them.

Those students who substituted dobbing for influence or power
were usually condemned as dobbers:

c3/32*   I don't like dobbing. I just reckon it is a cheap way
         of getting back. If you want to get them back then
         you should come back and slap them down.

Dominant students' serious dobbing of classmates sometimes
remained unsignified and unjustified. Classmates tended not to
notice dominant students' culpable dobbing. The contrast
between the signification of dominant and subordinate students'
culpable dobbing is shown most strongly by those occasions when

dominant students committed their own unsignified dobbing in the same sequence of actions as they signified subordinate students' culpable dobbing. The following quotation describes sanctions brought to bear by a very powerful student, b6/13*, against a subordinate classmate, b6/4, for dobbing. The narrator mentions incidentally while describing the reactions to the dobbing that b6/13* also dobbed but does not signify the act. The result is that although b6/13*'s dobbing has serious consequences for classmates, he remains untypified as a dobber even while he typifies and sanctions b6/4 as a dobber:

b6/15   b6/4 got a bit stirred and started crying and he went up to [the deputy principal] and told him and [the deputy principal] wanted to see b6/10 and b6/22 and they got into trouble. [The deputy principal] said if we do it again we will get the cuts and after that b6/13* and b6/22 and a few others wanted to get b6/4 and they were going to bash him up and they told him. b6/13* followed b6/4 down the road and b6/4 was getting scared and the next day he told [the deputy principal] again and [the deputy principal] came down and asked what was going on that afternoon. b6/13* said that b6/7 was going to bash up b6/4.

Indeed, b6/13* admitted that, under pressure from the deputy principal, he dobbed his classmates in with serious consequences for them:

b6/13*   The deputy principal came down and he threatened to thump us unless we said where b6/10 and them were and we said, 'They're wagging it', and he said, 'I know this much,' and then I said, 'I know more but I won't tell you because then I will get a biff in the ear from b6/10' and [the deputy principal] said, 'I'll straighten you out, if you don't tell me,' and then everybody else started to tell.

b6/10   And so they told him where we were and he came over and gave us four cuts.

Certain students were seen to dob for little or no reason. When subordinate students did so, they were signified as dobbers by dominant classmates who punished them. The strongly dominant student, b5/42*, has been shown in this chapter to be unscrupulous in dobbing. Despite his own acts of dobbing, he signified and legitimated his control by threatening other students who engaged in unjustified dobbing:

b5/55*   Some kinds like b5/33 especially if he sees you doing something he yells it out as soon as he sees it. He doesn't stop to think or anything and then b5/42*

> or somebody like that will threaten him and b5/42*
> will tell b5/33 to shut up or something and b5/33
> just goes on doing something else.

THE CAPTAINCY

The school delegated responsibility for controlling the class
between periods to a captain elected by each class. This captaincy is analysed below under two headings. First, student's
normative concerns with the captaincy are described as a
function of pressures from students and teachers. Second,
captains' use of controls to enforce their authority and dominant
students' use of the captaincy to legitimate and broaden their
control are examined.

Expectations of the captaincy
Teachers directly and indirectly put strong pressures on the
captain to control the class (see Figure 7.2). Teachers allocated
blame for class disorder according to whether the captain was
seen to be trying to control the class or not.

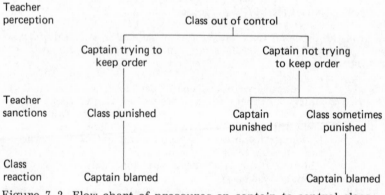

Figure 7.2   Flow chart of pressures on captain to control class

Captains were aware that they would be punished if seen by
teachers to be not attempting to control the class:

c3/41   c3/12* can't really control us all the time and she
           gets really mad because she gets the blame usually
           because she is the class captain and she is supposed
           to keep us quiet.

Thus even when unable to control the class, the captain made
an appearance of trying to do so to avoid being blamed by the
teacher:

b4/18*   b4/34 [the captain] will stand out the front and keep an eye on us if we are making a bit too much noise and [the deputy principal] comes along and he sees b4/34 out the front trying to keep us quiet then [the deputy principal] blows the class up and not him.

However, when the class was punished, students blamed the captain whether or not he had tried to keep the class quiet:

c4/35   We were all talking and Mrs Browning was late and she came in and was mad and c4/48* blamed c4/42 [the captain] because c4/42 never told her to be quiet.

c4/36   Half the class was sitting there working and the noisy ones were making the noise and they all blamed it on c4/42.

When the captain associated with stirrers, the principle of equity of universalistic enforcement of order conflicted with feelings of friendship. There were three outcomes of this conflict. The captain could isolate himself from his former stirrer associates and attempt to govern impartially. The captain could try to keep the class quiet while permitting himself and associates some licence. The captain could abandon attempts to keep order and misbehave with his associates. Outcomes of these three are examined below to demonstrate the normative expectations of the captaincy.

A former stirrer, b2/26, illustrates the dilemma of a captain with stirrer friends. In his case it was resolved by choosing to enforce order rather than associate with his friends. b2/26, aware of the potential conflict of principles, had resisted election. After his election his rule was opposed by his associates. Some classmates did not think that he tried hard enough to overcome this opposition:

b2/44   b2/26 didn't want [the captaincy] because he didn't feel like dobbing in his mates. He could be more strict. He's supposed to write the names up on the board [to tell teachers who had misbehaved] but his mates rub them off themselves, just kid more than anything.

Conflict developed as his former associates resented more and more strongly his efforts at control and as he became more and more annoyed with their resistance. A former associate said:

b2/22*   I might tell him to sit down and shut up when he's out front [of the class]. I say, 'It'll be alright, Beef. Sit down and control yourself.' He sometimes goes wild, flies off his handle and just about knocks you down.

Upset by continuing persecution at the hands of his former associates, b2/26 moved across the room to dissociate himself from them:

Q   Do you know why b2/26 moved across the room?
b2/15   I think they were bugging him too much. Every
           time he tried to listen they'd hit him with a ruler
           stirring him up.

Captains who remained loyal to misbehaving associates were attacked by other classmates for favouritism. For example, a student criticised her captain, c3/12*, because:

c3/48   c3/12*'ll warn you once and if you keep talking even
           if you are only whispering she will put it up [tell
           the teacher] whereas the people that are making a
           lot of noise and walk around outside she hardly puts
           any of them up because they are her mates.

Reflexively the universalistic imposition of order applied to the captain. Captains such as c3/12*, who permitted themselves some licence, were not considered fit to hold the position:

Q   What is c3/12* like as class captain?
c3/28   Not particularly good. She is always mucking around
           herself. She is talking and she tells everyone to shut
           up and you sit down then and she goes and puts the
           other kids' names on the board and then she mucks
           up in class and talks away and it is all right for her
           because she doesn't get any detention.

Control and the captaincy
This section discusses captains' use of sanctions to control class-mates. It first examines the effectiveness of captains' use of teachers' delegated sanctions. It then analyses the consequences of dominant and subordinate captains' attempts to use their own power or influence. Factors discussed are schematised in Figure 7.3.

Although teachers, by punishing the class or captain when a class was disorderly, created the conditions in which captains had to try to keep order, teachers on the whole did not second captains' efforts to keep that order. Captains were required by teachers 'to report any student who misbehaves'. Students, however, did not believe that teachers acted effectively on captain's reports:

b2/44   Mr Wordsworth just says, 'Don't let me catch you.'
           Stuff like that doesn't work.

Reporting misdemeanours was not only ineffectual in controlling the class but made the captain vulnerable to activation of the commitment against dobbing:

Q   How do you feel about being class captain?
a/14   It's just that you have to be so in between. You
can't take sides. Like about dobbing people in and
that's a hard thing to do. Many people have wanted
me to dob people in. . . . Whenever you dob a person
in you don't only get on the bad side of the person
you dob but you get on the bad side of the whole class.

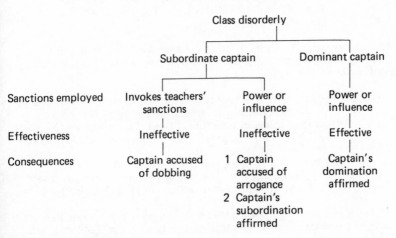

Figure 7.3 Captain's use of sanctions

Each captain's ability to control the class depended on his or
her influence or power. Powerful captains such as b1/23* had
few problems:

Q   How is b1/23* as class captain?
b1/47 He is all right. He keeps authority. He is big enough,
thumps you around if you do anything, get his book
and bashes you on the head.

By contrast, subordinate captains in boys' classes had their
control challenged by powerful classmates. When they attempted
to control the class, they were subjected to verbal and physical
abuse which affirmed their subordinate status:

I b4/52 The class captain [b4/34] is a bit too small. He can't
push them around to make them shut up. They just
give him back cheek.

II b4/37   b4/34 is all right but if he tells the teacher on b4/31* o
any of them for mucking around before the teacher gets
there they might go around knocking him around a bit.

In girls' classes the captain's authority was resisted by more
influential classmates. This is illustrated below by relations
between a captain, c3/12*, and her influential classmate, c3/14*.
c3/12*'s attempts to impose order annoyed c3/14*.

c3/18   She wrote c3/14* name [on the board to advise the
teacher of misbehaviour] and c3/14* was real wild.
Q   Did she write c3/14*'s name just for a stir?
c3/18   No, c3/14* was talking.

c3/14* persuaded others that c3/12's control was based on
illegitimate dobbing, and that she was herself the legitimate
controller of the class:

c3/21   When c32/1* is doing her job as class captain and
is always writing people's names upon the board,
c3/14* is always saying, 'Gee! There are some
dobbers in our class!' and getting at c3/12* but
she doesn't really dob.
Q   Does c3/14* keep the class quiet?
c3/21   If she is writing something or doing a ledger she
will insist that the class has to be quiet for her.

Classmates, talking about c3/12* as captain, mentioned her
failure to control the class and suggested that c3/14* would be
a better captain:

c3/55   I voted for c3/12* but I don't think so anymore
because she mucks around with the rest of the class
and doesn't shut them up . . .
Q   Would you like to see another class captain?
c3/55   Yes. I think c3/14* would keep them quiet.

Dominant students such as b5/42* and c2/18* were often
captains or allied with their captains. They used the captaincy
as they used other dimensions of classroom activity to make their
control manifest and legitimate, and to appropriate a source of
privilege.

c2/18*, as captain, resolved the contradictions in the captaincy
to her own advantage. She reacted pragmatically to demands
from the class and teacher. For instance, she and her classmates saw her job between periods as keeping the class and
herself out of trouble. From her desk she could see teachers
approaching the classroom. She used the information so gathered
to monitor noise:

Q   What is c2/18* like as class captain?
c2/41*   You don't even realise it.
c2/42*   The class captain is supposed to keep you quiet and
           she is the noisiest.
Q   She never tries to keep the class quiet?
c2/41*   Sometimes.
c2/42*   Sometimes.
c2/41*   Jokingly.
c2/42*   It all depends on which teacher we are having next.
           If it is a teacher that is going to get mad at them if
           they make a lot of noise she would but if it is a
           teacher that doesn't care or doesn't say anything
           if they do then she doesn't.

Similarly, her use of the requirement that captains obtain relief
teachers when rostered teachers did not arrive gained her
credit with the class, kept the class quiet, and avoided teacher
supervision and annoyance:

c2/28   c2/18* is a good class captain. When we have a lesson
           and our teacher is away if you muck around and make
           a noise [the deputy principal] will come over and he
           will know that you haven't got a teacher but c2/18*
           says to be quiet and don't make a noise and then we
           won't get a teacher and she won't tell.

Careful use of controls and legitimation of her teacher-given
authority by appeals to student interest meant that students
obeyed her, she did not have to dob students in for misbehaving,
and therefore could not be accused of favouritism.
     Other aspects of the captaincy showed c2/18* acting with an
authority few teachers could emulate. Students listened when
she required attention from the class:

Q   When c2/18* does try to keep people quiet do people
           listen to her?
c2/36   I don't think she tries to keep them quiet but
           whenever she says something everybody listens.

b5/42* was allied with his captain, b5/41*, who was also his
seatmate. b5/42* used this alliance to legitimate and extend his
control. He helped the captain control the class:

Q   What are your main difficulties as class captain?
b5/41*   You don't have to do much - only keep them in order.
b5/51*   It is easy when you get b5/42* to help you.

Like c2/18*, b5/42* warned and quietened the class by
announcing the approach of teachers:

b5/51*   b5/42* might be sitting out at the port rack [ledge

where school bags are kept on the verandah outside
the classroom], and the class is mucking around and
he just walks inside and tells them to shut up and
that because the teacher is coming.

His seat by the door was strategically located like c2/18*'s by
the window. Both positions permitted unobtrusive observation
of teachers' approach. Significantly only dominant students
legitimately act as 'cockatoo', or student warning of the
approach of teachers. Subordinate students' attempts to take
the role were seen as officious rather than helpful and met with
comments like 'I don't know why he does it. Nobody asked him.'

Alliance with the captain freed b5/42* from peer control. When
b5/41* quietened the rest of the class, b5/42* continued to make
a noise without the captain intervening:

Q   Is there anybody b5/41* lets get away with things?
b5/36   b5/17, b5/42* and all his friends but he keeps the
           rest of the class quiet.

ELECTIONS

Elections to decide minor class offices were controlled by
dominant students. Chapter 9 shows how b5/42*'s control of the
choice of a new leading actor determined the outcome of the
English play to his own advantage. As the teacher concerned
ruefully noted, b5/42* and his group generally determined
election and plebiscite results:

'I was trying to do a lot of democratic processes with them
and taking votes which worked to a degree but whatever way
[b5/42* and his friends] voted went because if anyone voted
against them they would be howled down.'

c2/18* similarly manipulated the teacher-sponsored classroom
politics to obtain what she wanted. Students who wanted another
result typically found themselves unable to resist her influence:

c2/13   I particularly wanted to be vice-chairman and I
           put my name down so that I could be elected . . .
c2/14   c2/18* and c2/17 gang up. They pick or nominate
           someone else and they pick the one that they want
           and all of them vote for that person and then we
           don't have a chance.

CONCLUSIONS

This chapter has examined students' use of teachers' authority
under two conditions, invocation by students and delegation by

teachers. It was shown that the sociological literature which suggests a total student ban on the student invocation of teacher authority, or 'dobbing', is based on a superficial use of informants' categorical statements. Dobbing is justified by any of a large number of possible interpretations of the reality. Control of the definitions of given acts of dobbing is in the hands of dominant students. These dominant students can then use dobbing as a sanction supplementing power or influence. Equivalent use of dobbing by subordinate classmates is condemned. Where the dobber does not attempt to justify his actions, the informing of dominant dobbers is never signified, and that of subordinate dobbers is condemned and punished by dominant classmates who became thereby guardians of student morality and interest. The overall result of dominant students' control of the definition of individual acts of dobbing is that the signified dobber is a subordinate student, dobbing when power is used against him. This subordinate dobber arrived at his status as dobber not because of the frequency of his acts but through inability to control the definition of the situation. Signification of students as 'dobbers' is thus an extension and legitimation of peer group control systems.

The delegation of teacher authority was examined under two headings, the position of captain and the control of elections. It was shown that successful occupancy of the captaincy does not depend on official formal sanctions. It depends on student controls being congruent with the position of the applicant. Subordinate captains were condemned by dominant classmates for not keeping order even as the latter caused the former their discipline problems. Use of informal sanctions by dominant captains ensured their successful occupation of the position. Thus the captaincy, either by lack of order under subordinate captains or the order under dominant captains, affirms and extends the peer group control system. The association of class punishments with subordinate captains and freedom from trouble with dominant captains further legitimates the peer group control system.

Universalism and particularism are ancillary issues in the analysis of the captaincy. The captaincy was the scene of conflict between universalistic pressure for equitable treatment of classmates and loyalty to associates. Successful resolution of this conflict depended on universalistic practices tempered by the particularistic co-optation of dominant associates to enforce order.

Chapter 8

Diffuse relations with teachers

This chapter examines students' initiation of diffuse relations with teachers. The topic is covered under four headings. It opens with a comparative account of the student concept of 'crawling' or ingratiating oneself with another. This is a motive which other researchers have shown is commonly imputed to students who initiate diffuse relations with teachers. The later sections of the chapter examine three areas in which students may expand the scope of their contacts with individual teachers. These are: students' intensive academic interaction with the teacher in class, students' offers to help teachers, and students' choosing to talk to teachers in any area beyond the ambit of lesson presentation.

The literature review in Chapter 1 suggested that students gave two opposed definitions of classmates' diffuse relations with teachers. Diffuse relations were either a sign of students' maturity or a sign of their dependence on teachers. The present research shows that students evaluate classmates' initiation of diffuse relations with teachers according to criteria of student dependence or independence, and that the application and activation of definitions of dependence and independence is, to some extent, controlled by dominant students.

Teachers' popularity was a second criterion used by students to evaluate the acceptability of classmates' initiation of diffuse relations with teachers. The ban on researching students' perceptions of teachers (see Appendix B) means that neither this topic nor the wider issue of the social construction of the popularity of teachers is discussed here.

'CRAWLERS' IN COMPARATIVE PERSPECTIVE

Previous research conducted in city schools and a competitive university setting (Becker et al., 1968: 99; Sugarman, 1973: 167; Werthman, 1971) redounds with terms such as 'brown noses' and 'ass-kissers', which denote and condemn students' efforts to ingratiate themselves with teachers. The pilot study for the present research showed students in metropolitan schools making a like use of the term 'crawler'. The comment given below from a metropolitan high school student encapsulates the most frequently expressed concerns:

'A crawler is someone who strives continually for the favour and

attention of the teacher. The trouble with crawlers is that they
are so busy with what the teacher thinks of them they forget
about the kids in the class. They always volunteer for extra
work and when they do something they make sure the teacher
knows about it. Also they make excuses for talking to teachers
after the lesson. In the class a crawler is considered to be
the lowest of the low.'

Goldtown students are shown in this chapter to express similar
concern with classmates' initiation of diffuse relations with
teachers and with the associated and despised role of crawler.
However, perhaps because of the particularistic and diffuse
values of the school's host community, expressions of these
concerns were weaker and fewer at Goldtown.

People who were generally knowledgeable about state high
schools but were still strangers to Goldtown High School clearly
expected a greater student concern with crawling than they
found. A newly arrived teacher commented:

'That is funny in this school. The kids don't go on so much
about crawling. They don't seem to notice it too much. Like
c3/26 is a bit of a crawler in science but I don't think the
kids here worry too much about it. Every other school I have
been at there has always been this word, "crawler". "Oh God!
Not a crawler!"'

The student whom classmates often dubbed a crawler was first
labelled by a visiting inspector. The students were less concerned than the inspector with that student's relations with the
teacher:

b3/25   Mr Chips and b3/14 are related and b3/14 was out
         talking to him and the inspector called him a 'crawler'
         so everyone called him 'crab' after that. . . . If he
         wants to go and ask the teacher something that is
         fair enough.

A few students accepted the definition of b3/14 as a crawler.
Most rejected it.

Like the strangers and newcomers, Goldtown students frequently stated that 'crawling to teachers' was not a major student
concern. They claimed either that all crawling had been prevented
by fear of sanctions or that imputations of crawling were 'just
for a bit of a stir. They have a bit of fun, but nobody gets
their temper up.'

None the less, Goldtown students did occasionally use 'crawler'
and similar terms to describe people who ingratiated themselves
with a superior. This superior could be a teacher, a dominant
classmate or, for girls with active and immature sexual interests,
a boy. The term, when applied to students' relations with
teachers, formed part of a consistent matrix of concern with

classmates' dependence and independence, a concern also evident in students' evaluation of other activities, such as stirring.

ACADEMIC STATUS AND INDEPENDENCE

The social construction of academic status was a focus of the struggle between teachers' and students' definitions of the situation. Students' awareness of this struggle led to teachers' definitions of high academic status being frequently followed by allegations that the student concerned was crawling. Intellectual and a concomitant social independence were often mentioned as prerequisities of classmates' acknowledgement of students' high academic status. Allegations of crawling and dependence were used to detract from other students' academic attainment.

Students asserted that true 'brains' had intellectual independence as well as high marks. Dominant students with high marks were attributed a greater intellectual independence than subordinate students with high marks. This supposed independence combined with high marks defined high academic status. In the following quotation, the informants compare two classmates with high marks, a subordinate student, b1/17*, and a dominant student, b1/24*:

b1/52   b1/17* studies like a tape recorder. He will switch on and he will say exactly what he has heard or read. . . .

b1/51   Whereas if b1/24* has read something he will put it in his own words.

These dominant students also demonstrated their intellectual independence by challenging teachers' knowledge on occasion. For example, two students said that a student was a 'brain' if:

b1/54   He's got something to add to the teacher.

b1/43   Like in science . . . the teacher said something, that was one way of doing it, and b1/24* said the other way is the wrong way, sort of thing.

The association of intellectual independence with the definition of a 'brain' was sometimes extended to include other types of independence. Academic performance combined with social independence became in some cases a requirement for respect:

Q   How do you get respect from other people in the class?

b4/18*   Knowing the work and not being like a goody goody all the time.

Recognition of academic status was sometimes facilitated by willingness to flout teachers' authority:

b4/21   b4/33 is pretty brainy.
b4/31*   Oh no, he is not, not really.
b4/21   He appears to be pretty brainy, doesn't he? He
          always has the top marks in the class.
b4/31*   I don't think he is really brainy. There are lots of
          kids who tend to stir and they tend to get good marks.

Students believed that it was possible to improve marks by crawling to teachers. Two methods of ingratiation to improve marks were 'checking' marks, and giving the teacher the kind of contribution wanted in classroom discourse. Students generally believed that an overly assiduous checking of marks and the associated acceptance of the teachers' definition of the situation constituted crawling. More checking, however, was allowed dominant than subordinate students. For example, the case of a dominant student, b1/32*, may be compared with that of the generally unpopular b1/17*:

I   b1/31 b1/32* always says, 'I am going to get another six
            marks' . . . He just goes out and crawls and then
            he gets a few extra marks.
     b1/36 Anyone will [crawl] to get extra marks.

II   b1/15 When the maths paper came back, b1/17* went
            scungeing for marks.
Q   Most people would ask for marks, wouldn't they?
     b1/15 Yeah, but he got three or four.
     b1/35 He once got half a mark and seemed real pleased about
            it and I said, 'Oh, half a mark! What a thrill!'

Possible condemnation of the dominant student's attempt to obtain higher marks, although associated with the pejorative term 'crawling', is neutralised by the assertion that everybody does it. By contrast, the subordinate student's attempt is derided and the pejorative meaning of 'scunge', discussed in Chapter 3, is unmitigated. b1/17* was extremely concerned with marks. He became the butt of frequent jokes and the focus of intense competition as a result of this concern:

b1/18*   I would like to wipe b1/17* off the map. . . . Actually
          in woodwork we told b1/17* that he had flunked and
          he nearly started bawling. Everything is as though
          his life depended on it. It doesn't really.

Another focus of allegations of crawling was contributions to classroom academic discourse. Unpopular but academically active students were commonly accused of crawling to teachers by producing the knowledge the teacher wanted. As a result these students' academic contributions were discounted by classmates. b3/26*, for example, held well-informed beliefs which contradicted the commonsense knowledge of classmates. His teachers

commented on how the clash of knowledge influenced b3/26*'s
relations with classmates:

> 'b3/26* is the victim of a certain amount of ridicule among
> the others. . . . b3/26* has these very independent
> ideas. . . . He is rather a supporter of sandmining and
> many of these kids have tendencies towards conservation
> and he will argue his position quite rationally and
> he is quite unconcerned that they don't agree with
> him.'

Different assessment of b3/26*'s academic contributions led to
allegations that he was crawling to teachers. Students knew that
the teacher who praised b3/26*'s defence of sandmining was a
conservationist and unsympathetic to sandmining. None the less,
b3/26* was accused of sycophancy:

b3/33	Everyone says b3/26* just crawls to Mr Mills and that.
Q	In what ways does he crawl?
b3/33	If we start talking about something in cit. ed. he will start talking about sandmines because his father is one of the bosses down there. Everyone will start yelling and say, 'Here goes b3/26* again!' and then everybody else starts saying things like, '[a sand-mining company], oh, they don't do this and they don't do that' and it gets him wild.
Q	Does he earn this?
b3/33	Probably he is trying to be honest but everybody just don't give him a chance.

OFFERING TO HELP TEACHERS

Students in evaluating classmates' help for teachers were
concerned with the formal position of the student, the manner
and frequency of selection for helping, and the imputed motivation of students in volunteering help or teachers in choosing
helpers (see Figure 8.1).

Students distinguished three formal student positions in
evaluating classmates who helped teachers. These were the
captain, the monitor and the ordinary student. Captains were
often expected by the teacher to do a wide range of jobs.
Monitors were given certain routine jobs such as cleaning the
blackboard. The monitors' and the captains' jobs were normatively
indifferent. Accordingly, only ordinary students' help of
teachers is considered here.

Students distinguished occasions when classmates volunteered
to help teachers from occasions when teachers chose who was to
help them. Volunteering or being chosen to help were each
socially problematic. Students who were asked by teachers to

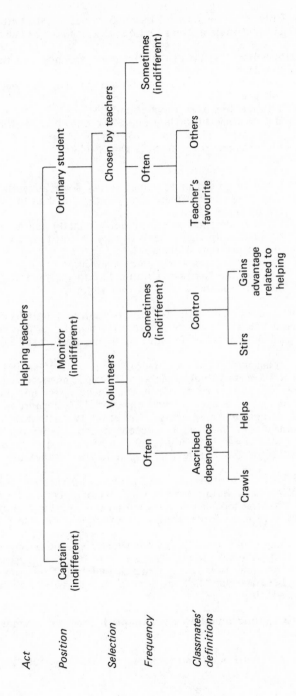

Figure 8.1 Students' evaluation of classmates' helping teachers

help were liable to be accused of being favourites. Students who offered to help had their motives critically examined by classmates:

c2/28 Teachers' pets will usually go on errands and things like that.

Q Do they offer to do the errands or does the teacher ask them?

c2/28 The teacher asks them usually.

c2/27* If it is something they need someone to trust they take them. They won't take us.

Q Do you ever offer to help the teachers?

c2/28 Yes.

c2/27* Yes.

c2/28 I like to go out of the room to get something for the class, like in English. Everything that has to be done I will go and do it.

c2/27* I like to do them but they don't usually ask me but I like to help them carry things or anything. Like I like to get out of class a lot.

Q Would anyone say you were crawling?

c2/27* They would just say I would like to get on the good side of teachers.

The problems associated with students offering to help teachers are discussed below. Teachers' choice of students to help was commonly a mark of teacher favour. It is therefore discussed in Chapter 10.

Students commonly attributed one of four kinds of motive to classmates who chose to help teachers. Two of these motives involve the wish to control the teacher. These were that the offer to help was motivated by perceptions of opportunities for private advantage or for stirring. The other two attributed motives assume that the students accepted dependence on teachers. These were that the students who offered to help were either crawling or felt it their duty to help the teacher as teacher.

The most often asserted and least problematic reason given for students offering to help teachers was that of private advantage connected with the job. Students such as the following found helping teachers more interesting than other available activities:

b5/16 They just want to get out there to do an experiment. Mr Lavoisier says, 'Who wants to help?' and most of the class put up their hands just to get out the front because else they are just sitting there and doing nothing.

Students also found ancillary advantages in helping teachers. For example:

c3/32* After we have had a class . . . we . . . just go for a

> walk and when we come back if we see our teacher carrying books or something then we carry books or something.
>
> Q   Why do you do that?
>
> c3/32*   So they won't rouse us too much for not being in the classroom.

Assertion that offers to help teachers were motivated by private advantage was, except among the few goody goodies, always an acceptable explanation. It is symptomatic of students' lack of concern with classmates' helping teachers that this explanation for helping was not generally challenged even when proffered by weak and unpopular classmates.

Less frequently, students offered to help teachers in order to stir them. Sometimes, as in the first example below, the stirring was in the offer to help. More often, as in the second example, it was in the 'help' given:

> I   Q   Why would you volunteer to help Mr Hogben?
>
>   b3/46* So we can stir him.
>
>   Q   How would volunteering help stir him?
>
>   b3/45* Because he don't like b3/46* and me because we stir him.
>
>   b3/46* We used to stir him up and he never liked it.

> II b2/14   b2/57 reckoned that he was going to help Mr Riemann. . . . We were kept in and b2/57 had this rubber band and bit of paper and b2/22* and them were standing outside and Mr Riemann went outside to them like to tell them to move away and b2/57 says, 'I'll get them away, sir!' and shot off this wad of paper and just missed Mr Riemann's head.

Attribution of stirring was a motive by all except goody goodies. To stir by offering to help the teacher involved confrontation between stirrer and teacher. It required individual responsibility for the stirring and so did not lead to class punishments. The acts of stirring were short lived and usually did not detract from or compete with valued lessons.

Offers to help teachers which were motivated by crawling and altruism usually acknowledged the ascribed superiority of teachers. Altruism helping of teachers was generally associated with respect for the position of teachers. Crawling assumed a diffuse teacher control best accommodated, not by the specific reciprocity implicit in perceptions of private advantage in helping, but by establishing a diffuse and qualitatively dependent relationship with the teacher.

Attribution of the motives of crawling and altruism depended on the perspective of the student. Hostile classmates might impute crawling as the motive for offering to help. The student concerned and his friends would claim that the offer to help was honest and unselfish.

Students imputed two kinds of goals to classmates accused of
crawling to teachers by helping them. These goals were either
diffuse in seeking the advantages, discussed in Chapter 10, of
a teacher's favourite, or, within the scope of a particularistic
relationship with a teacher, directed to the specific advantage
of receiving high marks. For example:

I   b4/51   b4/55 and b4/56* regularly volunteer, don't they,
            to help teachers. They think teacher's buddy,
            teacher's little boy. . . . [They help in order to get
            on the good side of the teachers.]

II b3/45   c3/36 tries to get in good with teachers so that she
            can get higher marks. She is always trying to get
            higher marks and beat everyone else and brag. She
            offers to carry books for every teacher or S.R.A.
            kits or something like that.

Students never directly approved classmates' crawling to
teachers by offers of help. Nonetheless, under two conditions
such crawling was tolerated. As is seen later in the discussion
of dominant students' diffuse relations with teachers, unsignified
crawling through increased interaction with teachers can lead to
increased respect from classmates. Students also sometimes
accepted classmates' crawling even when it was signified. For
example, dominant students in the academically competitive
class, 9b1e1, despised but tolerated b1/45*'s crawling to get
higher marks:

Q   How do you feel about b1/45* and b1/17* [volunteering
            to help teachers]?
b1/27   Well, that is their problem.
b1/32*   If they want to do it that's up to them.
b1/27   If they want to get in with the teacher real good.
Q   You don't mind them wanting to get in with the
            teacher real good?
b1/32*   No.
b1/27   They can be teacher's pet. That is okay for me.
b1/32*   If they want to get marks that way, let them.

Both b1/45* and b1/17* ascribed to themselves the altruistic
desire to help the teachers. b1/45* was aware of and uncomfortable with the other motive, that is crawling, imputed to his offer
to help the teacher:

Q   Do you ever volunteer to help the teachers?
b1/45*   Yes. Well I reckon - like Mr Riemann - he is sort of
            handicapped. I reckon he should be helped. He needs
            it. He can't do everything like we can. We can help
            and I reckon that we should do it to any teacher, like
            respect them.

b1/58*   Yes. I would do the same with Mr Riemann, help him
          with his books and that.
Q   Do you find people getting hostile if you do offer to
          help?
b1/45*   Yes. They reckon you are the teacher's pet if you do
          help. If you help too much they make fun of you.

When control was contested by students, the labelling of
offers to help followed the allegiance of the student concerned.
The conflict of c3/14* with c3/12* and c3/11* has already been
described with regard to the captaincy. This conflict carried
over into definition of c3/14*'s choosing to help teachers. c3/14*
regularly used lunchtimes to write homework on the board. Her
rivals for control alleged that she was crawling:

c3/12*   c3/14* helps the teachers in a way to get in good
          with them but the others do it just to get out of work.
c3/11*   c3/14* at lunchtime. We have got business principles
          after lunch and she will go and write up all the home-
          work on the board and Mrs Pitman comes in and says,
          'Who is the nice kid who put that up on the board?'
          and c3/14* goes, 'Oh, me!'

c3/14* and her interview partner were aware of these explanations
of that behaviour. They asserted however that their motives
were unselfish and in the interest of the teacher and class:

c3/14*   It is mostly jealousy in our class, jealous because I
          get better marks than them. You can tell that they
          are jealous can't you?
c3/56   Yeah.
Q   Who would show jealousy?
c3/56   c3/11*. Like c3/14* writes business principles up for
          Mrs Pitman because every time Mrs Pitman comes into
          the room she has got to write the same things up on
          the board and c3/14* just saves time cos Mrs Pitman
          gets real mad and the other kids don't help her.

It was a sign of c3/14*'s ascendancy that classmates generally
accepted her definition of her motive in helping and not her
rivals' alternative definition.

TALKING WITH TEACHERS

To interpret classmates' talking with teachers beyond what was
considered usual, students took into account the categories given
in Figure 8.2. They divided the content of discourse into
academic and social. Students gave no consistent statement of
the acceptability of each but were concerned with whether the
motive was genuinely academic or social, or only pretended. If

they decided that the motive was genuine, then they looked at
the interaction between student and teacher to see whether the
student was accepting dependence on the teacher or asserting
equality.

This section shows that students evaluate classmates' talking
with teachers by criteria of independence and dependence.
Talking with teachers is acceptable when it asserts student
equality by stirring or talking with teachers as an equal. Talking
with teachers is condemned when it shows acceptance of the
superiority of teachers. This acceptance of teachers' authority
is seen in crawling and a dependent though sincerely motivated
interaction with teachers.

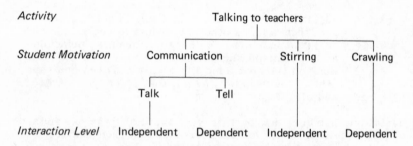

Figure 8.2 Students' evaluation of classmates' talking to
teachers

Of the alternative motives attributed to student-teacher talk,
students generally contrasted a genuine social or academic
concern or stirring with crawling. The independence of the
stirrer and the dependence of the crawler were antithetical.
Recognition as a stirrer thus precluded definition of students'
talking with teachers as crawling. For example:

Q   Would anyone say you were crawling because you
           talk to teachers?
b4/27   No. Our class is different because they seem to have
           all the stirrers . . . in our class. Like in a class
           where you have got stirrers and nonstirrers every-
           one gets a bit mixed up but in this class you know
           that they are not really crawling.

With this antithesis in mind, students, as in the following
example, often introduced an element of stirring into their talk
with teachers to forestall allegations of crawling:

Q   What's the difference between your talking to Mr
           Einstein and the others talking to him?
b3/42   It's a joke. You stir him a couple of times about seeing

> him up at the pub and then you talk about the lesson
> but they come up and say, 'Oh, sir! That was a good
> lesson! Can you explain this and all this?'

The stirring used in talking with teachers was comparatively
goodnatured. It embarrassed rather than annoyed the teacher.
As in the example below, the talk tended to focus on tacitly
shared mature interests:

> c1/53*   Miss Adler has a boyfriend. He helped her set up the
> doughnut stall and they tried to get her to talk about
> that and one day she came to school and was sunburnt.
> She had been down to the beach with her boyfriend
> and they tried to get her to talk about that and gee!
> did she go red?

Classmates rarely objected to such stirring. It never led to
group punishment, never seriously upset teachers, and, when
in class, only briefly interrupted work.
Within the domain of academic content, students judged whether
the classmate was genuinely interested by their knowledge of his
academic commitment and performance. A student known to be
interested and competent in a subject could talk to the teacher
concerned without being labelled a crawler:

> b1/22   b1/15 was talking to Mr Riemann a lot for a while
> when he had this special science book and all stuff
> like that [details].
> Q   No one would think that he was crawling?
> b1/22   No, because I don't think he likes Mr Riemann much
> and Mr Riemann lets him get away with everything
> and he is pretty good at science. He always gets
> good marks.

When students had established that a classmate had a genuine
academic or social concern for conversation with a teacher they
distinguished two levels of discourse. These, following a tendency
in students' descriptions of them, are called here 'talking' and
'telling'. 'Talking' was the admired ability in students to talk
with teachers as equals. 'Telling' was where students who were
too concerned to talk about themselves produced what classmates condemned as trivia in conversations with teachers.
c4/44* is representative of students who talked as equals with
teachers and c4/58* is representative of students who talked as
subordinates with the teacher:

> I c4/18   c4/58* is really goody goody to the teacher at the
> end of the lesson. She will go out and talk to the
> teacher and tell her everything that has happened
> in the school and in the class and all this.
> Q   Another person who likes talking to teachers is c4/44*.

c4/18   She just likes talking to teachers. She would talk to anyone.

II c4/43*   You – she talks to the teachers real easily.
c4/44*   But I get along with the teachers.
c4/43*   But you're game to talk to all the teachers as if you're a real close friend . . .
c4/44* c4/58*   doesn't talk to them freely. She wouldn't be game to. . . . She is always talking about herself.

Students' and teachers' perceptions of classmates' talking with teachers were not always the same. The frequent unequal conversation of certain unobtrusive subordinate students with the teacher remained unobserved and therefore criticised by classmates. c1/53* was such a student. More than any of her classmates, she told teachers of her private concerns. Her teachers complained of the incessant telling:

'c1/53* is a crawler. . . . She will come up and see you every five seconds. You turn around and there's c1/53*. She's asking you something. She drives you up the wall, almost parasitic. She just clings to the teacher. She tells you her problems. She tells you everything that is going on.'

Even her classmate most often willing and competent to condemn others' flaws did not perceive the nature of c1/53*'s relations with teachers:

c1/16*   If they stay behind they are genuinely interested in what they are talking about. Nobody has been accused of crawling.
Q   Who would stay behind?
c1/16*   c1/53* often stays behind to get more pointers on maths.

By contrast, when students had active claims to a status which was unacknowledged by classmates, their talking with teachers was remarked on and criticised. b3/26* is an example of this. He was seen earlier in this chapter to have claims to academic status acknowledged by teachers but not by students. As well as talking about academic interests, b3/26* talked with teachers about his private concerns. Teachers accepted this as proper. One, for instance, said:

'A few things he has told me – the home situation is not very supportive, Mum says she doesn't care if he comes home at all. . . . I find him a thoroughly worthwhile person.'

Classmates condemned b3/26* for social 'telling' in his relations with teachers:

I b3/33   b3/26* talks and sort of tries to make teachers feel
sorry for him.

II b3/45* b3/26* is always hanging around the teachers,
telling them every little thing that goes on.
b3/46* Any little thing, talks to them.
b3/45* He tells them about what has happened in classes and
things like that.

DOMINANT STUDENTS AND STUDENT-TEACHER RELATIONS

Dominant students tended to interact widely with teachers.
c2/18* and b5/42*, as dominant students, were prominent in
helping and talking to teachers.
 b5/42* was often named as offering to help teachers. He was
seen to monopolise the advantages of helping teachers. He may
have been sincerely concerned to help. One student asserted
that under the right conditions offering to help teachers
activated an alliance with him:

b5/31*   b5/51* will carry stuff [for teachers]. . . . He has
been doing it specifically to get in good with b5/42*
just so that b5/42* can beat me up if I hit b5/51*
again.

However, the most commonly imputed motive for b5/42*'s offers
to help was crawling. Only one student, a peripheral and
antagonistic member of b5/42*'s group, accused b5/42* to his
face:

b5/32*   If the teacher asks for anything, b5/42* is always
first on the spot. If he wants a red biro [ballpoint
pen], b5/42* is always out there and handing it out
to him. If the teacher wants something done, b5/42*
is always out there doing it. I called him a 'crawler'
once, and he just about started bawling.

This public accusation was covertly repeated around the class and
it was generally agreed outside b5/42*'s group that he was a
crawler. Despite this, b5/42* was able to publicly label two
students, including a conformist and conscientious brain, b5/57*,
as crawlers when they offered to help teachers:

b5/42*   b5/58 hangs round with b5/57*. They are both
crawlers. If teachers ask for something to be done,
b5/57*'ll go straight away and pick up the papers
or something . . . and we aren't in favour of doing
that. He'll just bound up and get the rubbish bin and
he'll go up and do it.

c2/18* is only comparable in a limited way because as captain she had unsolicited access to a wide range of jobs. None the less, her classmates said that she offered to help to obtain private advantage, to stir a disliked teacher, to disinterestedly help teachers, but not to crawl. Much of the help was of a kind that teachers accepted as responsible. In the school fete, for example, she and her deskmate looked after the class stall almost all afternoon, and afterwards cleared up.

b5/42* had the widest relations with teachers of any student in his class. He was one of very few students from any class to visit a teacher's home socially. He talked with teachers during lessons. This talk was social: about his shooting, sports and beach nudism:

b5/42*   I was talking with Mr Euclid about nudists. We were walking up the beach and there was this old bloke sitting there in the sand and – oh Christ! you have never seen anything like it and . . . there were a couple of sheilas and this old man he had binoculars with him and was having a bit of a perve [and so forth].

The talk occasionally edged over into stirring:

b5/42*   I said if I went over there I would probably shoot you [to Mr Riemann] and he got stirred up.

Classmates believed that b5/42*'s diffuse relations with teachers originated in teacher favouritism as well as in b5/42*'s initiation of them. Their total significance is therefore discussed in Chapter 10.

Classmates stated that c2/18*'s conversations with teachers were more as an equal, more friendly and more threatening than those of her classmates. Her talk was turned aggressively to the teachers' social interests:

Q   Who will . . . talk to teachers after class?
c2/43   c2/18*.
Q   Why does c2/18* stay and talk to teachers?
c2/43   Socially mainly I think. Like she says, 'Are you going to a dance?', she asks the teacher.

This equality of discourse intruded into lessons with playful comments, which were seen by classmates to include judgements on teachers and to interrupt lessons:

Q   How does c2/18* break up class discussions?
c2/14   She makes personal comments on how Mrs Milton does her hair or on the clothes she wears or the way she looks nice and sometimes c2/18* says Mrs Milton looks awful too.

This did not become stirring because the teachers generally reacted equably and because c2/18* was only familiar with teachers she liked. The initiation of diffuse relations with teachers were thus part of c2/18*'s merged clown and stirrer roles, discussed in Chapter 6.

Even when c2/18* disliked the other students she did not control classmates' initiation of talk with teachers. c2/24* had dobbed in c2/18* in an incident discussed in Chapter 7 and had been attacked by c2/18* for other reasons. Despite this, c2/18* when she saw c2/24* talking as a dependent with teachers, put no pressure on her. c2/18* said of c2/24*'s talking with teachers:

c2/18*	c2/24* is always being a real goody goody in class. She goes up to the teachers after lessons and talks to them. . . .
Q	What is the difference between the way c2/24* goes up and talks to the teachers and the way other girls do?
c2/18*	She is a little pet towards lessons and all that is going on. . . . She wants to find out more about the lessons than we want to find out. She wants to be the top of everything.

c2/24* acknowledged that she talked a lot with teachers out of class. She said that she experienced no pressures from c2/18* or any other students when she did talk with teachers:

c2/24*	Maths. I like maths. I like our teacher. If you ever want to learn anything she will teach you separately and she will keep at it until you really know it. And I just like to talk to Mrs Russell as a person. . . . I used to talk with Mrs Pitman but don't now, usually about home and everything like that. . . .
Q	Do you find any pressure from other girls when you talk to teachers?
c2/24*	No. [Two rephrased probes also answered negatively.]

CONCLUSIONS

Goldtown students paid comparatively little attention to classmates' initiation of diffuse relations with teachers. When they did, they judged the propriety of this interaction by determining whether the students concerned were asserting their independence by controlling and manipulating the interaction, or whether the students concerned were accepting and extending student dependence on teachers. In evaluating academic attainment, students praised classmates who showed intellectual and social independence. In evaluating classmates' offers to help teachers, the wish to obtain diffuse advantage as teacher's favourite and the intrinsic desire to help were condemned as connoting acceptance of dependence on teachers, and stirring and hope of specific advantage were praised as showing student independence. In evaluating classmates' talking with teachers, students were similarly concerned with whether the classmate was accepting dependence on teachers or asserting student independence. A genuine concern to communicate was interpreted according to the level of the exchange: students who tacitly accepted dependence on teachers were condemned and students who tacitly claimed equality of interests with the teacher were praised. Students who pretended a wish to communicate with teachers were seen either to be stirring, and thus asserting independence from teachers, which was generally praised, or to be trying to gain diffuse advantage as teacher's favourite, which was generally condemned as acceptance of dependence on teachers.

Dominant students tended to be conspicuous in talking to and helping teachers. A favourable interpretation was usually given of their activities, and they appropriated many of the advantages of helping and talking to teachers. These dominant students could generally assert the propriety, when challenged, of their initiation of relations with teachers, and could often challenge successfully the propriety of classmates' initiation of relations with teachers. However, dominant students did not always enforce definitions of the propriety of their own behaviour or condemn and limit other students' initiation of diffuse relations with teachers.

Chapter 9

Students' construction and management of academic status

Chapter 1 showed that researchers have often assumed that academic work is students' principal classroom performance dimension and one in which students consider themselves successes or failures according to teachers' judgements. Against this thesis, it was suggested that connotations of dependence on teachers might qualify students' acceptance of academic work as a performance dimension.

Later chapters have shown the importance of the norm of independence in students' relations with teachers and in definitions of performance. These chapters have also shown that dominant students usually control applications of the norm of independence. Chapter 2 indicated that there were no upper limits to the amount of academic work considered proper, but Chapter 4 showed that commitment to work could become a problem when it precluded the sociability within the peer group which is implicit in mucking around. Chapters 6, 7 and 8 have shown the value students place on independence in their interaction with teachers. Chapter 8 showed that students tended to value academic performance which was seen as independent of teachers' control. In each case dominant students controlled the definitions of independent and dependent action.

This chapter argues that high academic status has two origins: students' construction of definitions of academic status and teachers' imposition of definitions of academic status. It is shown how students' perceptions of academic status within these origins are largely determined by the interests of dominant students. The discussion below shows that when students' academic status as defined by teachers and students' control status are incongruent, academic status tends to remain unsignified. In its place, dominant students construct their own definitions of academic status.

HIGH ACADEMIC STATUS

Management of high academic status defined by teachers
Students with lower academic status as defined by teachers often resented subordinate classmates' claims to respect for higher academic status as defined by teachers. The dominant students did not openly resent the subordinate students' high marks. However, as in the example below, they condemned the subordinate classmate who attached any significance to the high marks:

141

c1/11*   c1/47 thinks she is real smart. But you name it she
          is good at it. That's the worst part.
c1/12*   It is just the attitude when she is in lessons. She is
          good at them and she knows it.

Students named four circumstances under which claims to high
academic status as defined by teachers became significant in
classroom interaction. These were signification by teachers, by
classmates, by the student concerned, and by performance
inside the classroom. Signification by teachers, by classmates,
and by the student concerned is discussed immediately below to
demonstrate how subordinate students with high academic status
as defined by teachers manage their relations with their classmates. Performance inside the classroom is more immediately
relevant to students' construction of alternative definitions of
academic status and is discussed in the second part of this
section. The conditions for subordinate students' successful
management of teachers' definitions of their high academic status
are schematised in Figure 9.1.

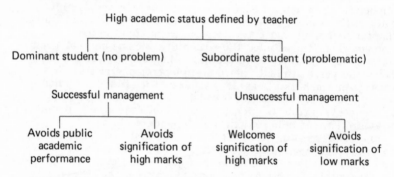

Figure 9.1 Management of high academic status

Teachers advertise high marks
Subordinate students' successful management of imposed high
academic status demanded real or tacit negation of the high
academic status consequent on teachers' advertising it. Actual
negation, involving intentional lowering of marks obtained, was
rare and confined to girls. More commonly the subordinate brain,
like c2/46* in the following example, tacitly negated high
academic status by showing embarrassment at teachers' allusions
to it:

c2/25   c2/46* doesn't want to be shown off and being the
         smartest she doesn't like being told.
c2/36   If the teacher says, 'Well, there was one good mark'

everybody will turn around and say, 'Yeah, that's
c2/46*.'

Subordinate students who disliked teachers' signification of their
imposed high academic status were liked and respected by their
classmates.

A small minority of teachers openly resented certain students
obtaining high marks. When this occurred the student concerned
had no problems of academic status management. An example
is c3/32*, who was accused by the teacher of not working, of
knowing too much and knowing too little. c3/32* annoyed the
teacher by minimising the apparent amount of work done and by
refusing to use her knowledge to aid the teacher in instructing
the class:

c3/21   In cit. ed. all the time c3/32* says she doesn't know
        and she has got the top marks for cit. ed., Mrs
        Machiavelli is always going mad at her telling her she
        knows the work.
c3/22   'And if you tried a bit more you would know a lot
        more and come top in cit. ed.'.

When c3/32* did come top in citizen education Mrs Machiavelli
publicised her high marks but refused to concede graciously
her high academic status. Mrs Machiavelli's open resentment of
c3/32*'s high marks led to allegations that she was victimising
c3/32*:

c3/31   c3/32* gets picked on by Mrs Machiavelli - cos Mrs
        Machiavelli said when c3/32* got first in cit. ed. this
        semester, she said, 'Little Miss Know-All got first'
        and all this. I don't see why Mrs Machiavelli should
        hate c3/32*. She is a good kid.

c3/32* did not advertise her high academic status. Her relations
with the teacher precluded connotations of dependency associated
with imposition of high academic status. This status was therefore unproblematic.

Classmates advertise high marks
Often lower academic status students signified classmates'
imposed higher academic status. Even good natured compliments
and teasing from friends embarrassed subordinate brains. The
accepted response of subordinate brains when their imposed
academic status was signified by friends was to indicate, as in
the following example, that they did not welcome the signification:

c2/27* c2/46* doesn't like telling us her marks. She thinks
        I just want to know because she is the best.
c2/28   She doesn't think she's the best but she thinks if
        she tells us we will call her 'smart' and that. . . .

c2/27*   We will say it jokingly but she is smart. She is miles
         better.

More often it was hostile classmates who deliberately made
subordinate brains, like c4/31*, uncomfortable by alluding to
their marks:

c4/31*   Just because I came top in home economics in the
         mid-semester exams c4/48* keeps calling me a –
         I wasn't even going to answer her – 'Look there
         goes smartypants!'

The student advertises high marks
Close friends commonly 'skited' or boasted about marks received:

b4/31*   We say, 'I bet I get a higher mark than you' and all
         that and then he'll say, 'I'll beat you the next one.'
         Just ordinary stuff.

There were three conditions for the acceptability of skiting
about high marks. Skiting needed to be confined to associates
and among these associates needed to be seen as joking, and
laying no claim to a higher academic status. These conditions
are illustrated in the following discussion:

Q   Do you find anyone skiting about marks?
b2/42   Yeah. I think it's b2/54. Usually he carries on about
         how he's beaten everyone. Everyone else does it
         though. I know I do it too.
b2/41   That's among friends – a bit of a joke. Someone tells
         you what they got and then if you did better you can
         say, 'I beat you.'

Subordinate brains had problems in joining in the normal classroom exchange of information about marks. Their initiation of
such exchanges, by enquiring about a classmate's marks with
the expectation that the classmate would respond with a reciprocal
enquiry, was invariably seen as skiting. The resultant comparison of marks constituted signification of higher academic status
by the brain. This, as in the following example, was always
condemned:

b1/56   He's a skite. He came first and he would let anyone
         know. He would say, 'Where did you come?' and of
         course you end up by telling him the truth and if
         you came about eleventh he'll say, 'Ah, beat you!
         Came first!'

Even the brain who did not display overt pleasure at receiving
higher marks could be condemned for initiating comparison of
marks:

c4/34   If c4/31* gets higher she asks you, 'How much did you get?' and you ask her and she has got higher marks and she sort of secretly smiles to herself.

Subordinate students with normally high levels of marks were also expected to reduce their claim to high academic status by freely acknowledging their occasionally lower marks. Failure to do so was condemned:

c3/11*   Every time c3/18 gets a test back she looks at her marks and if she gets a high mark she will say, 'Oh, yeah! What did you get?' and if you get a low mark she will say, 'I got so-and-so.' But if she gets a low mark she won't say anything. She just sits there and you ask her marks and she won't tell you.

Rules governing students' signification of their own high marks were either not activated against dominant brains or were interpreted elastically. For instance, skiting about high marks by a dominant brain, such as b4/31* in the following example, was understood to be a 'joke'. It was therefore not to be taken seriously:

b4/42   b4/31* gets high marks and goes around skiting, saying what high marks he's got and goes around beating everybody and that. Most of the time he's only fooling around.

Fooling or not, b4/31* as a dominant student was able to use high marks to signify his high academic status in a manner not permitted to subordinate classmates.

Other actions by subordinate students which assumed academic superiority were unacceptable even when couched in terms of helping others or of praising classmates' performance. Subordinate brains' unsolicited offers to help classmates were, as in the following example, taken as assertions of academic superiority. They were therefore resented:

b2/15   If you haven't done an experiment he will try and tell you about it. We want to do it ourselves.
b2/28*   You get sick of him thinking he knows how to do it. He's a real brainwave. It makes you feel good when you beat him in exams.

By contrast, although it was not generally expected that dominant brains would help classmates, when they did it was favourably mentioned. b1/24*, for example, was named as a good neighbour because of his willingness to help:

b1/26   b1/24* helps us and he is pretty brainy and if you can't figure anything out he will always help you.

Dominant students' creation of high academic status
Most dominant students had high academic status. Those dominant students who lacked high marks selected and defined what constituted academic performance and controlled public aspects of academic attainment. They thereby gave themselves high status.

c2/18* and b5/42* were typical of dominant students in their ability to create high academic status. c2/18* and b5/42* had marks which were two thirds and one third respectively down their class order of achievement. Despite c2/18*'s low marks, many classmates considered her a brain. Even patently poor performance did not detract from her academic reputation. She was named as best class debater although, as she admitted, in the most recent debate she 'had got nothing prepared for it so [she] got zero'. When her class divided into small groups to produce plays, her group failed to produce a significant play. None the less, a class consensus stretching even to the opposition goody goody faction agreed that:

c2/23   c2/18* can do anything in acting. She will just apply herself to it but most of us, we can't.

She was consequently the student in her class most often chosen on a drama sociometric criterion.

b5/42* was not top in any school subject. None the less, classmates believed he came top and termed him a brain. He was seen in many respects to be a model student. He was believed to contribute well in class discussions, to do extra work on assignments, to be quick to discern teachers' mistakes and to be the first to answer teachers' questions.

One way that dominant students created high academic status was by controlling public academic behaviour. Students used public academic behaviour of classmates to construct academic status. Students, such as b1/18* in the following example, who had high marks but did not participate in academic discourse tended not to be seen as 'brains':

Q   Brains of the class?
b1/24*   b1/18* is not too bad. I had forgotten about him because he is quiet. He is completely different in that a quiet person is not normally brainy and that is what he is.

Dominant students, by limiting classmates' contributions and optimising their own, could monopolise this constituent of academic status.

'Calling out', making unsolicited contributions, was one method by which dominant students maximised their contribution to classroom academic discourse. 'Calling out' by dominant students also limited other students' contributions. In this way, c2/18* limited her class brain's contributions. The brain, c2/46* commented:

c2/46*   Usually other girls say things and I don't get any
          chance to say anything. c2/18* just says the answer
          and usually I don't bother.

However, even c2/18*'s associates did not recognise that calling
out by c2/18* stopped c2/46* making academic contributions:

c2/27*   c2/46* has worthwhile things to say, but she doesn't
          talk too much.
Q   Why not?
c2/27*   I don't know. She just wants to listen.

Students generally held the universalistic principle that all
students should be given an equal opportunity to participate in
class discussions. c2/18* selectively activated this principle and
so quelled other students who called out. These included, as in
the example below, rivals for leadership. The rivals were
publicly shown to be unable to control classroom interaction, and
their efforts to construct a definition of their high academic
status were thwarted:

c2/36   c2/41* always seems to be calling out answers.
          c2/18* just yells out, 'Here she goes again!' and
          one day in class c2/41* yelled out something and [the
          teacher] said to her, 'c2/41*, I wish you would wait
          until it is your turn', and c2/18* said, 'Yes, c2/41*'
          in a real sour way.

c2/18* also raised her academic status by using associates'
knowledge to supplement her own in class discussions. One of
her friends said:

c2/28   If c2/27 and I say something and c2/18* hears it she
          will go ahead and say it. She will put up her hand
          and say it aloud and she will get it right.

Even when c2/18* did not answer, she still tried to impress
classmates with her knowledge:

c2/41*   There are times when the teacher can't remember
          something and remembers it later and c2/18* says,
          'I know that' as if she knew it all the time.

b5/42*'s calling out, whether completely unsolicited by the
teacher or in response to questions undirected to particular
students, similarly limited other students' contributions while
optimising his own:

Q   If you see [a teacher] has made a mistake on the
          board [what would you do]?
b5/55*   I would stick up my hand and tell him but b5/42*

and the ones that are like him as soon as they see
a mistake they go, 'Sir! That's wrong!', and they
yell it out so that everyone can hear.

b5/42* also dissuaded subordinate classmates from contributing
to class discussions by defining their efforts as unwarranted
claims to academic status. He commented on his relations with
one such student:

b5/42*   b5/55* thinks he knows a lot about things and we
just tell him to shut up or sit down or something.

The victim gave a similar description of how b5/42* prevented
him joining in classroom discourse:

b5/55*   If the teacher actually asks me a question, I will get
up and answer it but if he asks the class a question
I prefer to sit down because b5/42* and them like
the opportunity to go mad always.
Q   What sort of things do they say and do?
b5/55*   It is not so much what they say but they probably
torment you about it for a week or so. They thump
or knock you over, not to hurt you, just to torment
you. They just think that you are trying to be smart
so they do things like that to you.

On other occasions, b5/42* limited classmates' contributions by
labelling their performance as poor while tacitly asserting his
own superiority:

Q   Some people make fun of what you say in class?
b5/26*   Yeah, b5/42*. He does a lot of that.
b5/25   He says all comments if you say anything, calls out,
'bullshit!'
Q   Would you ever keep quiet because of b5/42*?
b5/26*   Yeah. I hate him.

Students often cheated to obtain pass marks. They rarely
cheated to obtain high marks and were usually condemned when
they did so. However, dominant students were more likely than
their classmates to cheat to obtain high marks. c2/18*, for
example, regularly copied friends' work. b5/42* appropriated
classmates' work. A classmate told of one occasion:

b5/47*   b5/42* was supposed to do a project and when he
didn't do his he went over to Room G1 and he tore
out the name of somebody else and put his own on
the back and wrapped it up and gave it in as his own.
I seen him do it and he said, 'If you say you seen it,
I will thump you.'

Dominant students in cheating did not incur the stigmatisation as 'cheats' which was often suffered by subordinate students who cheated.

Dominant students minimised the significance of subordinate students' high academic status. c2/18* did this by activating problems of academic status management. Her rivals for leadership commented:

Q   Who might tease c2/46* about being a brain?
c2/42*   c2/18* always goes, 'Ooh' every time she gets a good mark.
c2/41*   She goes, 'Ooh, that's a good mark!' or something like that.
c2/42*   She is just being sarcastic.
c2/41*   Wishes that she could get it most likely.

b5/42* more subtly ignored the class brain's high academic status. Instead, he dwelt on the brain's negative attributes. These included not stirring and, perhaps more important from b5/42*'s perspective, not acceding to b5/42*'s definition of the proper time to stir and breaking b5/42*'s monopoly on relations with teachers:

b5/52   b5/57*'s a goody goody, doesn't muck up much.
b5/42* Always likes to be on the same side as the teacher's on. We all get round stirring some day and will go around stirring the one teacher and [the teacher] will all get savage and b5/57* will just sit there and be a little goody goody and then he will get off and we will all get into trouble. He doesn't carry on when we start.
Q   He seems to get good marks?
b5/42* Yeah. He is brainy and he knows everything.

The contrast between b5/42*'s control of the definition of academic status and the consequences of another student's failure to control the definition of academic status illustrates the circularity of control and academic status. Each was given the principal part in their class play as a tribute to reputed acting ability. Each, having put little effort into mastering the part, then left it. In leaving the part, b5/42* preserved the reputation of a competent actor:

b5/55* b5/42* was a good Tarzan. He could do quite well, like you would expect a Tarzan to be.

Classmates accepted as valid b5/42*'s reason for deserting the part:

b5/33   b5/42* didn't like getting around with b5/16 dressed as Jane.

b5/42* then effectively condemned the play to failure. This was done by ensuring the election of an incompetent subordinate successor to the part:

> b5/46   Once b5/42* didn't want to be Tarzan for the play, [his group] suggested b5/26* and then they said, 'Those that want to vote for b5/26* put up their hands' and b5/42* put up his hand for b5/26* and nearly the whole lot put up their hands. A typical vote, you know.

b2/22*'s similar desertion of the principal part in his class play destroyed his academic reputation and pretensions to power. At the time I asked:

> Q   How do people feel about the play?
> b2/37   Good.
> b2/57   I reckon it should be a good one if they all take part.
> b2/37   Now that b2/22*'s out of it.

His successor, before seen as a quiet and conscientious brain, was admired for his performance in a play which was eventually chosen for presentation on Speech Night. As a result of this successful performance, he became the only brain in the research population who derived influence from academic status without it being buttressed by power or other source of influence. His capable acting excited comparison between him and b2/22*:

> b2/42   It is okay to have a few good kids in the class. b2/28* is playing Cripple in the play.
> b2/41   He's only had a couple of weeks to learn and he has done a good job and he even acts like he is a cripple and he goes around like he was and everything.
> b2/42   He took the job over from b2/22*. b2/22* wasn't very good. He couldn't learn his lines fast enough.

b2/22* tried to define his successor as a crawler, a cheat and an isolate, who used illegitimate methods to obtain high academic status:

> Q   Anyone who goes out of their way to help teachers?
> b2/21   b2/28* I suppose.
> b2/22*   He tries to crawl for answers too, looks up his books and everything to find the answer. He sits by himself anyway.

These attempts to denigrate b2/28* and discount his academic performance failed. Even b2/22*'s associates, such as b2/55, denied the charges:

> Q   Anyone who does help the teacher more than others do?

b2/55   b2/28* seems to co-operate, helps teachers by telling
other people to keep quiet.

Q   No one would think that he was crawling? Or goody
goody?

b2/55   No. He usually mixes well with all the kids.

Failure to control the definition of academic status led to b2/22*
losing academic status. This loss of academic status led, in turn,
to loss of control:

Q   Who would you try to keep out of your group?

b2/37   Probably b2/22*. He'd mess it up. He'd try to take
the whole thing over. Like this play here, he didn't
want to be the cripple so he tries to be the producer.
That didn't work.

LOW ACADEMIC STATUS

Low marks tended to attract contempt. Low academic status
students had a variety of ways in which they could try to amelior-
ate their position. From Figure 9.2 it can be seen that they
either attempted to control or accepted teachers' definitions of
academic performance. If they attempted to control teachers'
definitions of academic performance they did so either by rejecting the teachers' definition of the significance of academic performance or by modifying or suppressing its significance among
classmates. If the students accepted the teachers' definition of
academic performance then they attempted or did not attempt to
improve their low academic status. The consequences of each of
these alternative reactions to teachers' imposition of low
academic status are discussed below. It is argued that students
cannot afford to accept teachers' imposition of low academic
status, but that they are unable to counter it directly. Successful
management requires modification or suppression of the significance of low academic status as defined by teachers.

Rejection of teachers' definition of the significance of low marks
Students, in attempting to reject teachers' definitions of the
significance of low academic status, either inverted the academic
status system, or substituted an alternative performance dimension,
or blamed the teacher for the academic failure. The most frequent
of these reactions was to invert the academic status system by
boasting of low marks. This kind of boasting was far more common
than boasting about high marks. It did not convince classmates:

Q   Does anyone skite about marks in your class?

b2/13   Apart from being the lowest. I don't see what there is
to skite about though.

Q   Who might skite about getting low marks?

b2/13   b2/24 laughs and jokes. He got eleven per cent in

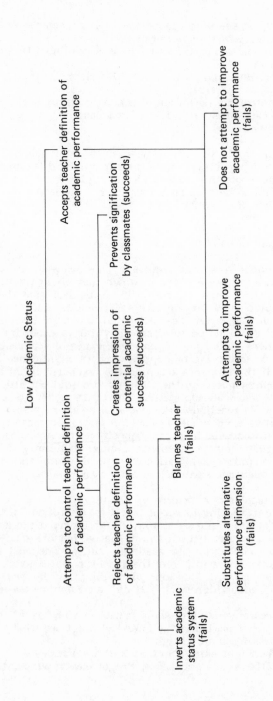

Figure 9.2 Management of low academic status

maths. Oh hell! I wouldn't be joking about it.
b2/28   I think he says it but he doesn't really mean it. He's
not that happy about it. I'm sure I wouldn't have been.

Students were similarly unimpressed by classmates' efforts either
to blame teachers for their failure or to erect substitute performance dimensions. Each was, as in the example below, taken as
confirmation of low academic status:

I c4/23* If they get 'two' or something in maths they go mad
with the teacher because they reckon they didn't
learn anything.

II b2/46 b2/22* usually stirs because he doesn't know his work.
You know he mucks up because he can't cope with his
work.

These findings show that teachers' imposition of low academic
status cannot be confronted directly by students. Attempts to
reject low imposed academic status by challenging the teachers'
authority or by blaming the teacher each fail.

Modification of teachers' definition of significance of low marks
Modification of teachers' definition of the significance of low marks
was a more effective strategy than rejection. Modification, however, was rarer than rejection. The most common form of
modification was to define the possession of low academic status
as advantageous.
A group in 9c3d2 exemplifies students who were untroubled
by low academic status and able to joke freely about it among
themselves. Two of them continued this joking in the interview:

Q   Does anyone stir you when you don't pass?
c3/33* I'll kill you.
c3/32* So long as you don't hurt me.

Low academic status satisfied and even promoted c3/33*'s adult
career aspirations:

c3/23* c3/33* hates school.
c3/31   She says when she leaves school she is going to be a
dropout.

c3/33* did little schoolwork. She avoided classmates' definition
of her not working as laziness by having them see it as successful manipulation of teachers. Her management of low academic
status allowed her to minimise class work and the assignments
expected of her by teachers. It also avoided confrontations with
teachers:

c3/18   She just sits there as if she is a bit dumb. She doesn't

do anything and when [the teacher] asks a question,
'I don't know.'

Continued failure to do homework led teachers to feel that
attempts to enforce homework were wasted effort:

c3/33*   I just won't do it and she never bothers me again.

c3/33* asked teachers questions to show that she would like to
do the work and to legitimate her doing none (cf. Hargreaves,
1975: 149-150). Asking these questions was another way of
demonstrating to classmates her control over teachers:

c3/23*   c3/33* just doesn't feel like doing it so she puts up
          her hand and, 'Mrs Euclid, I can't do this sum. Can
          you help me, please?' and Mrs Euclid has got to come
          trudging over and shows her how to do it.

Despite self-presentation as a low academic status student,
c3/33* left teachers and classmates with the impression that
she was intelligent and that if she wished she might have
earned high marks. Classmates easily integrated the two aspects
of c3/33*'s presentation:

c3/52*   c3/33* - in most of the subjects she just acts dumb
          but she is pretty smart really.

Teachers less often understood c3/33*'s use of low academic
status. One commented:

'A real birdbrain. She asks some of the most ridiculous
questions yet incredibly she could be quite good at work. She
has astounded me in various areas of shorthand and this type
of thing. She can read it back when none of the other members
of the class can.'

c3/33*'s low academic status became an object manipulated by
classmates as well as herself in order to bemuse teachers.
Another of her teachers said:

'c3/15m is always saying to c3/33*, "You are an idiot." They
can't believe some of the things she says. . . . I often wonder
whether it is all an act cos my brain can't take it after a time.
You can spend fifteen minutes explaining to her how to weave
and then you can turn around and in two minutes flat she has
made a horrible mess and then you wonder whether anything
went in and then everyone turns around and knocks c3/33*.'

Students' comments were designed more to annoy the teacher
than to deride c3/33*. Her goals were not shared by all
classmates but her management of low academic status and of

teachers earned general respect.

Prevention of signification of low academic status
In the lowest stream male class, powerful students prevented
their low marks being signified by subordinate students.
Subordinate students' attempts to signify the low academic
status of powerful classmates, such as b6/13* in the following
example, were quickly crushed:

Q   How did you feel about getting the [low] marks in
      maths?
b6/13* Some of the real pansy guys in the class think you're
      a real dumb twit. You soon fix them. Go and hit them
      a couple of times.

This power policy was backed by a statement of an ideology of
the uselessness of much school academic knowledge and related
qualifications:

b6/13* You go out into the world and get a job – you go into
      town, 'I want a quarter of this' or something like this.
      Some of those things in maths you have c + a = b, you
      don't go downtown and say, 'a + s worth of this'.
b6/10   A lot of jobs you don't need that. You don't need a
      junior pass. My brother, he's not very brainy and
      he got a job at Cooper's sawmill and they just asked
      him if he wanted to learn and he just said, 'Yeah.'

b6/13* concluded with a comment on the ignorance of teachers
who stress the importance of school marks:

b6/13* A report card is only to show how well you have been
      doing but sometimes teachers make a real big deal
      about it. They think it's really important.

Acceptance of the significance of low marks
Two types of student did not contest teachers' definition of the
significance of the low marks given them. These were students
interested neither in improving their marks nor in managing their
low academic status and students with low academic status who
persevered in attempts to improve it within the bounds of
teachers' definitions.
    Low academic status with no attempt to improve or manage
the status led to rejection by classmates. These low academic
status students were blamed for low academic commitment rather
than lack of ability or low marks:

b1/35   b1/27 and b1/28 don't know anything. They just
      don't care. They don't know the work what is going on.
b1/36   You do a bit of work but b1/28 doesn't study for exams
      and I think that is childish.

These students sat alone or with someone similar. They were
either sociometric isolates or formed isolated dyads with someone of similar academic status and commitment. They were even
excluded from the mucking around which was the normal student
alternative to work and the principal form of sociability:

> b2/31   I might talk for a while, bit of a joke . . . , just
> talking really, not listening to the teacher. It's just
> human. Really everyone does that.
> Q   What about people who wouldn't sit back and chat?
> b2/31   Most of them do. b2/38 wouldn't. He's detached from
> the rest of the class, sort of thing.

The low academic status students with the most problems were
those who accepted the teacher definition of the significance of
their low academic status and who persevered in their academic
commitments. They were condemned both for trying to work and
for not trying to work. c1/23*, at the bottom of her class
academically, exemplifies such students. She differed in one
respect from similar low academic status students. Although
her low marks were constantly publicised, her classmates did not
as constantly tease her about it:

> c1/43   People just out of curiosity say, 'What did you get,
> c1/23*?' - this sort of thing - not to sneer at her -
> to make sure they are not the lowest I would say.

Unlike subordinate brains, c1/23* with low academic status
could enquire freely about others' marks or skite about her
occasional higher marks without causing offence:

> c1/51*   c1/23* is really happy when she gets a good mark.
> Very happy about it. She comes and tells you about it.
> 'I got nine out of ten' or something. The way she does
> it she doesn't really skite. She is just so happy that
> she has passed.

However, her slow mastery of academic work combined with the
wish to learn caused her considerable social problems. Her
attempts to learn were resented by students who saw the obtrusive
desire to learn impeding the proper progress of the lesson. The
propriety of conformist low academic status students' efforts to
master work were judged not by their need to know but by the
pertinence of the question to classmates. Accordingly, c1/23*
was condemned when she asked teachers questions:

> c1/45   c1/23* is kind of dead.
> c1/38   If she asks a question in school it will be a really silly
> question that we have already talked about and then
> that is when everyone starts saying those things about
> her.

Even private requests for help were refused and resented because they interrupted classmates' work:

c1/14* c1/23* bugs you sometimes when you are in the middle of working out a sum and she wants a chat with you while you are doing something and you are just concentrating and you have to go to tell her to turn around.

Q Why does she want to chat?

c1/14* She needs some help. She might get stuck.

Although some academic work is a prerequisite of academic success, the converse is also true. Low academic status students find it impossible to work when they fall too far behind with work and attempts to obtain help are repulsed. Their almost universal rejection on sociometric work criteria was induced both by perceptions of low academic performance and by activation of work norms:

Q Is there anyone you would try to keep out of the group?

c1/42 Probably c1/23* because she wouldn't work, I think.

c1/41 I don't think she would put much work in it.

These illustrate how observations of her not completing desk-work and homework diffused to all work settings. She felt that she could contribute to group work. Although classmates did not value her contributions, students who had worked with her reported her more earnest than other group members:

Q You said c1/23* was pushing to get work done?

c1/55 Yes. I think most of the time she is going mad at c/18 and c1/17* . . . c1/18 and c1/17* are always talking about boys and so she goes mad on them and says, 'Hurry up and get your work done.' Sometimes she will get really mad and throw her pen down.

Thus low academic status conformist students were accused, usually correctly of not working and, incorrectly, of not wanting to work. What began as a disability was condemned as voluntary deviance from work norms.

The chief problems of low academic status students were not seen by them or classmates to be related to low academic status and conformity. Every low academic status conformist was a social as well as a work rejectee. Classmates shunned them in every classroom and work situation so that they sat alone and did not mix with classmates in the playground. The reasons given for shunning low academic status conformists always included personal hygiene with accusations, such as the following, that they were unkempt and vermin ridden. No other students were so accused:

c1/52*   c1/16* is real nasty to c1/23*.
c1/51*   One day c1/16* asked for a pencil or something and
          c1/23* went to give her one and she wouldn't take it.
c1/52*   As if there were germs on it or something.
c1/51*   And so she took one off someone else.
c1/52*   Sometimes c1/23* sits behind us . . . and you get all
          scratchy and they reckon that she has got fleas and
          everything on her.
c1/52*   Mrs Goethe picked c1/23* to go out to the front and
          c1/47 and c1/48 and everybody else were telling c1/23*
          to sit down.
          'Oh, we don't want the germy old things up front'
          and they were going on and c1/23* went and sat down
          - she was crying.

c4/23* and b5/47*, who were also low academic status conformists, were similarly accused of being unkempt:

I c4/28   c4/23* is dirty. She picks her nose and that.
  c4/14   c4/23* looks as if she never has a bath. Sometimes
          you see her with dirt in her hair. It's all knotty.
          Sometimes she smells as if she has been up in the cow-
          bales and never came home to have a bath.

II b5/24   b5/47* is awful I reckon. He never washes his hair.
  b5/13   He smells.
  Q   He is dirty?
  b5/24   My oath! Ever since he first came here, the first day
          from Fishingtown.
  b5/13   The first day on the bus.
  b5/24   They called him 'Grub' and that was it.
  b5/13   Yeah. On the bus.
  b5/24   Ever since.
  b5/13   Everyone calls him it.

The negative attributes were extended in the case of b5/47* to allegations of homosexuality and in the case of c4/23* to allegations of theft:

c4/41   Everybody thought it was c4/23* but they became
          unstuck and it was c3/36. [The teachers] said that if
          anyone knew anything about it we were to say it and
          everybody at once said c4/23* whether they knew it
          or not, which they didn't know because it wasn't her.

These allegations were a rhetorical reality (Marsh, Rosser and Harré, 1978: 83-114; Willis, 1977: 194-199) which described the attitude of others to the low status conformists. Empirical foundations of the accusations were not apparent to the interviewer. Moreover, when conversation in interviews moved from a rhetorical to a factual mode the accusations were frequently modified or denied. Some, like c4/58*, rejected the allegations:

c4/58*   They said c4/23* had nits and all that and she didn't.
c4/56*   [rationale for rejecting c4/23* on the English socio-
            metric] I don't think anyone in the class likes c4/23*.
Q   But why don't you?
c4/56*   I don't know really. I just don't like her for herself.
Q   What makes you feel unhappy or uneasy with her?
c4/56*   I don't know. I think it is because no one else does.

Interestingly the class sexual minorities who were outside
normal classroom interaction did not share the class consensus
and could not perceive the empirical base for it. These students
made comments like:

I c4/45m   Strange c4/23* gets left out. I think it is because in
             Grade Eight all the Grade Eight boys used to torment
             her. They used to call her . . .
c4/46m   'Stinky'.
Q   Does she smell?
c4/45m   c4/46m No.
c4/46m   I don't know why everybody doesn't like c4/23*. . . .
             She hasn't got anything wrong with her. She isn't
             ugly. She isn't that ugly.
c4/45m   She's not ugly at all.

II Q   Is there any girl in the class whose uniform looks a bit
             smarter or shabbier?
c1/58m   I wouldn't say shabbier than anybody but a lot of
             people pick on c1/23* because I suppose . . . they
             want someone to pick on. Well, c1/23* takes it all in
             her stride and she is okay.

CONCLUSIONS

This chapter has confirmed the central importance of academic
status. Academic status is a symbolic reality no student can
ignore.

The significance of academic status is mediated and determined
by students so that it reinforces and legitimates students'
control systems and ideologies of independence from teacher
control. This is seen in student constructions of high academic
status which tend to identify acceptance of teacher definitions
with crawling and assertion of student definitions with stirring
and mucking around. It is also seen in the difficulty subordinate
students had signifying their high academic status when defined
by teachers, and the ability of dominant students to create
definitions of academic status.

Students were unable to counter directly teacher definitions of
academic status. None the less, it was important for the students

concerned that they construct an alternative interpretation of their low academic status. Most successful were attempts to define low academic status as student manipulation of teachers. Least successful were assertions of the significance of alternative performance dimensions and reactions which admitted the validity and significance of the teacher's imposed definition of low academic status.

Overall, dominant students determined the use and construction of academic status. Dominant students could not ignore this symbolic reality. Its use and management was a prerequisite of the maintenance of control but successful exploitation of high academic status was a preserve of dominant students.

Chapter 10

Teacher particularism

Students discerned two kinds of occasion when teachers established particularistic relations with teachers and so departed from universalistic performance treatment of students. These occasions were the favouring and victimising of students.

This chapter first considers students' evaluations of teachers' favourites, then examines students' attitudes to the alleged victimisation of students by teachers, and concludes with a description of dominant students' control and use of definitions of favouritism and victimisation. Earlier chapters have included accounts of talking to or helping teachers, stirring, outside activities, goody goody behaviour and the construction of academic status. These are all factors related to teachers' favouring or victimising students. Case studies in this chapter are continued from these earliest accounts.

This chapter describes how dominant students appropriate use of universalistic norms governing interaction with teachers. Dominant students are shown to monopolise legitimated teachers' favour. They do this by controlling definitions of the qualities in students which students believed should be recognised and rewarded by teachers. Dominant students are also shown to control the activation of allegations of teachers' victimisation of students and thereby to draw favourable notice to themselves.

TEACHERS' FAVOURITE

Goldtown students applied the terms 'teacher's pet' and 'teacher's favourite' to students who were alleged to be favoured by teachers. Students commonly referred to three bases for teachers' selection of favourites. Teachers were supposed to find their relations with well-behaved, co-operative and intelligent students rewarding. Teachers were also supposed to find rewarding the establishment of reciprocal, particular relations with students reputed to be difficult for teachers to handle. Third, teachers were often perceived taking as favourites students they knew outside the classroom or with whom they shared outside interests. Students judged the legitimacy of teacher's favour by consider- ations of whether the student concerned had earned it. It thus depended on whether students shared the teacher's evaluation of the student. These attributed origins and consequent types of favouritism are discussed and schematised in Figure 10.1.

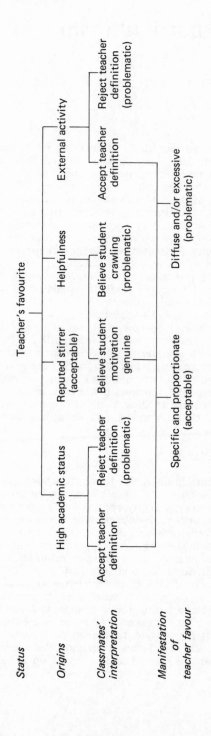

Figure 10.1 Teacher favouritism

Virtuous students as favourites
Hard work, intelligence and co-operation with teachers were
supposed by students to be separately and interactively sources
of teachers' favour. Within these parameters students' discrimination of the equity of favour reflected students' status systems.
For example, public recognition by the teacher of high academic
status was shown in Chapters 8 and 9 to be problematic for
subordinate students and a resource for dominant students.
In Chapter 8 it was shown that classmates' interpretation of
students' helpfulness was often related to the control status of
the student concerned. This section shows that, when two
conditions were met, students legitimated teachers' favouring
students whom they saw as diligent, intelligent and helpful.
These conditions were that teachers and classmates agreed on
the classmates' qualities and that the manner of favouritism
corresponded with the perceived attributes of the favourites. It
is shown that these conditions resulted in frequent challenges
by students to the propriety of teachers' favouring subordinate
students, and in classmates' acceptance of the propriety of
teachers' favouring dominant students.
    A hardworking brain was generally regarded as a legitimate
favourite. The advantage received and the attention granted
were sometimes resented. They were not considered improper
unless the truth of the teacher's perceptions, in terms of which
these favours were granted, was challenged. For example:

b1/22   [b1/45* and b1/17* are teacher's pets.]
b1/32*   I think they earn the right sometimes because they are
         good at work. They always work well and b1/45*
         always jokes with teachers and that. They always get
         good results so it is just normal to be teacher's pet.
         [b1/32* is not annoyed by this favouritism.] Doing an
         experiment they say, 'Oh, I'd like to do that' and they
         put up their hand and the teacher always says, 'Right-
         i-o, b1/45* or b1/58*,' or something like that. I would
         like to participate in the experiment too but those kids
         are always participating. . . . Mr Gauss favours
         b1/17* a bit. He lets him talk on for a while about
         theories that he has made up and that.
b1/22   I don't really know. I suppose we can talk about other
         things if we argue like what he has done and what we
         have done. I suppose that we can talk on like that for
         a while.

The right of such students to receive privileges was sometimes
contested on the grounds of their qualifications. They could be
accused of presenting themselves to teachers in a way that
falsely enhanced their academic performance:

b1/21   b1/45* a crawler - poses in front of the teacher some-
         times - especially in front of Mr Kingsley, same pose

as Mr Kingsley puts on in front of us. . . . The
reason b1/45* is copying him is so that he can get
friendly with him.

They could, independently of their self-presentation, be alleged
not to have the qualifications teachers attributed to them:

b1/44   In English b1/45* is a bit of a pet . . .
b1/17*   Sometimes I get a bit annoyed with b1/45* because he
         gets a heap of acting parts and I like acting too - and
         he overacts too much.

In Chapter 8 it was shown that students often offered to help
outside the classroom for extrinsic advantages which were not
considered proper by teachers. Teachers, therefore, tended to
become cautious in which students they chose for certain jobs.
A goody goody commented:

b3/26*   The teachers took b3/25 and me as favourites but only
         to the extent that if something could be got then I
         would get it because he could trust b3/25 and a few
         other things. That was the main thing, you see.
         Things could get pinched quite easily.

Classmates had a different perspective. Students seen as responsible by teachers were often seen by classmates as crawlers or
goody goodies. The qualities of students which led to their being
chosen by teachers to help were often condemned by classmates.
A goody goody described the divergence of perspectives in the
following terms:

b3/23   If the teacher thinks [you have a sense of respons-
         ibility] obviously the kids wouldn't because if you get
         a good report from the teacher you don't always get
         a good report from the kids because they might think
         that you are crawling or something and I don't crawl,
         I can assure you of that.
Q   What do you mean by 'crawling'?
b3/23   Well, if you try to be responsible and not to muck
         around and all this the kids say you are a pansy,
         a crawler, a teacher's pet. But I don't see any point
         in acting stupid and scoffing off at teachers and
         everything.

The term 'teacher's pet' was sometimes extended to refer to
obsequiousness as a characteristic teachers desired in students.
c3/14*, herself seen in Chapters 2 and 8 to be diligent and ready
to help teachers, condemned classmates as 'teacher's pets' in
the following terms:

c3/14*   c3/58, c3/48, c3/47 and c3/57 are not really popular in

the class. Everyone hates them because they sit down
the front and they don't stir – you know teacher's pets
– that's c3/48* and c3/47 anyway. c3/57 and c3/58
talk a bit but not much.

Q 'Teacher's pets?'

c3/14* They stay behind after class and talk to Mrs Curie
sometimes or they try to get on the good side of the
teacher all the time.

Q How would they do that?

c3/14* They stay behind and talk to the teacher.

c3/13 They always do their homework, learn it and study it
and things like that.

c3/14*, however, was herself accused by classmates of being
improperly favoured by teachers. She had the common problem
of a contested definition of qualifications in the core area of
favour:

c3/17 c3/14* is the pet of the whole class.

c3/18 She knows the answers.

c3/17 We know them too but Mrs Pitman never listens to us.

Other of her difficulties resulted from teacher's favour which
went beyond the specific domain of justified favour. Teachers
allowed her to escape unpunished with actions that would have
had classmates in trouble. Teachers allowed her an autonomy,
denied to classmates, in deciding the pace of her work. These
inequities led to some hostility and allegations that she was
improperly favoured:

c3/18 Some kids can say almost anything to teachers whereas
other kids wouldn't dare to. c3/14* gets away with
most things she says. Sometimes she gives back cheek
but the teachers take it all in good with her.

c3/17 And sometimes we have journals for homework and we
just have to do the journals she does the whole lot.
One time we did the whole lot and it was alright for
her to do the whole lot. . . . Mrs Pitman would say
[to us], 'I told you only to do the journals. What if it
is wrong? Blah! Blah!' And then she would say to
c3/14*, 'Have you finished? You can start the next
one.'

c3/18 'That is very good, c3/14*', and we are there fuming.

Teachers widened c3/14*'s authority to matters normally decided
by class discussion and vote. This caused her more problems:

c3/41 Mrs Pitman asks c3/14* everything. In the Flowershow
Mrs Pitman asked what she thought we would do for
the Flowershow so we did c3/14*'s idea and all that
sort of thing.

c3/14*'s problems were exacerbated by not using her influence, as other dominant students did, to define positively the teacher favouritism. She professed her status as teacher's favourite unwelcome but did nothing about it:

Q   Do you sometimes feel you are the teacher's favourite?
c3/14*   Sometimes. Like Mrs Pitman looks at me. When she
           doesn't think something is right she will look at me
           and you sort of shrivel up because you know every-
           body thinks you are a pet.
Q   What can you do about it?
c3/14*   There's nothing you can do about it.

Stirrers as favourites
Teachers sometimes assumed a particularistic, diffuse responsibility for the progress and wellbeing of girls stereotyped by
teachers as troublemakers. The stereotyped troublemaker who
accepted the reciprocal role behaved and worked well for that
teacher. The special attention granted c4/48*, otherwise the
harshest stirrer in her class and the most influential member of
her clique, led to her becoming in this way a teacher's pet:

Q   Do any teachers have favourites in your class?
c4/44*   Mrs Sappho does. c4/48*.
c4/43*   Yes. c4/48* because Mrs Sappho can control c4/48*.
           She gives her extra attention, doesn't she?
c4/43*   c4/48* and Mrs Sappho - they keep on talking to each
           other all the time.

Such students did not find that their status as teacher's pets
was a problem. Indeed they activated the status required for
the advantages offered:

c4/17   c4/48* talks herself out of getting detention, that is
           with Mrs Sappho too. She went up to detention the
           other day and said, 'Gee, you smell nice, Mrs Sappho,'
           and everyone looked at her but she got away with it
           without a detention.

Even such assiduous courting of teacher's favour remained
unproblematic. As was shown in Chapter 8, the status of stirrer
precludes labelling as a crawler or goody goody.

External interests
Relations with teachers outside the school and interests in
outside activities which were shared with or known to teachers
were seen by students to lead to two possible manifestations of
teachers' favour. These were higher academic attainment and
familiarity with teachers in the classroom.
      Higher academic attainment as a perceived consequence of
outside association between student and teacher was rare and

never legitimated. The connexion between significant high
academic status and high control status, which was demonstrated
in Chapters 8 and 9, resulted in only subordinate students being
said to benefit by higher marks because of outside association
with teachers. In alleging favouritism students used, as in the
example below, their knowledge of the work performed and the
association of student with teacher:

b2/28* b2/56* got '29' for his book and the average was about
'22' and I reckon that other people in the class were
worth more than him and a lot of people in the class
thought that it was just because Mr Atlas boards at
his place.
b2/15 And they seem to think that the teacher could have
told him what to study and that - the main points.
b2/28* '29' for a book is a big mark.

Accusations of favouritism more frequently followed teachers
acting familiarly with students consequent on outside contact.
Signs of familiarity were teachers' calling boys by the first
name in a school where they were customarily called by surnames,
and teachers' asking students, either male or female, about their
outside activities. Classmates objected to the attention the
teacher gave these students when others were thought to have
an equal claim to that attention. For example:

Q How can you tell that Mr Gauss favours b6/15?
b6/11 You can tell.
b6/12 Praising him when football first started. He asked
b6/15, 'Are you playing football this year?' He didn't
ask any of the other kids. He just asked b6/15.
b6/11 I reckon all the kids should be equal to a teacher.

The subordinate students thus selected for favour either
continued to be attacked as teacher's pets or took steps to end
the status. The subordinate students could end their unwelcome
status by increased mucking around and stirring in the relevant
teacher's period. This misbehaviour, as in the example below,
decreased the teacher's favour. The misbehaviour also countered
any allegations that the favourite had bought that favour by
being a crawler or goody goody:

b4/23* I used to be Mr Parson's favourite for a while because
I played golf with him in a student-teacher match.
b4/24 And he called b4/23* [by his first name].
b4/23* Sometimes he used to call me [first name] but now he
usually says [surname].
Q How did you feel about being his favourite?
b4/23* I thought it was alright but I didn't really like the
idea of calling me [first name] and all this. I would
rather he treated me like the others so I misbehaved

a bit. I didn't really misbehave a lot - just annoyed him.

STUDENTS 'PICKED ON' BY TEACHERS

Teachers' 'picking on' students was the mirror image of teachers showing favouritism. Students' perceptions of victimisation and favouritism originated in comparisons of treatment meted out for equivalent behaviour. Both were often seen to occur in the same context. For example:

> c3/14* Mrs Euclid picks on me because I talk too much but
> there is all these other kids up the front. They talk
> all the time and she doesn't say anything.

Students alleged a similar breaking of universalistic justice in victimisation and favouritism. However, in the case of victimisation the student instead of receiving unequal advantages, was disadvantaged compared with classmates. Perceptions of victimisation were usually concerned with the accuracy and even-handedness of teachers' imputations of pupil misbehaviour and the equity of consequent punishment. Two minor themes in allegations of victimisation were sexually specialised. Some male would-be stirrers said that they had been victimised by teachers who lowered marks in retribution for stirring. Girls occasionally alleged that some teachers victimised certain students by showing their dislike without actually punishing. The distribution of students' allegations of victimisation as discussed below are depicted in Figure 10.2.

Students' allegations of teachers' victimisation of students followed the pattern described by Hargreaves, Hester and Mellor (1975: 171-251). Students saw teachers using stereotypes of students to identify culprits and allocate punishments. For example:

> c4/21   [Teachers] have just got it in for me because you see
> as soon as they start getting a bad name it goes round
> the school and [they] take it for granted that you are
> bad so they just act down on you as if you are bad.
> . . . If you stop for a couple of seconds to discuss
> something say in maths you don't understand it
> properly, like c4/22 might be able to help me a bit or
> I might be able to help her, Mrs Newton will ask me
> how much work I have done and even though I have
> done a fair bit it is still not enough sometimes.

Students' discussion of instances of victimisation took into account whether students shared the teacher's stereotype, accepted the teacher's attribution of blame, or accepted the equity of punishment. They considered either or both the

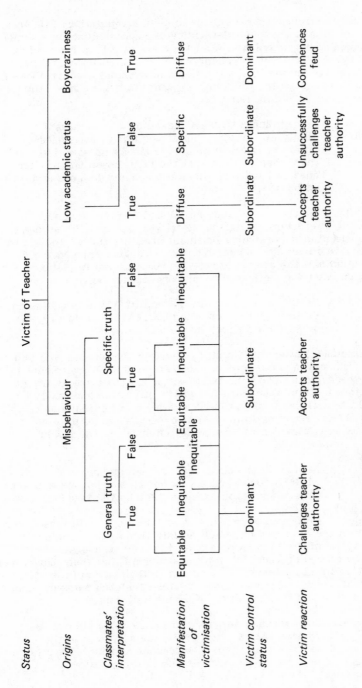

Figure 10.2 Teachers' victimisation of students

immediate circumstances and the student's reputation. Students did not always challenge the justice of misattribution on specific occasions when it followed what they saw as a true typification. The general truth of the allegation outweighted its occasional falsity. The mixing of the typified and immediate reality allowed classmates, as in the following comment, to believe that students were being picked on fairly:

> Q　　Any students that get picked on by teachers?
> b6/12　b6/13* all the time. Sometimes fairly, sometimes unfairly. Because he always mucks up sometimes and then when he does that the next lesson the teacher goes and tells the other teacher and he goes and picks on b6/13*.

Victimisation by extra punishment had few consequences for student interaction among the majority of subordinate students who accepted it passively. Dominant students turned the victimisation to advantage. They, like b2/22* below, enjoyed the attention and the chance to activate commitments to justice against what was defined as arbitrary teacher behaviour:

> b2/28*　Mr Boyle, said, 'Shut up' and b2/22* didn't shut up. He just kept on and then b2/22* started to say, 'Why do you always pick on me all the time?'

Sometimes, students directly controlled the teacher who had discriminated against them or a classmate. Public statements to the teacher comparing the treatment of students almost always led to more equitable treatment of the students concerned. It could lead either to the student who had been threatened with punishment escaping unpunished, or the favourite who had so far escaped punishment now being punished by the teacher. For example:

> Q　　Anyone in the class ever dobbed anyone in?
> c4/38　c4/48* would when she is not allowed to talk and she sees other people talking she tells the teacher.

Students' control of allegations of victimisation is discussed more fully in the next section which deals with dominant students' management of status as pets and victims of teachers.

The rare allegations by would-be stirrers that their marks had been reduced by teachers' reactions to their attempts to stir were discounted by classmates. Instead the classmates explained the allegations as the skiting of a failed stirrer:

> b5/42*　Just because he gets a low mark for a subject he thinks, 'Ah, I must have made a bit stir in that subject.' He thinks the teacher knocks his marks down because he is a stirrer. He is really stupid.

No competent stirrer thought that teachers discriminated against him by granting lower marks.

Girls accused some teachers of diffuse victimisation of certain of their classmates. This was shown not by unfair punishments but by statements the teachers made in class. Three types of girl were believed to be the occasional objects of such victimisation. The victimisation of nonconforming girls with high academic attainment which was not accepted by teachers was discussed in Chapter 9. Low academic status conformist rejectees, such as c1/23*, were another focus of victimisation:

c1/25   c1/23* [is picked on a lot]. The moment she says
         something Mrs Tennyson immediately jumps down her
         throat.
c1/24   She says 'What do you mean, c1/23*? You are just
         raving on as usual.'

Such girls received some sympathy from classmates. However, their usual passive acceptance of teachers' authority ensured that they neither resisted nor exploited their status as victims.

Girls with mature and active sexual interests were another focus for victimisation by teachers. Both their interests and their talk about these interests could provoke the teacher. c1/11* and c1/12* whose sexual interests were discussed in Chapter 5, were victimised in this way:

c1/23*   Mrs Pitman picks on c1/11* and c1/12* [because] they
         talk a fair bit in class but they don't talk to the
         extent that they have to be shifted or anything but
         Mrs Pitman always thinks that she has the right to
         do this but the kids aren't really talking that much.
         She is always picking on them.

c1/11* and c1/12* although potentially influential made no use of being victimised. They did not publicly challenge teachers' arbitrary exercise of authority. When other such girls with mature and active sexual interests chose to exercise their high influence diffuse feuding with teachers resulted. This is discussed in the next section.

DOMINANT STUDENTS AND TEACHER PARTICULARISM
Dominant students were especially prone to favouritism and victimisation because they tended, as a result of their conspicuous activities, to be known by teachers directly and through reputation. This teacher particularism, whether expressed in favouritism or victimisation, had a similar function in classroom interaction. It focused attention on that student. As such it afforded a resource for the celebration of the importance of dominant students.

All teachers who taught c2/18* had a broad knowledge of her

derived from staffroom discussions and administration opinions.
A member of the administration commented that she was 'a sly,
bad type', 'a liar and you can trust nothing she says'. Her
form teacher commented: 'They reckon that she has improved
this year. I would hate to have seen her last year.' Many of
her teachers were aware of c2/18*'s sexual reputation. Even
sympathetic teachers, such as her form teacher quoted again
below, believed that her sexual interests, which as was shown in
Chapter 5 were a strong source in class control, isolated c2/18*
from classmates:

> 'c2/18* is . . . not a social leader because of her relationship
> with boys. Exactly what her relationship with boys is I am not
> prepared to say but obviously she finds an interest in boys
> that many of the other girls don't. Perhaps they have the
> interest but they aren't about to show it.'

Students generally knew of c2/18*'s sexual reputation among
Goldtown adults, and the malicious use certain teachers made of
it. This victimisation became part of the rhetoric which
surrounded c2/18*'s sexuality:

> c1/13* Mum reckons that she is a real nice kid.
> c1/14* Some old people don't give her a chance.
> c1/13* They build up a story and the story becomes bigger
> and bigger and bigger and only a little happening.

c2/18* was herself aware of how certain teachers used her
sexual reputation:

> c2/18* I just don't get on with Mrs Beeton.
> c2/17 She kind of rubs c2/18*'s nose in the ground, throws
> her name round a lot. I don't like the way they talk
> about c2/18* in the staffroom. . . . That is why c2/18*
> doesn't like her and that is why I don't like her.
> c2/18* . . . but Mrs Beeton thinks that she is high and mighty
> in society and the whole school belongs to her - the
> way she goes and talks about everything. She talks
> about anyone.
> Q   Would you say she picks on you then?
> c2/18* I deserve to get picked on sometimes but not all the
> time. . . . In her class I go around just like any other
> class. She knows I ran away last year and she blames
> me all the time.

Classmates perceived that Mrs Beeton selectively activated
aspects of teacher imposed order against c2/18*. This was
believed to be unjustified victimisation:

> c2/36 Mrs Beeton always [picks on c2/18*]. c2/18* just says
> one little thing to somebody else and she says, 'c2/18*

up the front. Come and sit near me.'

c2/18*'s response to the perceived victimisation was to go out
of her way to stir the teacher:

c2/18*   I like to get Mrs Beeton mad. I like to see her mad.
Sometimes rocking the chair or singing out works.

She often preserved the appearance but not the intent of conformity in order to annoy Mrs Beeton:

Q   Who does ask teachers questions during lessons?
c2/36   c2/18* [asking teachers sensible questions].
c2/25   In home economics she asks questions to annoy.

Occasionally the cold war broke into open conflict:

c2/11   c2/18* really got into trouble. She was giving Mrs
Beeton back cheek and she got sent into the dressing
room and she wasn't allowed to come out until the end
of the lesson and Mrs Beeton really yelled at her.

As was shown in Chapter 5, c2/18* was an acknowledged but
good tempered stirrer with other teachers. Her studied management of teachers' attempts to control this stirring led to a
negotiated settlement or a tacit recognition by teachers of her
importance. Privately c2/18* accepted her typification as a
stirrer and, except with Mrs Beeton, the specific attribution of
most acts of misbehaviour. None the less, she responded to
teachers' accusations with 'backchat', that is, claims of
innocence and allegations of victimisation:

c2/21   Mrs Wells will say, 'You are talking, c2/18*' and
c2/18* will just say, 'No, that was c2/17' and c2/16
will say, 'No, that was someone else', and Mrs Wells
will say, 'Shut up' and c2/18* will say, 'You are always
blaming me.'

Thus teachers if they intervened to stop the noise had either
to accept an accusation of injustice unrefuted or engage in
disputation which would disrupt the lesson. Most of the time
they unwillingly tolerated the disturbance, and so gave her
a special licence to misbehave in the classroom. A teacher
commented:

'c2/18* seems to think it is a good thing getting into trouble
so I just ignore her most of the time. It is just if she is
getting too rowdy for the class that I have to tell her to be
quiet but otherwise I just ignore her. It is the only method
that works because the more attention she gets the worse she
gets.'

Classmates perceived that c2/18* was being treated as a favourite who escaped unscathed with actions that would have had other students in trouble. These actions included talk which asserted social equality. The talk was familiar to an extent which bordered on stirring:

c2/13   c2/18* comments on how Mrs Wells does her hair or on her clothes she wears or the way she looks nice and sometimes c2/18* says Mrs Wells looks awful too and Mrs Wells just lets her go along with that.

c2/14   She tells c2/18* to stop it and c2/18* just keeps going and Mrs Wells lets her off.

Teachers also recognised that c2/18* was being treated as a favourite. They granted c2/18* recognition as in some respects a social equal, her condition for according them co-operation. This favoured treatment was an immediate consequence of c2/18*'s status as stirrer and clown, and of her claims to sexual maturity and her willingness to initiate talk with teachers. Her form teacher commented:

'This year I have a relationship that works. c2/18* will work well during periods with a minimum of supervision but five minutes before the end of the period she wants a little bit of attention and she figures you should be prepared to give it to her at that point. . . . She likes to tease . . . but she will keep this till the end of the period when she knows I am relaxed and the lesson is over with and then she will come out with the comment that will bring the house down and she waits for my comment which will perhaps do the same. For example, one day before the end of the typing period [my husband] walked by the window there and I waved at him and c2/18* said, "Ah, Mrs Pitman, you are waving at men." But I said, "He's my man. I am entitled to wave to him." But this is the kind of comment she will come out with.'

b5/42*, too, had arrived at a position in the class where most of his teachers either wanted, or decided it was politic, to establish particular relations with him. Teachers' decisions to associate with him followed from an awareness of his power over classmates, his monopolisation of academic contributions and helping of teachers, from his efforts to demand teachers' attention and from his sporting and external interests. His teachers commented:

I   'b5/12* tends to try in class, the one that they take most notice of. He sets a decent example to the rest of the class.'

II   'Obliging, comes in his own time to help with timber; makes a lot of noise, could do better, treated as an adult.'

III   'A pretty good kid in terms of personality, got tons of
          confidence. He must get on pretty well with his parents
          and he can go off fishing and so on. He has developed
          a personality and maturity all of his own. I get tons of
          co-operation out of him.'

IV   'One of the oldest in the class by far and physically the
          biggest – and plays in the first football and cricket and
          is generally recognised as the class king – what b5/42*
          says, goes. . . . . I get on well with b5/42*.'

V   'Occasionally he likes to take things into his own hands
          and goes his own way but most of the time he is good
          and I have tried to cultivate a good friendship with
          b5/42* for self-preservation as well as getting into the
          peer group friendship thing.'

One teacher who acknowledged b5/42*'s class dominance saw the
use that b5/42* made of his talking with the teacher and had
considerable reservations about his work commitment:

'b5/42* is topdog there and he wants everyone to look up to
him. He doesn't do much work at all. He just more or less
talks to you as an elder.'

Some students believed that the high academic status, shown
in Chapter 9 to be attributed to b5/42* by classmates but
unacknowledged by teachers, was the cause of his favoured
status with teachers:

Q   Do you think any of the teachers have class favourites?
b5/32* Mr Gauss.
b5/31* b5/42* is pretty good at maths and that's about it.
b5/32* Mr Gauss is always coming over to talk to b5/42* and
        b5/41*.

Other students agreed with the attribution of favoured status
to b5/42* but gave another explanation:

b5/47   I don't really know why b5/42* – because he is older
        I think. Mr Gauss lets him off more things and while we
        are doing work Mr Gauss will be talking to him. Like
        he went down to Noosa and told about the Noosa nudes
        and things like that.

The principal opposition to the favour given to b5/42* came
from classmates outside his group. Where they saw inequity in
the treatment of b5/42* and their friends, particularly in the
awarding of punishments, they complained. b5/26*, whose conflict with b5/42* over dobbing was described in Chapter VII,
recounted how the principle of equity was invoked on one occasion:

b5/26* Mr Austen lets b5/42* off a bit all the time. . . . The
other day b5/52 got into trouble because of not handing
his project in and b5/42* didn't have his in and we
were all talking and we were telling Mr Austen how
b5/42* hadn't got his in and why he had to pick on
b5/52 and all that. . . . Mr Austen just let b5/52 off.

b5/42* did not allege that he was victimised by teachers, but
did turn a classmate's victimisation to advantage. b5/42* usually
spoke of b5/33 with contempt. However, he associated himself
with b5/33 in the context of resistance to victimisation and an
accompanying challenge to a teacher's authority:

b5/42* Mr Heraclitus came up and pushed him around and he
just turned around and said, 'I am fucking sick of you
and I don't like you doing this to me. I am going to see
[the deputy principal].' And Mr Heraclitus wouldn't let
him so at the end of the period b5/33 went and saw him
because when Heraclitus pushed him he hit his head on
the desk and he had a big egg. You could see it in his
hair. . . . He's a stirrer. He will stir whoever he likes.
He will tell them off as soon as he wants to.

CONCLUSIONS

Students legitimated favouritism when the specific manifestation
of favour was commensurate with their perceptions of the specific
performances of the student. Agreement on the performances of
teachers' favourites only occurred regularly when the favourite
was dominant or when the favourite, as with some brains, maintained a becoming modesty. When agreement did not exist the
favourite was pressed by classmates to deny his special status.
When there was agreement the favourite's claim to status and
respect was reinforced by the teacher's attention.

Victimisation was seen or alleged by students to occur when
teachers attributed misbehaviour to the wrong student, or
punished one student for an offence but not others also committing
it.

The problem of being victimised by the teacher was resolved
by the reactions of the victim. Students who challenged the
propriety of the teacher's imputation or punishment of the
offence tended to escape without penalty and gain respect from
classmates.

Generally, it was dominant students who challenged teachers'
allocation of blame and punishments and in so doing escaped
punishment. Subordinate students accused of an offence tended
to accept punishment passively. The challenge to teachers'
imputation of blame brought favourable notice to dominant
students and was often interpreted as successful stirring.

Classmates tended to see dominant students as foci of teachers'

favouritism and victimisation of students. Whether the definition
of the situation activated was that of favouritism or victimisation
the dominant student emerged tacitly as an equal with the
teacher. If the dominant students were favoured they seemed
accepted as an equal by the teacher. If they were victimised,
they successfully challenged the dependence of student on
teacher. In all cases, the interaction between student and
teacher kept classmates' attention focused on respected qualities
of the dominant student.

Chapter 11

Students' evaluation of classroom seating position

Earlier chapters have demonstrated that students in each school class vary widely in control status, normative commitments and performances. This chapter shows that the definitions of advantage and disadvantage students attach to sitting in each classroom locality are informed by normative commitments. A study of the consequent seating patterns permits an analysis of the situational conditions which produce congruence of some normative commitments and control status in individual students, and the incompatibility of other normative commitments and control statuses.

Previous research on spatial distribution of classroom inter-action has been largely concerned with how location affects individual students' interaction with teachers. Teachers have been shown to communicate more with students sitting in the front and centre of the room (Adams and Biddle, 1970; Bate, 1973; Koneya, 1976; Lundgren, 1972). Students who are more active in class discussion tend to sit in the front and centre of the room (Bates, 1973; Koneya, 1976).

Researchers have been less concerned with other values informing students' choice of seating position. Dale (1972:51) alludes to a 'backrow brigade' of what in Australia would be called 'stirrers'. Stebbins (1973) describes how the relative empirical closure of the classroom is mitigated at its boundaries by outside diversions. This chapter shows that patterns of student seating are more complex than suggested by other researchers.

SIGNIFICANCE OF CLASSROOM SEATING POSITION

Almost all students ascribed some significance to their choice of seating area. This significance went beyond perceptions of territoriality and wishing to retain deskmates to wanting a particular location in the classroom. Only one student, b1/18*, initially denied any significance to his present area of seating. He was also the only student initially to resist the request to be interviewed. His distinct and isolated position in his class was reflected in his choice of a back corner to sit in.

Most students remained seated in the same area of the class-room. Only one student, a clown, moved freely across the room so that it was impossible to identify him with one seating position:

b3/15   b3/46* is up there sometimes in the front. He's like
a rabbit going from hole to hole.

Teachers were a minor determinant of seating position. Some
teachers insisted on students remaining in the same position
through the year. They thus preserved the original social
structure of the classroom peer group. More frequently, teachers
disrupted ongoing student interaction by separating troublesome
seatmates and redistributing them to what the teachers perceived
as strategically preferred areas of the classroom. For example:

Q   Why do you sit at the back?
c4/23* That is where the teacher shifted me because I don't
       muck up or anything. They try to get the stirrers up
       the front.

It required a determined teacher to enforce a seat change over
a prolonged period. Students shifted by teachers tended, like
c3/11* and c3/12* in the example below, to return to their home
seats as the teacher forgot or could no longer be bothered to
impose the seat change:

c3/41   A lot of kids like c3/11* and c3/12* get shifted around
        because they talk all the time but they always end up in
        their own seats.

With these exceptions, students chose or were constrained by
pressures from peers into a classroom seating position.

SALIENT CLASSROOM PHYSICAL DIMENSIONS

Two physical dimensions were frequently mentioned when students
discussed classroom seating position. The more often named was
from the front of the classroom, the area immediately facing the
teacher and blackboard, to the back of the classroom, the area
furthest from blackboard and teacher. The other frequently
named dimension was from the classroom periphery to the centre
with the periphery including places by the walls and windows on
the sides of the room and, for some purposes, the back wall. Two
areas of the classroom received special consideration: the extreme
back corners and the seats immediately by the door.

Front to back - academic commitment and relations with teachers
Students' perceptions of advantage and disadvantage associated
with sitting near the front of the room usually included proximity
of teacher and blackboard as teaching agents and teacher as a
controlling agent. In discussing implications of sitting in the
front row, students stressed visibility of the blackboard and
audibility of the teacher and the greater opportunities for one-
to-one interaction between student and teacher.

Students who, like b1/58*, combined strong academic commitments with a dependent definition of academic attainment preferred to sit at the front:

> b1/58* I like being up the front because I can hear the teacher.
> Q   It doesn't worry you having the teacher right over you?
> b1/58* No, I prefer it.

Students generally agreed that at the front there was an uninterrupted and close view of the board which rendered it more visible. At the back of the room, conversely, the union of distance and teachers' bad writing often left the blackboard unreadable for students:

> b4/46* Sitting at the back of the room some people reckon that
>   it is a good position but it's not really because you
>   can't see the board in case the teacher has small writing
>   or something you can't see it. It just looks like a mess
>   of scrawls at the back and if you are down at the front
>   sometimes you can make it out.

Students also saw the front of the room as a place where, for better or worse, one-to-one interaction with the teacher on academic topics was more likely. Some specially diligent or goody goody students, such as the following informant, welcomed this opportunity:

> Q   Why would you like to sit at the front?
> c4/31* Because it is closer to the blackboard and it is closer
>   to the teacher.
> Q   Why is it better to be close to the teacher?
> c4/31* Because they can hear exactly what you say. You see
>   sometimes they misunderstand what you said because
>   they can't hear your voice properly when you talk quiet.

Less diligent students, like c1/13*, were appalled by the prospect of teachers giving them individual attention:

> c1/13* The kids that are up the front get asked a lot of
>   questions, don't they? I was sat up the front for one
>   German lesson and the board seemed so close and the
>   teacher so big that I would rather sit at the back.

Immediate supervision by the teacher of the students at the front compelled less diligent students to do more work:

> Q   How much work did you get done after you were sent to
>   the front?
> b3/45* You had to. You really had to because the teacher was
>   right there and if you didn't you got a whack!

Conversely, students at the back could reduce or avoid work:

b4/17* When it comes to homework too some people down the
back don't do their homework and there is about three
problems to go. The teacher comes down to mark towards
us and meanwhile b4/18*·is writing away, doing his
homework.

b4/18* I have just got time to write out a few problems for
homework. There is a lot and you just write out a few
notes and you say you couldn't do it and he says, 'You
tried so it is all right.'

Students moved from the front to the back of the room in order
to pass from an area of compulsory attention to schoolwork to an
area in which they had more freedom to select their commitments.
For example:

c3/22 c3/56 hates it up the front. When anybody's away she
goes and sits in their place.

c3/21 Anywhere up the back.

Q   Why do you think she dislikes sitting up the front?

c3/22 Well, I don't think she's much for schoolwork.

Even some keen workers, such as b3/23 and b3/24*, resented
continuing supervision by teachers of students in the front row:

b3/23 I hate sitting at the front because the teacher is always
looking at what you are doing. I hate teachers looking.
I don't mind them looking at the end product but I
don't like them looking at what you are doing.

b3/24* Yes, I don't like them watching over me when I am
working. They give me the willies. You make a mistake
and they blow you up.

Against the general pattern, a few students thus believed that
they would do more work at the back away from teacher supervision. For example:

c1/25 I hate people standing over me and watching all the
time.

c1/24 Yeah.

c1/25 You put your hands over your work and wait for him to
go away and you write something and you scratch
around hoping that he will shove off.

Q   You don't worry sitting at the back you won't get as
much work done as you would at the front?

c1/25 I think that I would get less work done sitting at the
front.

Subordinate brains often avoided the front of the room where
their ongoing interaction with teachers drew attention to their

academic attainment. c1/27 was one such subordinate brain:

c1/53* c1/27 was sitting with me then but she doesn't like
sitting right up the front so she moved back to sit
with c1/26. Because she got first in the class award
and all the teachers used to pick up her book and mark
all the others because she was always right so she
shifted up the back so they couldn't pick up her book.

Just one seat from the front students experienced a different
interaction with the teacher from those sitting in the front row.
The board was still visible and the teacher still audible. However,
students felt less controlled by the teacher although the teacher
was close enough to preserve quiet in the students' vicinity and
to enable them to work without distraction:

I Q   You sit one row from the front. How would you feel if
        you were actually sat in the front row?
b2/44 I wouldn't like it. I like to have a bit of protection. If
        you're in the front you can't do nothing, you're in the
        front line. Normally the teacher just looks along the
        front line.
Q   Supposing you were at the back?
b2/44 I wouldn't like that too much either, missing too much.
        Some of the teachers don't speak too loud and you
        can't understand them and you get carried away about
        mucking up and talking to each other.

II b2/33 I wouldn't mind sitting about half way. You can still
        talk a bit without getting a clip under the ear from
        [a teacher] and you can hear a lot better. Like at the
        back with b2/22* is right next to me and all those guys
        are always talking.

The progression from the front to the rear of the room embodied
the dimension of academic work to mucking around described in
Chapter 4. Students did not see the continuum of activity from
the front to the rear of the room as from academic activity to
nonactivity. They saw the continuum as from a dependent academic
commitment and interaction only with the teacher to student
independence and the possibility of interaction with classmates.
Mucking around became possible with distance from the teacher:

c3/24   c3/23* and I got into trouble too much and so we
        shifted back because we got caught doing too many
        things.
c3/23* Everybody flies to the back of the room and takes the
        backseat so they can muck around.

Conversely, mucking around became impossible as the student
sat nearer the front. This was a result not only of proximity to

the teacher but also of having fewer class neighbours:

   c1/55   The kids who sit at the back are the sort that sometimes like to have a real natter with their mate when the teacher is not looking and up the front it is easier to see the blackboard.

   c1/56   You don't want to muck around when you are up the front because you sort of know the teacher is one step away from you. I think that I picked the front because I didn't want to have everyone mucking around whereas if you sit in the middle there, there are girls there whereas if you sit up the front there is nobody in front of you and you don't muck around.

A few of the students found that the back had some of the disadvantages for mucking around offered by the front row: visibility to the teacher and isolation from classmates:

   c3/24   I was sat before [in the back corner]. . . . I was getting a bit sick of the back. It is alright except that it is hard to see at times and the teacher can spot you if you are leaning back on your chair but if you stay in the middle or second back row if you are leaning back on your chair the teachers can't notice you so much because there are so many kids.

Mucking around among boys and sexually focused activities among girls were shown in Chapters 4 and 5 respectively to define student groups and status. The freedom associated with the back enabled boys, such as the following, to engage in competitive mucking around:

   Q   What are your reasons for sitting at the back?

   b5/32* The teacher can't see you and he hardly ever comes up here to see us mucking around, eating or throwing things around.

   b5/31* Fighting a little bit.

The same freedom permitted girls to pass notes and talk about boyfriends:

   I c1/17* Up at the front it's as if the teachers are always kind of looking at you and, yeah, you are too close and you can't really talk when you want to and that. You feel that they are going to jump on you. At the back you can talk quite a bit.

   II c2/16* At the back people can send notes to you, not at the front, because the teacher is always looking down on the desk or you can't talk across because they can see you talking whereas at the back they can't see you talking.

Power and influence were thus associated with distance from the teacher, and inversely related to academic commitment, when academic commitment connoted unconditional acceptance of teachers' definitions of academic status combined with a desire for intensive and subordinate interaction with teachers. The next section of this chapter shows that patterns of students' interaction, independent of any reference to teachers, promote a correlation between sitting at the back and high control status.

Perceptions of advantage and disadvantage sometimes became more complex as students saw teachers anticipating student knowledge of the classroom. Some students avoided sitting in areas of the classroom which could have led to their being stereo-typed by teachers as students who stirred or mucked around rather than worked:

> b2/38   The teacher looks at the back if you are sitting . . .
> but when you sit in the middle you know you are all
> right. . . . It is just the attitude that teachers have got
> to people who sit in the corners at the back. They
> think you are going to stir.

Students knew that teachers sometimes changed their positions to forestall students taking advantage of their respective locations in the classroom. Often teachers moved to the back of the room to be near the students. Thereupon, other students, especially those in the left front area, became invisible as far as the teacher was concerned. Students sitting there, like the following, could take advantage of this invisibility:

> b4/21   Like b4/57, they [throw chalk] behind the teacher's
> back. You don't expect it to come from them. They
> throw it and you look around and see them laughing . . .
> b4/31* They get out of it because the teacher doesn't think
> they are likely to do it and they do it.

Certain teachers reversed the significance of the back and front of the room by standing at the back. Students who were con-scious of their resultant vulnerability at the rear of the room sat further forward. Two such students commented:

> Q   How would you feel if you were sat at the back?
> b5/53 No different.
> b5/54 Yeah, but you have to do your homework then. Some
> teachers pick on those at the back. They think you are
> going to stir.
> b5/53 Some teachers generally stand near the back so they
> can't see what we are doing out the front.

Students sometimes took into account their knowledge of other students' knowledge of the classroom. This research has illus-trated how students often dislike or despise 'goody goodies' and

'crawlers', that is, students who because they accept dependence
on teachers tend to sit at the front of the room. Students who
wished to avoid stigmatisation by classmates and negative stereo-
typing by teachers, sometimes chose, independently of any
normative commitments, to sit in the middle rows of the classroom:

b3/38   You sit at the front and everybody thinks you are
         crawlers. You sit at the back and the teacher thinks
         you are stirrers so you sit in the middle and you are
         just sort of so-and-so.

Front to back – seating and control
Two aspects of the relationship between classroom seating position
and control status have already been examined. One was the use
of projectiles shown in Chapter 4 to unite powerful students across
the front left and back corners of the classroom and to signify
the subordination of students in other areas of the room. The
other, discussed in this chapter, is that distance from the
teacher at the back of the room allows students to engage in
such control creating activities as talking, passing notes and
competitive mucking around. This section examines three further
aspects of the relationship between classroom seating and control.
One is the establishment of influence through knowledge of
classmates' activities. Another use of knowledge of classmates'
activities is to control others by dobbing or by threat of dobbing.
Lastly, students immediately forward of others in a column of
desks are shown to be prone to picking on, or at a disadvantage
in competitive mucking around.
    Students in all classes generally agreed that an advantage of
sitting at the back of the room was the possibility of keeping
informed of classroom events, where significant classroom events
were understood in terms of students' interaction. Especially
among girls much of the knowledge was associated with creation
of influence. Girls at the back used their knowledge of classmates in front to deride them and their behaviour. Those girls
who were concerned with the exercise of influence became aware
of the back as a vantage point in a fight and of the vulnerability
of students further forward:

c2/13   I have always sat at the back. You can see everything
         and when you are up the front if you are having an
         argument with someone I think they are looking at you
         all the time. They are talking about you and so I like
         to sit at the back where you can see everything. . . .
         We can see everything and you get a wide view. There
         are some kids that just don't know half the things I
         know.

This was one of the most consistent aspects of girls' classroom
interaction. However, there were exceptions. 9c4 differed from

the other girls' classes in that sexually interested girls did not
dominate the less sexually interested and conformist students at
the front. In that class, classmates sometimes felt uncomfortable
when they saw the influential conformist students at the front
talking about them:

> c4/31* c4/44* is always picking faults with everyone. You can
> really tell it the way she looks at the class and the way
> she really looks at you and whispers, 'ooh'. They look
> around the class and they whisper to one another and
> they pick fault with everyone else and what they do.

Students at the back can see when their classmates sitting
further forward misbehave. This knowledge of classmates'
misbehaviour frequently led to dobbing, shown in Chapter 7 to
be a mode of students' control of classmates. Students who were
the objects of dobbing by classmates behind them often found it
unwelcome. Some decided to move back:

> c3/33* I would prefer to sit at the back corner.
> c3/31 You can eat chips better.
> c3/33* c3/23* behind - she will dob you in, 'c3/33* is eating
> chips' or something.

Students consistently picked on those sitting immediately in
front of them. For example:

> I c4/48*If we are stirring [c4/58* and c4/57*] we'll put our
> feet on the chair and push.

> II c3/33* I kick c3/44's chair - boong - she says, 'What do you
> want?' I says, 'Can I have a lend of your book?' and she
> gives it to me and again - boong - 'This is the wrong
> one', and she ends up by getting really mad. That is
> why she has moved her chair forward.

Others of a multitude of techniques for annoying students in
front included, 'kick them, hit them', 'get them up the arse with
compass', 'throw ink at them, write on their clothes', 'put water
in their bags and on their book', 'flick paper in their hair,
pushing their chair'. These annoyances were more fun for the
students sitting behind than the students on whom they were inflicted. Students sitting in front found it very difficult to retaliate
effectively. This was because of the direct physical relationship:

> b5/53 If they should sit behind you they will hit you in the
> back with a ruler.
> Q   What can you do back to them?
> b5/53 You can't really do nothing to them.
> b5/54 Sometimes just slap them one.

The physical disadvantage was exacerbated by teacher intervention:

> b2/56* If b2/46's sitting in back of me, he hits me across the
> head and when I look around I get hit by Mr Lavoisier.

Students thus often preferred to free themselves from assault
by sitting at the back of the room:

> Q   Supposing you were sat right at the back?
> b5/35 That would be better because nobody would pull your
> chair out and that.
> b5/36 It would be all right because nobody would be able to
> put chalk or anything down your back.

Periphery to centre
The walls and windows of the classroom form a distinctive
environment for students. This section describes students'
perceptions of advantage and disadvantage in sitting on the
periphery or in the centre of the room.
   Windows and walls were boundaries for interaction. They
allowed students sitting near them to isolate themselves from
classroom interaction:

> b1/18* When you are alone in the corner you seem to be alone
> sometimes and can do a fair bit of work.

Occasionally the physical comfort afforded by the boundary let
students relax and so, like the following informant, work better:

> b1/21 I do my best work when I am comfortable and that is
> when I am leaning against the wall and swinging on my
> chair.

Although the type of classroom described in the present study
is termed 'closed', inputs across its physical boundaries sometimes motivated students to choose to sit or not to sit on its
periphery. Apart from better ventilation and lighting, students'
major consideration in choosing to sit at the side of the classroom
were the view outside and possible interaction across the boundary. For example:

> I b4/27 Everyday this crow lands outside the window and it
> will sit there and we are amazed because a crow is a
> pretty crafty old bird and he won't get so close usually
> and this one just comes in and shits at the window - we
> throw a bit of lunch at him sometimes.

> II Q   What can you see?
> c3/37   The canteen and on top of B Block and across.
> Q   What is on top of B Block?

c3/37 Room B4.
c3/38 Her boyfriend.

Other enticements included 'people wagging it [truanting]', 'if
the weather is sunny or cloudy', 'penguins every r.i. day
[clerics arriving for religious education]', 'trees, dirt, etcetera'.
Some students aware of these distractions preferred to stay
away from the periphery:

Q   You wouldn't like to sit by the window?
c1/24 I'd go for the centre any way. I don't like to be
       distracted from my work.

The door, another part of the classroom physical boundary,
beside offering ventilation and view, allowed speedy entry and
departure. Students in seats near the door frequently reported
that they liked to leave in a hurry at the end of the teaching
period: some for specific purposes: 'so I can see a boy', 'so I
can get down to the pingpong table', 'tuckshop', and some more
general, 'I'd go insane if I stayed there any longer'. Seats near
the door, along with seats by the windows in some classrooms,
afforded early views of approaching teachers. This gave rise to
the specialised role of 'cockatoo', which was discussed in
Chapter 7:

b1/52 I am always looking out for the teachers. I am the
       cockatoo because I always sit closest to the door.

These seats presented special difficulties for students eager to
study because of external distractions such as 'noise from the
verandah', and because with the largest windows on the opposite
side of the room, 'much of the board is shiny'.
Analysis after the completion of interviewing showed that
although girls who sat in the extreme right hand column of desks
resembled those who sat in the extreme left hand column, the
equivalent male populations differed in two important respects.
The right hand column of desks was fully occupied but pairs of
desks on the left, except for the front and back corner seats,
were usually occupied by only one student. Boys on the right
hand side, except for the front corner and occasionally the back
corner, were always members of the dominant group. Those in
the left central seats were almost always isolates, rejectees, or
had exceptional social characteristics. They included, for
example, those students who combined low academic attainment
with low academic commitment, and b2/28*, the sole student in
the research population to derive general status from high
academic attainment, independent of power or influence. It may
be hypothesised that powerful students sitting on the right hand
side of the room see that area as furthest away from teachers
based at their desks in the left forward corner of the room and
that these boys are more interested in what is going on inside

than outside the classroom. However, these questions were not asked and students did not volunteer information that these dimensions were or were not critical.

COMBINATIONS OF FACTORS

Students' perceptions of advantage and disadvantage associated with the physical dimensions of the classroom in combination prescribe for each student a preferred seating position. The consequences of combining these factors are illustrated in the following extracts from interviews:

I c3/18   I get a headache at the front.
  c3/17   She can't sit up the front because it hurts your eyes and in the middle you get the glare from both sides of the door.
  c3/18   And I just like it up the back.
  c3/17   It is good in the back corner.
  c3/18   . . . It is next to the windows. You get a lot of air in here and it is not right next to the door where all the classes go by.
  c3/17   Where there are not so many people behind you really. . . .
  c3/18   I hate people sitting behind me because they always put their feet on my chair and kick you or put their feet on your dress or something.

II Q   How would you feel if you were sat in the middle of the room?
  c1/41*   Terrible. If I didn't look out of the window, I would be looking out of the door.
  Q   How would you feel if you were sat right at the front?
  c1/41*   I would hate it.
  c1/42   I hate sitting right at the front because the teacher's right there.
  c1/41*   And Mrs Goethe if you are just talking she hits you on the arm or on the head and it gets annoying. I would rather sit where I am.
  Q   What about the back corner?
  c1/42   I don't think that I would like to sit up the back corner. The tree is in the way. You can't see out because of the tree . . . . You can't see the board very well.
  c1/41*   Even where we are sitting most of the glare comes through and you can't see very well.

III b2/41   I'd rather sit up round the first three rows in the middle. If you're at the back that's where all the stirrers sit so you get copped with them. But if you're right up the front and you haven't done your homework you get caught. I like the middle because you can't

see the board properly from the sides or you might
end up by staring out of the windows.

IV c1/38   I like sitting exactly where I am now. If I had the
choice I would sit where I am now . . . . Well, mainly
why I sat there was to be close to the door and get
out real quick so I can get to the tuckshop and also
beside a window and I can see everything that goes
on outside. Then you are sort of close to the front
and close to the back so the teacher doesn't see
everything you do.

CONCLUSIONS

This chapter has shown that the seeming uniformity of classroom
experience conceals a clearly distinguished gradation of strength
of teacher control and student independent action. The front
tends to be associated with strong teacher control and opportunity
for attention to imposed academic knowledge. The rear tends to
be associated with reduced opportunity for attention to imposed
academic knowledge but also with freedom from teacher control,
freedom for student interaction, and freedom for the development of control in student interaction. Students have to
choose between intensive academic interaction with the teacher
and the establishment of influence or power in student interaction.

The movement from the periphery to the centre has less
significance. High academic commitment is equally associated
with the periphery, where students may separate themselves
from the distractions of student interaction in the centre, and
with the centre of the room, where students may remove themselves from the distractions of outside events.

Chapter 12

Conclusions

This chapter is in two parts: conclusions and questions for
future research. The conclusions summarise the major findings
of the research and, using these findings, discuss some recent
criticisms of Parsonian theory. Next they look at some implications of the research for educational administrators, teacher-
educators and teachers. Questions, suggested but not answered
by the present research, are then discussed. These include
questions raised by comparing findings from the present
research with those from other recent studies of classroom
interaction, and questions derived from macrosocial implications
of Parsons' theory of schooling.

NORMS AND CONTROL IN THE CLASSROOM

'The Feral Classroom' has shown that an adequate analysis of
classroom interaction requires attention to students' norms
originating in and intruding into the classroom. It has also
shown that students' controls are important in determining the
use of these norms. Dominant students used determinate sets of
norms whose origins were inside and outside the classroom.
These norms were areas and legitimators of control.

Dominance and subordination in peer interaction was the major
axis of differentiation between students. Dominant students took
classroom norms as cultural objects subject to manipulation and
selective application. Subordinate students experienced classroom norms as taken-for-granted or an imposed reality. Dominant
students controlled the definitions of performance and conformity
whose use was a necessary condition of the legitimation and
hence of the maintenance of control.

The most pervasive intrusion of values into the classroom peer
group and the major source of differentiation between male and
female peer groups concerns the controls used by each sex.
Power was boys' chief control. Attempts to use other controls in
boys' classroom interaction either supplemented power, or, if
exercised by less powerful students, were seen as illegitimate
and evidence of subordinate status. Influence was the main
control in girls' classroom interaction. Dominant girls' use of
power was supplementary to influence. The attempts to exercise
power made by girls without influence were either seen as
illegitimate or were not understood and were given no significance.

Thus, there were three levels of determination of the use of controls and norms by students. The successful use of controls was determined by sex-specific norms which dictated that girls exercised control through influence and activation of commitments and that boys exercised control through power. Exercise of these controls determined definitions of conformity within the bounds of norms which governed those aspects of classroom interaction which were not directly related to the construction of power. However, the operation of these norms legitimated dominant students' control.

Power, performance and norms in boys' classes
The use of power in boys' classroom peer groups determined the centrality and negotiability of each performance dimension as well as the definition of performance in each. The most central performance dimensions, beyond the ineluctable power dimension itself, were those which indicated power. In so far as pushing around, picking on, and, to a lesser extent, competitive mucking around directly indicated power, they were a non-negotiable reality with limited normative rules governing their application. Inasmuch as competitive mucking around, and, to a lesser extent, pushing around and picking on were distant from the establishment of power, they were shaped by norms, whose immediate selection and application was subject to the exercise of power by dominant students. These relations between the construction and use of power and the definition of success are summarised in Table 12.1.

Academic status was shown to be a reified academic performance dimension. Under most conditions dominant students controlled the definition and signification of high academic status but could not construct high academic status out of low marks and incompetent performance. It is indicative of the potential identification of high marks with dependence on teachers that dominant students only granted high academic status to those students who were acknowledged to be academically independent of the teacher.

Academic status, because of teachers' constant assessment of students' work, was an important performance dimension. It was usually associated with power. Almost all dominant students, as a result of their control of the definition and signification of academic status, were publicly said to have high academic status and associated intellectual independence.

Students could not directly contest teachers' definitions of low academic status. Successful management of low academic status as defined by teachers required that the student redefine it as manipulation of relations with teachers. Passive acceptance of teachers' definition of low academic status led indirectly to greater rejection and stigmatisation for the student concerned than challenges, even if unsuccessful, to this definition.

Performance as a stirrer was less important for boys than academic status. High academic status was in almost all cases a necessary precondition of high power, but a significant proportion of very powerful students were not stirrers. However,

Table 12.1 Boys' construction and use of power and success

	Fighting ability	Competitive mucking around	Challenge to teacher authority	Academic performance
Manifestation	1 Occasional fights 2 Pushing around 3 Size	Competition based on specific ways of giving pain	Challenges to teacher power signalled by teacher anger and student amusement	1 Classroom performances 2 Signification of status by student concerned, classmate or teacher
Part in Construction of Power	Results in power when used to construct a normative order	1 Signifies minor differences in power 2 Creates patterns of association based on major differences in power	No part	No direct part Legitimates power
Specific Performance Dimension	Yes	Yes	Yes	Yes
Use of Power	Punish classmates	Powerful students control definition of propriety	Powerful students control definition of propriety	Powerful students control activation of teachers' definitions, and construct alternative definitions of success
Successful Performance Requisite for Power	Yes	Yes	No	Yes
Direct Relevance to Teachers	Teachers generally unaware. Independent of teachers	Teachers generally unaware. Independent of teachers	Assertion of student independence	Teachers often unaware of alternative definitions of performance. Alternative definitions associated with assertions of independence

powerful students always controlled definitions of the success and acceptability of stirring. This control was as much motivated by the wish to avoid unwanted consequences of stirring as by the wish to monopolise a performance dimension.

Boys placed little emphasis on performance in outside activities. Respect for the external performances and associations of a male student were a function of that student's power inside the classroom.

Some external activities intruded indirectly on classmates attention. Often teachers who admired a student's external performance initiated with that student a conversation focused on the performance. Classmates who agreed with the teacher's assessment of the external performance saw the conversation as a mark of the teacher's recognition of the maturity and accomplishment of the student concerned. Classmates who disagreed with the teacher's assessment of the performance saw the favour as improper. Classmates' assessment of a student's external performance depended on that student's control status. Thus, judgements of the legitimacy of teachers' favouring a student on account of external performances ultimately depended on the student's control status.

Clowns were outside the cycle of power controlling the definitions of performance and conformity and the definition of performance and conformity legitimating power. There were some indications that powerful boys controlled the definition of clowning and that clowns took seriously clowning as a performance dimension. None the less, there were important differences. Classmates tended to evaluate clowns and treatment of clowns by qualitative criteria. The considerations of performance and normative acceptability which governed the actions and treatment of other students were suspended for clowns. Clowns, although exercising some specific control in the classroom, were not powerful. They were exceptional in boys' classes in exercising control through influence.

Influence, particularism and performance in girls' classes
The most important differences between girls' and boys' classroom interaction were related to the centrality of influence rather than power as a control, and to the importance of particularism. The uses of influence and the realisation of particularism are summarised in Table 12.2. Power and its indices were absent or had an altered significance which was related to the establishment of influence. Competitive mucking around and pushing around were unimportant. 'Fighting' and 'picking on' were transformed into the creation of influence and not of power.

Girls' groups and status systems were structured by particularistic loyalties which transcended or determined most classroom activity. At the bottom of girls' status systems were those who remained loyal to same-sex peers and teachers and expressed distaste for classroom expressions of sexual interests. Above them were girls with an interest in boys but who had not established

Table 12.2 Girls' particularism and use of influence

	Sexual interests	Talking, mucking around	Challenge to teacher authority	Academic performance
Manifestation	1 Sexually active girls value independent classroom life 2 Sexually inactive girls value close relations with teachers	1 Focus on boys 2 Communication in the peer group	Respect given to girls who achieve a friendly but authority-denying relationship with teachers	1 Classroom performance 2 Signification of status by student concerned, classmate or teacher
Relation to level of influence	Sexual maturity is a necessary condition for the exercise of influence	1 Medium of exercise of influence 2 Communication defines groups	Success of challenges related to influence of student	Successful management or construction of academic performance a condition of exercise of influence
Particularist dimension	Yes	Yes	Yes	No
Uses of influence	1 Define status of own sexual interests 2 Attack other girls' sexual interests 3 Defend other girls' sexual interests	Influential girls define the status of these activities	Influential girls define the status of these activities	Influential girls control activation of teachers' definitions and construct alternative definitions of success
Direct relevance to teachers	Teachers aware of and hostile to girls with active and mature sexual interests	Teachers generally ignore until it too openly competes with academic work	Influential girls open communication with teachers	Teachers often unaware of alternative definitions of performance. Alternative definitions associated with assertions of independence

a long lasting focus of attention on any one boy. These girls, within broad groups defined by level of sexual interest, had other girls as especially close if temporary friends according to shared acquaintance with or interest in a particular boy or group of boys. They looked down on girls with no professed interest in boys, and in turn were looked down upon by girls with mature sexual interests. The girls with mature sexual interests formed closed dyads in which they intensely discussed their boyfriends. Having mature sexual interests, they had high influence. Forming closed dyads, they did not as regularly exercise their control over their classmates as did boys with equivalent power. When girls with mature sexual interests did extend control over their classmates, it was often in terms of arbitrating disputes over sexual interests and advising on sexual problems.

Girls with active sexual interests valued friendly but independent relations with teachers. They despised sexually inactive girls' friendly and unequal relations with teachers.

Girls' construction and management of academic status formed a similar pattern to that found among boys. Each was similarly concerned to assert the significance of an academic status system congruent with control status. Each, therefore, was concerned, when student control status and teachers' definitions of academic status diverged, to minimise the significance of teachers' definitions and to construct an alternative academic status system.

The strength of particularistic loyalties is shown by the degree to which uniform styles of behaviour are associated with each focus and with each level of activity and maturity within each focus. It is also shown by the persistence of groups formed around a common particularistic focus even when, as infrequently happens, the classroom behaviour of members of the group is conspicuously different.

PARSONS AND HIS CRITICS: GENERAL COMMENTS

Parsons' work is now receiving some favourable attention in the British sociology of education (Davies, 1976; Demain, 1981). However, a conventional wisdom has long been strongly critical of assumptions supposed to underlie Parsons' theory. Many of these criticisms are based on misreadings or ignorance of his work. The present research, by an application of Parsons' action theory as incorporated in models of the family, school and peer groups, disputes two of these criticisms which relate to his use of the concepts of 'norm' and 'socialisation'.

A prominent criticism of Parsons has been that he 'portrays a model of man as a puppet or cultural fool constrained completely by agents or mechanisms of the system' (Erben and Gleeson, 1977: 83; cf., Daw, 1970; Giddens, 1979: 52; Wrong, 1961). Sarup (1978) specifies 'norms' as the constraining agents of Parsons' social system:

> In Parsons' work . . . there are binding normative patterns
> which compel human behaviour. There is conformity to norms
> and roles: meaning (*sic*) are fixed and not negotiated. In such
> a society, physical force is not required, social conformity
> acting as a form of soft coercion. (Sarup, 1978: 177)

Becker (1969), in an accusation conceptually related to perceptions of the normative subordination of actors, alleges that
Parsons places 'too much emphasis on consensus in social
interaction' and that 'his scheme of society (is) a harmoniously
disposed social system'.
Other sociologists' comments are more guarded and qualified.
Wilson (1971) associates Parsons with the normative paradigm.
None the less, he notes that for Parsons 'internalisation is never
perfect, and the actor need not be regarded as merely 'pro-
grammed by his culture' and the social system is 'incompletely
integrated and thus displayed tendencies towards unregulated
conflict, tension and patterned deviance'. Ahier (1974) and
Robinson (1981) reject an often alleged antithesis between the
models of man in interpretive and Parsonian sociology. Ahier
speaks of how studies in the style of the new sociology of
education illustrate 'the active alternative to the *supposedly
passive* (my italics) model of man posited by Parsons' (Ahier,
1974: 212).
These criticisms are based on a partial reading of Parsons.
Undoubtedly, Parsons places great emphasis on the problem of
order. This is not because he takes it for granted. It is because
he sees any kind of social order as problematic and challenged
by competing individual interests (DiTomaso, 1972; Menzies,
1977: 110-115; Parsons, 1937). Parsons and his colleague Bales
(1955) in their description of socialisation and interaction
processes do give a model of socialisation by which the child is
socialised into conformity with the parents' wishes. This model
is defensible on two accounts. A model of socialisation is required
which takes into account the dependence of unsocial babies on
adults (Bourricaud, 1971: 98-108) and which takes into account
the degree to which social reproduction and cultural transmission
occur in our society (Giddens, 1979: 96-130). Even within this
framework, Parsons does not adhere to the crude form of
functionalism sometimes imputed to him. Bourricaud notes of
Parsons' concept of socialisation that:

> Socialization does not teach the individual any particular form
> of behaviour. It teaches him, rather, how to orient himself
> relative to his actual or potential partners in the interaction
> process by laying down a frame of reference in very broad and
> general terms. (Bourricaud, 1981: 115)

As children grow older and begin to attend school, they move
into a condition of increased autonomy. In so far as the school is
an agent of cultural transmission and social reproduction, the

process of socialisation will remain in the pattern of an unsocial-
ised inferior being socialised by a social superior. However, the
process of 'double contingency' in social interaction (Parsons,
1951: 36–45) also becomes important. The reactions of each
person in interaction depend on the contingent responses of the
others in that interaction, and these responses then become
sanctions (Parsons, 1951: 38). The definition and control of
sanctions become a central part of the operation and construction
of the normative order. This normative order comprises the
symbol systems which make communication possible and a set of
mutual normative expectations.

It is the latter model of interaction and mutual socialisation
that has been used in 'The Feral Classroom'. Students' norms
and values were shown to originate in group reaction to the
exigencies of the classroom. The significance and operation of
norms was shown to be also a consequence of students' establishment of control according to values which originated beyond the
classroom.

'The Feral Classroom' has demonstrated that control and
normative perspectives can be integrated in Parsonian sociology
by regarding norms as symbolic resources which are used by
dominant students. Dominant students were shown to control the
activation, selection and application of norms to their own
advantage: it cannot be said, in Sarup's terms, that norms
compelled dominant students' behaviour. Notably, however,
potentially dominant students experienced problems when they
neglected to control the operation of norms.

PARSONS AND HIS CRITICS: THE MODEL OF SCHOOLING

Specific aspects of Parsons' model of schooling have also been
widely criticised. Among the critics, Marsh, Rosser and Harré
(1978) have most nearly shared the concern of the present
research with the description and explanation of the independent
classroom life of students.

Marsh, Rosser and Harré emphasise the extent to which
Parsons assumes that schools socialise students to become adults
whose values are compatible with willing occupation of roles in an
industrial society. They recognise the growth of nonacademic
values and skills inside the classroom. They separate, as does
Parsons, his analysis of the peer group from his analysis of
the classroom:

> Parsons believes that in the schoolroom the children acquire
> their attachment to the larger social order of adult society
> which is reflected in the methods of giving and getting
> encouraged in school. As schooling goes on there is a pro-
> gressive revelation of the selective role of the school vis à vis
> the labour market, bringing children into an asymptotic relation
> to 'real life', for which it provides the apprenticeship. Accord-

ing to Parsons, criminality arises in the feral life of the playground.

We would turn this position upside down. The social structure of the society of the classroom seems to us as well adapted to be the nursery of crime as it is of 'good' behaviour. The distinction between real and apparent achievement, if only it can be concealed from the teacher, and suitably managed by a child, provides the opportunity for rewards to be achieved just as well for cheating as for genuine achievement. The possibility of achieving the semblance of virtue by working at standing high in the teacher's estimation, seems to us a perfect nursery for the acquisition of the criminal or exploitative view of the social world. (Marsh, Rosser and Harré, 1978: 3)

Marsh, Rosser and Harré's criticisms are well founded. Parsons has not integrated his models of schooling and peer group to describe student interaction as an end in itself or to describe the growth of the value of structured and intelligent manipulation of the imposed structure of schooling. Marsh, Rosser and Harré's (1978: 31-32) 'unofficial' theory of schooling gives a valuable account of students' 'rules of disorder'. However, it overemphasises the teacher as focus of student interaction and does not offer a model of schooling to interpret and explain the students' construction of reality.

Marsh, Rosser and Harré's error lies in their rejection of Parsons' theory along with what Parsons has done with that theory. Parsons' model of schooling as elaborated by Parsons (1959) and Dreeben (1968) ignores the structured resistance to teachers' authority implicit in the model. Marsh, Rosser and Harré have described this structured resistance to teachers' authority. However, they have left Parsons' model of peer group interaction where Parsons left it: outside the classroom. They have thus failed to see that it offers a model of patterns of peer interaction in the classroom which determine the significance of student conformity to teacher authority and student resistance to that authority.

'The Feral Classroom' has presented a picture of students defining the significance of schooling according to peer interaction which is itself to some extent shaped by sexual values. Teachers' actions become symbolic resources to be defined and used by dominant students. The pattern of interaction in the classroom ensured that students who wished to attend to teachers were generally subordinated to classmates who had a commitment to independence from teachers.

This picture of the classroom is new. Previous theoretically informed studies have examined classroom interaction from an educationist or from an imposed ideological viewpoint. These studies have largely ignored the independent significance of the peer group. Those studies which have left themselves open to the students' perspectives have lacked adequate theoretical models to interpret their findings. It is a virtue of Parsons' models of schooling, peer groups, sex roles and control that they have admitted an openness to data while offering a structure for analysis of those data.

SOME EDUCATIONAL IMPLICATIONS

The findings of 'The Feral Classroom' have many immediate implications for adults concerned with education: teachers, educational administrators, and teacher educators. The argument given in this section proceeds in three stages. The structure of schooling produces certain well-defined problems for teachers and students. There are determinate steps which teachers and other concerned adults may take to remedy these problems within the structure of schooling. However, a basic solution needs to have regard to the practices of teacher educators and policies of educational administrators that ensure that these problems persist and that teachers too often do little effective to cure them.

The findings as informed by the theoretical perspective offer teachers and administrators a bleak picture of the conventional classroom in the junior high school. This picture covers a wide range of issues. These include student indiscipline, oppression of students, and the irrelevance of many teacher practices.

The findings are not peculiar to Goldtown High School. Goldtown teachers were, on the whole, conventionally competent and pleasant people. Some were, by almost any standard, excellent. Goldtown students were more amenable to control and more friendly with their teachers than were students in most metropolitan schools. The problems are a consequence of the experience of schooling, and not of the special circumstances of Goldtown High School and its community.

Students' resistance to teachers' authority is structured by the experience of schooling itself. In these circumstances teachers who suffer discipline problems or resent the constant need to impose on students should not blame themselves or the students. The responsibility lies with the administrators whose unthinking use of traditional classrooms and groupings of students has largely ensured that discipline problems are rife.

The research has shown that individual teachers have a number of options open to them in achieving effective control of the classroom. Conflict between dominant students and teachers is a likely but not a necessary part of classroom interaction. Dominant students' interests are not necessarily incompatible with those of teachers. Dominant students are more interested in achieving a legitimate control over their classmates than in flouting teachers' authority. If teachers can create a definition of classroom order and learning which is compatible with dominant students' interests then there are no discipline problems. The dominant students will enforce the order the teachers want upon misbehaving subordinate students, and will define positively classroom learning activities.

Teachers may find it difficult to accept the need to achieve this alliance with dominant students. The well-behaved but subordinate students are ignored while positive attention is given to the independent and dominant students. Paradoxically, the teacher who wishes to exercise effective control must renounce immediate control and direct assertion of the desired moral order. Teachers' control needs to be mediated by students' control, and teachers' desired moral order must work with dominant students' perceptions of a desirable social order.

Teachers' effective use of student control systems was illustrated in 'The Feral Classroom' by the operation of the captaincy. So long as the teacher's use of the captaincy was compatible with dominant students' control of the class, the captain kept order for the teacher. Similar considerations applied to the control of stirring. Dominant students controlled and limited the stirring for those teachers who were defined by their students as punishing disorder and teaching worthwhile lessons.

Teachers generally do not have the knowledge which would let them use student controls. They are too concerned with their subject matter and their order to know students' values and social structure. Students value teachers who know their subject matter and appreciate teachers who keep order. But, teachers who wish to impose this order and communicate this knowledge must know which students are in control, how they exercise this control, and how they legitimate this control.

A misguided emphasis on curriculum and presentation of lessons in teacher education is to some extent responsible for secondary teachers' lack of knowledge of classroom social structure. When the categorisation of student-teachers by discipline loyalties teaches them the overriding importance of their knowledge of French irregular verbs, the Great Plains of North China, and the love-life of amoeba, they are misled. When student-teachers, by their experience of micro-teaching and practice-teaching, are taught that a fixed order of lesson planning is more important than knowledge of classroom social order, they are deceived. Teacher education needs in its syllabus to take more account of classroom peer interaction. Teaching practice should give student-teachers an extended opportunity to become acquainted with their class members as well as to present lessons.

Teachers might also learn to respect the kinds of learning being disseminated in the peer group. Teenage sexuality, for example, seems peculiarly difficult for adults to adjust to: a prurient interest on the one hand is matched on the other by a determination to ignore a hard-to-miss reality. Schools do not address the issues which confront most Grade Nine girls: how to obtain the attention of boys; how to behave on dates; 'two-timing'; how to cope with being 'dumped' by a boy; how to behave with classmates' boyfriends. These topics were widely discussed in the classroom. Arguably, knowledge so gained was more germane to the girls' present and future concerns than, for example, the love-life of amoeba.

'The Feral Classroom' has shown that teachers, instead of aiding the development of these kinds of knowledge, fight against girls' socio-sexual maturity. Teachers objected to aspects of dress which indicated sexual maturity: make-up, jewellery and perfume were all banned. Certain teachers found the girls with mature and active sexual interests so distasteful that they victimised these girls. Even sympathetic teachers usually did not discern the importance of girls' status systems based on these definitions of maturity. As a result, teachers were constantly feuding with influential girls, and combatting some major pressures for harmonious and happy classrooms.

Teachers might also take into account the unhappy lives led by some children in each class. These include students low in power or influence who were generally persecuted by their classmates. They also include students who did not manage their low or high academic status competently.

There were two ways in which teachers might alleviate the plight of subordinate students. One is to discuss with these students the construction of power and influence and attempt to give them some competence in interaction. Another is to work with dominant students. 'The Feral Classroom' has shown that girls respect classmates who exercise their influence in the interest of classroom harmony and integration. Parallel findings, not discussed in 'The Feral Classroom', show powerful boys protecting subordinate classmates from students attempting to exercise an unlegitimated power. These tendencies to look after the interests of subordinate classmates could have been greatly strengthened by any adult who had the knowledge and the concern to intervene. It is a drawback of the extreme specificity of student-teacher relations in the junior high school that few teachers have either this knowledge or concern.

Academic status, whether high or low, offered subordinate students great and complex problems of role management. Teachers and administrators who impose the structure which exaggerates the significance of specific academic performances are responsible for this problem, but do nothing about it. The problem could be ameliorated by discussing their classroom management of high and low academic status with the students concerned. A more basic solution would be to reduce the constant classroom emphasis on public, specific and relative academic performance. School and teacher emphasis on the importance of marks was a consequence of the structure of schooling and perhaps of teachers' general ignorance of the conditions of work in their students' communities. Students saw much schoolwork as neither enjoyable in itself nor serving any purpose in their adult roles. They saw teachers' emphasis on marks as irrelevant to the general conditions of obtaining employment in Goldtown and Kimberley. These conditions were because of the students' particular relations with the employer or because of the employer's diffuse knowledge that the student concerned was a 'good worker'.

Teachers' ignorance of their students' communities is largely ensured by their training and by state education department policies. It is a very rare teacher-education course which pays adequate attention to specialist problems of the nexus between schools and their host populations. The people in charge of Australian state school systems too often reward for administrative convenience those teachers who transfer readily across disparate communities rather than those teachers who are prepared to make a commitment to one community. When teachers' training and educational administrative policies change, teachers will begin to be able to use adequately their own and their students' knowledge of the community.

Solutions to the problems discussed above all suggest a reduction in the specificity and performance aspects of student-teacher interaction. This would run counter to the degree of subject-based specialisation which has been the mark of high status education in Western societies. Efforts to restructure education to reduce performance and specific student-teacher relations would meet very wide resistance.

FUTURE RESEARCH

Two attractive features of Parsons' theorising are his use of analytic universals and the extent to which it includes a general model of society. Each of these features suggests questions for further research. A third source of questions is the necessary limitations of any research conducted by a single researcher on a single population.

'The Feral Classroom' has described members of a single grade in a single school during the few hours that could be spent with each student. At most, my experience of any single class stretched over a month of interviewing with the students extending that experience by recounting their knowledge of their own history. Yet the model tested and developed in 'The Feral Classroom' covers patterns of socialisation into the family, and into the school over the fourteen or fifteen years before the children were interviewed. At their best the findings can only suggest the explanatory utility of the models of schooling, peer groups, and sexual roles advanced and tested. To do more would require at least a cross-sectional study of children of all ages in a defined population. A longitudinal study of a cohort of children from before the time they begin school to the time they leave school would be ideal.

No attempt was made in the research to explain recruitment to each of the strongly differentiated roles of the classroom peer group. Background information collected during the research and accounts by students hinted at some explanations. An adequate explanation would require longitudinal research.

Evidence in 'The Feral Classroom' has been presented in the form of excerpts from interviews. Such evidence has the advantage that it, in a limited way, brings the reader directly into communication with the students. It is hoped too that the examples of conversation give the reader a sense of the reality of the classroom, and this sense of the reality of the classroom will bring to life the dry bones of a largely analytic argument.

Such use of extracts of conversation removed from the context in which they occurred has been convincingly criticised. A trivial though true accusation is that the reader is unable to determine the criteria used to select the evidence used to illustrate the exposition. This accusation is trivial because the reader is almost universally dependent on a faith in the integrity of the research. A more basic criticism is that isolated selections of conversation lose meaning determined by the social context in which they regularly occurred (Leiter, 1980: 106–157). This criticism has been to some degree met by the system of coding and indexing individual students' comments. This places each quotation in a context of the student's identity in the class, and of the action described in the context of total classroom interaction. A criticism that it is difficult in interviews to elicit taken-for-granted aspects, action has been met in two ways in 'The Feral Classroom'. It is met to some extent by the researcher's role as 'strangers' as informants: these included social isolates, visitors and newcomers in the classroom. A fourth criticism of the use of interviews in research is that the analysis tends to be of talk about action and not of the action itself. This problem is discussed in Appendix A.

A method such as Mehan's (1979) 'constitutive ethnography' would have met some of these objections. This method involves observation of lessons to allow an exhaustive analysis of rules in operation in the various social contexts of the lesson. Mehan uses Schutz' (1953) 'postulate of adequacy' to validate the descriptions of rules. This postulate requires that the actor whose actions are being described accept the description of his activities.

A study which employed such a research method would add useful detail to the findings of 'The Feral Classroom'. For instance, Chapters 8 and 9 described how students construct academic status through their control of the opportunity to participate in the lesson, and their control of the definition of the quality of the participation. However, this analysis has not, as Mehan did, explored the rules by which teachers decide which students should contribute to the lesson (Mehan, 1979: 85–125). As a result, 'The Feral Classroom's' examination of students' construction of academic competence through capable use of teachers' rules is incomplete (Mehan, 1979: 126–171).

Constitutive ethnography, however, has its own failings. The postulate of adequacy does not take sufficient account of the structure of relations between researcher and informant. Informants too readily assent to the researcher's description of their rules. Hargreaves and his colleagues (1976) similarly employed the postulate of adequacy to validate their description of the rules teachers use to decide who and when among the students may contribute to the lesson. Their formulation of the rules differs in significant detail from that of Mehan (Hargreaves et al., 1976: 81). A satisfactory account should exhaustively describe, as Mehan has done, the rules operating in a domain of observed action. It should also leave itself open to informants' unprompted statement of these rules.

The research in 'The Feral Classroom' has been couched in terms of a model which should apply to all organisations making similar demands upon a population. If the theoretical statement is valid, results from other schools will more or less resemble those from Goldtown, with differences because of distinctive features of the school system and of the population being researched. Similar studies in schools which did not share Goldtown High School's rural background, or with specialised social class recruitment would be valuable.

The variables used by Parsons to construct models of sex roles, peer groups and schooling have also been employed by him in describing a range of adult roles. These roles include adult roles in the family (Parsons and Bales, 1955) and adult roles in Western industrial society (Parsons, 1971a, 1971b, 1976). This congruence of variables helps his attempt to offer an explanation of how:

> the school functions to internalise in its pupils both commitments and capacities for successful performance of their adult roles, and . . . how it functions to allocate these human resources within the role structure of the adult society. (Parsons, 1959: 297)

The present research suggests that if acceptance of a role in the school implies commitment to an acceptable adult role in society, then Goldtown students will accept the broad orientations which ensure adequate occupancy of adult roles. However, any analysis which uses simplistic definitions of 'dependence' or 'independence' as outcomes of schooling misses the complexity of students' occupancy and use of their classroom roles. Different students in the same class will have radically different patterns of interaction with their peers and with teachers, and different attitudes to schoolwork. Willis (1977) and Thomas (1981) have described some continuities between commitments in school, and commitments to and occupancy of adult roles among sections of the school population. Further research is required on continuities between commitments in school, and commitments to and occupancy of industrial, unemployed, domestic and subsistence adult roles.

Comparative studies of schools and other organisations with varying degrees of structured specific, performance and universalistic relations would be of considerable theoretical and practical interest. One focus would be on the degree to which patterns of student classroom interaction are determined by homogenous recruitment, and specific performance and universal-

istic formal relations. The second focus would be on the continuities between roles in different styles of schooling and the
occupancy of adult roles.

Research on the degree to which peer interaction is determined
by the formal structure of relations should go in two directions.
An extension in one direction would examine schools where diffuse and particularistic relations are important, and teaching
groups are age-heterogenous. Another extension would be to
examine peer relations in circumstances which are theoretically
similar but occurring under otherwise different circumstances.
An example would be the social relations of Papua New Guinean
villagers employed as labourers at a large mine. The structure
of relations within their villages of origin resemble those in the
family, and the formal demands of them at work and the structure
of authority relations at the mine resemble those in the school.

The second focus of interest would examine the consequences
of different styles of schooling for commitments to adult roles.
For example, it has been argued in 'The Feral Classroom' that
students in the conventional structure of school often learn to
evaluate their formal setting and to structure resistance to that
setting. It was suggested earlier in this chapter that structured
resistance to school authority was likely to be less important
in schools with alternative formal structures. The degree to which
conventional rather than alternative patterns of schooling produce structured resistance to imposed conditions of work is of
theoretical interest. It is also of practical interest to conser-
vatives, liberal reformers, and radicals.

Appendix A

Student interviews

A variety of research methods was used according to their efficiency and effectiveness for the purposes at hand. The principal method was interviews with students. This appendix describes the structure and order of the interviews, the justification for using this research method, and the sociometrics which were used to elicit the classroom social structure.

THE INTERVIEWS

The preparation of interviews with each class followed the same pattern. A teacher who had good relations with that class introduced me to the class. I informed students of the purpose and procedure of the research. Students were given a small questionnaire in which they were asked to write their names, and nominate classmates whom they would like as interview partner, and classmates with whom they would prefer not to be interviewed. This information was used to select interview partners for each student, order the sequence of introductory and principal interviews, and to form sociograms of each class.

The introductory interviews
The introductory interviews were conducted with pairs of students from each clique distinguished on the interview sociometric. Information from these interviews was used to construct an interview schedule grounded in the social reality of that class but comparable with schedules used in other classes. Questions asked covered the topics of: perceptions of group activities in English and whatever other school subjects were potential sociometric work criteria; student seating patterns; academic norms; playground and out-of-school activities of class members.

These informants were also asked to describe each classmate. This information allowed the tentative placing of each new set of interviewees in the classroom social structure delineated by the findings of the interview sociometric.

Lastly, these interviews gave representative students a chance to ask questions about the research. I was able to discover and sometimes correct their preconceptions regarding it. The introductory informants thus became sponsors for my multiple entry into the class through each clique (Kahn and Mann, 1952).

The principal interviews
The principal interviews were organised to balance largely
incompatible goals. On the one hand, open responses were
encouraged. On the other hand, it was necessary to avoid con-
tamination between different replies, and to ensure comparability
between classes. The following schedule details topics covered in
each interview. The order of discussion of topics varied according
to the flow of students' interests in the interview:

1   Informants' perceptions of the purposes of the research.
2   Check of background details obtained from school records.
3   Interview sociometric.
   (a)   General considerations in choice and rejection of
       classmates.
   (b)   Specific reasons for choices on the interview socio-
       metric.
   (c)   Specific reasons for rejection on the interview socio-
       metric.
4   Either Prior acquaintances in class from primary school and
     Grade Eight;
     Or Difficulties in moving into a new district and school.
5   Relatives in class and school.
6   Exchange of visits to home of classmates.
7   English sociometric.
8   Lunch-time activities and companions.
9   Second work sociometric
   (a)   Previous experience in area of second work sociometric.
   (b)   Specific reasons for students chosen on the second
       work sociometric.
   (c)   Specific reasons for students rejected on the second
       work sociometric.
10   Descriptions of interaction with deskmates and immediate
     class neighbours.
11   Descriptions of interaction with more distant classmates.
12   Reasons for location in the classroom.
13   Sexual interests.
14   Expected age of marriage.
15   Work norms
   (a)   Discussion of those who are seen to do a lot of school-
       work.
   (b)   Discussion of those who are seen to do less schoolwork.
   (c)   Discussion of those who are seen to join more in
       teacher-sponsored class discussions, who volunteer
       answers to teachers' questions and who ask teachers'
       questions.
16   Expected age of leaving school.
     Expected and desired activities after leaving school.
17   Discussion of the students' school subjects under the
     following headings –
   (a)   The student's reactions to his marks obtained on the
       last semester results.

(b) Perceptions of the utility and interest of the subject matter.

(c) Perceptions of the relevance of high marks in the subject.

18 Perceptions of high academic status students.

19 Perceptions of low academic status students.

20 Discussion of ways students help each other academically
(a) Legitimacy of styles of help.
(b) Who helps whom?

21 Things for which students obtain respect.

22 Skiting (boasting)
(a) What forms of skiting are there?
(b) Who skites about what?

23 Power in the classroom.
(a) Toughs.
(b) Sissies and sooks.
(c) Who 'can't take a joke'?

24 'If you don't understand [names of three subject masters], what do you do?'

25 'When lessons get boring, what do you do?'

26 'When people start to muck around, what do you do?'

27 Dobbing (informing)
(a) 'Have you ever dobbed anyone in for any reason?'
(b) Supplementary question if answer is incompatible with information derived from earlier interviews or other sources.
(c) 'Who has dobbed others in?' 'How do you feel about it?'

28 Helping teachers
(a) 'In what ways have you helped teachers?' 'Why?' 'How did other students feel about it?'
(b) 'What students often help teachers?' 'How do they help them?'
'What are their reasons for helping them?' 'How do you feel about their helping them?'

29 Talking to teachers
(a) 'Do you talk to teachers after class? In little or big lunch? Out of school?' 'What do you talk to them about?' 'How do other students feel about you talking to them?'
(b) 'Which students often talk to teachers after class? In little or big lunch? Out of school?' 'What do they talk to them about?' 'How do you feel about their talking to teachers?'

30 Class captaincy and vice-captaincy
(a) Either 'How do you feel about the job [student named] does as captain?'
Or, if the respondent is captain, 'What's it like being class captain?'
(b) Either, 'How do you feel about the job [student named] does as vice-captain?'

Or If the respondent is vice-captain, 'What's it like being class vice-captain?'

31   Teacher favouritism.

32   Teacher victimisation of students.

33   Perceptions of students 'who never do anything wrong'.

34   Stirrers and stirring. Their activities, the rationale, the consequences and class reactions.

35   Students picked on or teased by classmates.

36   Interview conclusion

(a)   'Is there anything that has been left out of the interview if I am to understand how you feel about other people in the class?'

(b)   'Do you feel that the questions have over-emphasised any part of the classroom life?'

(c)   'Are there any questions that didn't make much sense or you couldn't see any purpose to?'

(d)   'What questions embarrassed you or made you feel uncomfortable?'

(e)   Either 'How did having a friend present alter how you felt about coming up for the interview?'
Or 'How did you feel about coming up for the interview by yourself?'

(f)   If students are in pairs: 'What answers did you alter because you had a friend present?'

37   After the interview

(a)   Continue listening and talking to the students and record any extra comments they make.

(b)   After the students have left, record impressions of student uniform according to the following criteria:
If girls -
- are they wearing make-up, nail polish, perfume, bangles, necklaces, rings, ear rings?
- are they wearing their tunics without belts, bloused, hitched at the shoulders?
- are they wearing exceptionally long or short tunics?
- are they wearing leather shoes, canvas shoes, or thongs?
If boys in summer uniform -
- are they wearing their socks pulled up or lying down?
- are they wearing their shirt tails tucked in or lying out?
- are they wearing hair that is exceptionally long or short?
- are they wearing regulation school shorts or 'stubbies'?
- are they wearing canvas shoes, leather shoes, or thongs?
If boys in winter uniform -
- are they wearing hair that is exceptionally long or short?

- are they wearing a tie with their top shirt button
done up, a tie with the top shirt button undone,
no tie?
- are they wearing leather shoes, canvas shoes, or
thongs?
- are they wearing school blazer, regulation school
pullover or a non-regulation pullover?

Validity of the interview data
The use of interviews has been criticised as offering a study of
informants' verbal behaviour in an interview setting rather than
a study of the social interaction it purports to describe (Brown
and Gilmartin, 1969: 288; Phillips, 1971: 2-6). In the present
research the many interviews in each class all focused on the
same set of actions, offered concurrent validation of students'
statements. However, students' different interpretation of the
same event or actor did not invalidate their statements. Instead,
the different responses were often evidence of socially structured
differences in their definitions of social reality.
    Interview data has been said to be invalid because the social
structure of the interviewer-interviewee interaction largely
determines interviewee responses (Phillips, 1971). Although the
structure of interviewer-interviewee relations remained consistent
through the series of interviews, its importance was reduced by
the policy of interviewing students with chosen companions
(Lofland, 1971: 88). Students who talk alone with the interviewer
are reported by Becker (1958) to give different information
when accompanied by fellow students. This finding suggests
group interviews may aid research into public knowledge, the
domain with which the present study is concerned. A bonus
associated with the use of group interviews is that interviewees
are more likely to respond freely (Labov, 1972: 189).
    Interviewing in dyads probably contributed to students' will-
ingness to be interviewed. All students were free to refuse to
be interviewed. None refused. Only one, b1/18*, was reluctant.
Students interviewed in dyads expressed satisfaction, but the
occasional student who was not an isolate but had to be interviewed alone stated a preference for an interview partner.
    The interviews were standardised in so far as some comparison
between students and between classes was required, but non-
standardised in so far as account was taken both of the distinctive
place of each student in his class and of aspects of student
culture peculiar to that class. Subtle differences of wording
were unlikely to miscue the students who were always strongly
involved in the issue under discussion (Cantril. 1947). Indeed,
use of a sympathetic vocabulary differentially employed according
to the classroom concerns of the students responding may be a
prerequisite of a valid response (Labov, 1972; Oppenheim,
1964: 65).
    Similar considerations apply to use of a free sequence which
allows the flow of interview responses to determine the order of

topics discussed, for:

> No fixed sequence of questions is satisfactory to all respon-
> dents. The most effective sequence for any respondent is
> determined by his readiness and willingness to take up a topic
> as it comes up. (Richardson et al., 1965:48)

Presumably, informants find conversation easier when it follows
their pattern of thought and are more likely to be motivated to
respond if it is felt that the interviewer is actively listening.

Order of classes interviewed
The prime consideration determining the order in which students
were interviewed was that intensive knowledge of each class
was needed during the interviews for contextual grounding of
questions and responses. This ability to ground the interviews
depended on recent contact with the class. Therefore each class,
except for absent students, was interviewed in sequence.

The classes were interviewed in the following order: 9b6, 9ad1,
9c4, 9b4, 9b2, 9b1e1, 9b5, 9b3e2, 9c2, 9c1, and 9c3d2. Initially
it was planned to study classes in an order which balanced high
and low stream status and sex. However, the number and frank-
ness of descriptions of their sexual interests by girls in 9ad1 and
9c4 suggested the wisdom of finding a chaperone. The remaining
girls' classes were left until the end of the series of interviews
when a suitable chaperone was found.

A second consideration which modified the order of classes
interviewed was access to drama, debates or other public performances of a class. During these performances, I sat next to,
and talked with students from that class about the performance
and behaviour of their classmates. My observations, mediated
through informants' perceptions of these performances and more
ordinary lessons, were used as background for interviews.
Because access to public performances was occasional, I took
advantage of it when it occurred and interviewed that class while
my memories were still vivid.

Order of interviews within classes
The main series of interviews in each class was ordered according
to information derived from the introductory interviews and the
interview sociometrics. Principal objectives of the ordering of
interviews were to obtain allies among the dominant students in
each group, to avoid identification with any group (Kahn and
Mann, 1952; Vidich, 1955) and to maximise the advantages of
openness early in each series of interviews and of greater interviewer information later in each series. Interview order was
sometimes changed to avoid embarrassing social isolates or to
take into account students' wishes to be interviewed or not to be
interviewed at a particular time.

The series of interviews with each class began with pairs of
middle status members of each class clique. The central part of

the series included the dominant students, low status dyads, and isolates. Wherever possible, isolates were interviewed in couples with their closest class associate. Each series of interviews concluded with pairs of central but not dominant members of the principal cliques. These last interviews were used to confirm or modify earlier findings.

SOCIOMETRY

An important base of the analysis of classroom interaction was the responses to the six sociometrics: that is the positive and negative responses to the interview and two sociometric work criteria. The findings given in the body of the book are derived solidly from analysis of species of interaction associated with well defined sociometric structures. Sociometry was chosen as central for analysis of classroom interaction because of its compatibility with Parsonian theory (Blau, 1972; Moreno, 1952: 153; Sugarman, 1968), the stability of the social structures elicited by sociometric responses (Blyth, 1960; Glidewell et al., 1966), and their relationships with a large number of variables (Secord and Bachman, 1968: 232-257).

It has been alleged that sociometry does not represent group relations. Hargreaves (1972: 307) and Potashkin (1946) deny that sociograms represent social structure because the test elicits perceived or desired as well as actual relations. High status students usually nominate their actual associates. Low status students may make unreal choices of people whom they admire but with whom they rarely interact. However, inability to fulfil choices has little significance. Sociometric choices denote reference groups which are related to actors' values and which determine specific goals and definitions of situations (Blau, 1962; Bradley, 1974; Cheyne, 1972; Gnagey, 1961; Kidd, 1958; Kounin, Gump and Ryan, 1967; Lott and Lott, 1960; O'Hanlon, 1964; Secord and Bachman, 1968: 363-413).

A sociometric criterion is the overt focus of a sociometric question. It is often distinct from the considerations which inform a respondent's choice:

> for instance, if asked in a school classroom to give the names of those (a student) would really prefer to *study* with, he might give on the criterion two names of individuals with whom he wishes to be for companionship. (Jennings, 1950: 19)

The relation between the sociometric criterion and the concern of the student parallels, with the right choice of criterion, that between teacher intentions and student use of the resulting classroom situations (Cusick, 1973: 64).

Use of negative sociometrics has been criticised. It has been alleged that it is difficult to elicit rejections (White, 1961) and that reports of rejections are artefactual because 'most people are not actively interested in those with whom they do not associate' (Northway, 1952:5). However, students are forced to mix with classmates some of whom they would prefer to ignore and others of whom they actively dislike (Harper, 1968: 225). Moreover, the constellation of values, activities and labelling associated with high rejection is more intense and stable than with high acceptance (Croft and Grygier, 1956; Harper, 1968; Muldoon, 1955). The more pertinent the deviation is to goals of others in the situation defined by the sociometric criterion, the greater the rejection of the deviant (Emerson, 1969: Schachter, 1951).

The sociometric criteria

Three sociometric criteria were used in the present research with a free number of choices and rejections on each (Eng and French, 1948; Holland and Leinhardt, 1973). The criteria were choice of interview partners and two classroom work situations which the introductory interviews for each class had shown constituted a meaningful situation for students in that class.

The interview sociometric has been discussed in this appendix in connection with the ordering of interviews. It does not refer to a classroom situation but has a validity, unshared by the other sociometric criteria, because students knew it was to be used to distribute them (Moreno, 1952). Further, the considerations students used in choosing interview partners had wide relevance. Almost universally, students chose classroom associates or 'mates' as partners. A very few students mentioned aspiring to know the other student and once a student was nominated as a joke.

A few students did not choose each other when they were, by their own and others' reports, closely associated either inside or outside the classroom. This failure to choose usually resulted from ambivalent feelings towards the associate not chosen. An example is the case in Chapter 5 of a girl whose alleged sexual promiscuity caused her companions to reject her on sociometrics. Such instances of ambivalence have special interest because they underline key classroom social structural variables.

It was intended to use English and mathematics as sociometric work criteria. These criteria were chosen because the subjects are taught in all Queensland Grade Nine classes. They are also subjects in which the preference and performance of each sex tends to differ. Boys tend to do better in and prefer mathematics and girls tend to do better in and prefer English (Bakan, 1966; Garai and Scheinfeld, 1968; Keeves, 1972; Keeves and Radford, 1969; Kolesnik, 1969; Keeves, 1972; Keeves and Radford, 1969; Kolesnik, 1969; Maccoby, 1966; Martin, 1971; Oetzel, 1966).

Mathematics could not be used consistently as a work criterion. Four classes were cross-set for mathematics and so students had different and not comparable target populations. Where possible, a science work sociometric was substituted for mathematics because sex differences in the interest in performance in science are similar to those in mathematics (Keeves, 1972; Keeves and Radford, 1969; Kolesnik, 1969; Oetzel, 1966). Science, however, was not taught in all girls' classes. Substitute female school subjects were either individually performed such as typewriting and therefore offered no sociometric use or, like home economics, involved split classes and halved target populations. Compromise alternative work criteria were chosen for each class, aiming to optimise identity of the target population and meaningfulness of the criterion for each class.

The English sociometric was specified to producing and acting in a play. This sociometric appears to be similar in meaning from class to class. This similarity may be illusory. Previous experience in comparable workgroups influences pupil considerations in choosing workmates (Pearce, 1953: 249).

The Grade Nine classes' experience differed considerably. For example, 9b2's play was considered good enough to be acted before parents on the school speech night. 9b5, on the other hand, at the time of the interviews, had been rehearsing a play for over a term. Class leaders had withdrawn from the play and, as was shown in Chapter 9, condemned it to failure. Despite this lack of uniformity between school classes, no other subject-based criterion would have offered any advantages.

The validity of sociometrics which do not require students to make a choice with real consequences may be questioned (Moreno, 1952). In one instance, validity was tested. A mathematics teacher submitted a sociometric for seating in her subject one week before interviews with that form began. There was only one difference in choices on her sociometric and the research sociometric. This indicated that the interview setting and absence of real consequences of choices did not greatly alter students' choices.

Analysis of sociometric data
Sociometry has been used elsewhere to measure specificity, diffuseness, particularism, universalism, and social status and to define groups. Only the sociometric definition of groups is used here. This section explains the omission of the former measures and the use made of the latter.

Previously used statistical techniques (Criswell, 1949; Gardner and Thompson, 1956; Katz, 1953) were found in the present study not to describe students' control status. Summed or vector measurements of status would not have indicated the status of such powerful and influential students as b5/42* and c2/18*. On the interview criterion, for example, both b5/42* and c2/18* were rejected more often than chosen, and both came below the class median in number of choices received. Students' descriptions of decision-making and the exercise of control were not related to quantitative sociometric measures but were related to groups and places in groups as indicated by sociometric analyses.

The argument for the statistical analysis of sociometric data to measure specificity and diffuseness is stronger. Choices are

more specific and universalistic where students employ work
rather than social considerations in evaluating sociometric work
criteria (Criswell, 1949). Students with high achievement needs
are more likely to make different choices for social and work
criteria, presumably when the work criteria promote performance
considerations (French, 1955; Mehrabian, 1968). A simple and
plausible measure of specificity/diffuseness in students' relations
with connotations of universalism/particularism and quality/
performance rests on a comparison of the choices and rejections
made for the interview and work sociometrics.

Despite its appeal, the sociometric statistical analysis of
specificity/diffuseness was not used. This was for two reasons.
The different significance of the sociometric work criteria used
in each class means that the comparison of apparently similar
sociometrics is invalid. Further, the present research shows that
major classroom activities are outside the explicit domain of the
sociometric criteria. Thus, a comparison on the basis of the sociometric structure elicited by these sociometrics would be an
invalid description of the core concerns of the students.

Researchers have also given sociometric interpretations of
universalism and particularism. Populations with highly skewed
sociometric choices are said to have universalistic values as
actors choose partners without regard to particular relations
(Blau, 1962, 1964). Conversely, reciprocated sociometric choices
are said to be an index of particularism (Ausubel, 1970: 349;
Scarr, 1964; Schumuck, 1973). However, the present research
has shown that an important particularistic focus, sexual interest,
lies outside the classroom. Although Chapter 5 showed cohesive,
closed dyads based on common sexual interests in girls' classes,
attribution of an internal particularism to these groups would
often be mistaken. The research also produced evidence, cited in
Chapter 4, that these groups changed with a change in boyfriends. An overall statistic would conceal the difference between
such groups and the tight particularistic groups, associated with
girls whose sexual interests, if any, did not intrude into the
classroom.

These statistics have been used to show the significance of
certain roles within classes but not to make overall comparisons
of classes. There are three examples in 'The Feral Classroom'
of the use of this statistic to describe specialised roles. These
are the description of the specific, performance values of clowns,
the description of successful and unsuccessful controllers of
the meaning of academic performance, and the description of the
diffuse particularism of girls with low or concealed sexual
interests.

Sociometric analyses define groups by measures of concentration of choices in an area of a sociometric network delimited by
boundaries of sparser concentration of choices (Alba, 1973:
115). Groups have been defined in the present research by
defining concentrations of choices in each class's sociometric
network of choices. The most useful statistic for isolating groups

within sociometric networks (Alba and Guttman, 1971a, 1971b; Peay, 1974) employed modified versions of Luce and Perry's definition of a clique: 'A clique is a group of individuals, every two of whom has chosen each other and excluding no one who has chosen and been chosen by every member of the clique' (Luce and Perry, 1949: 96). Researchers found this definition too strict because 'a friendship group may lack but a few friendships to achieve completeness and hence be found wanting as a clique' (Alba, 1973: 116). The definition has been relaxed in two ways. Firstly, unreciprocated choices may be taken into account. Secondly, the concept of 'power graph', 'a graph in which two points are connected when they are within some fixed distance of each other in the original graph' (Alba and Guttman, 1971a: 2), has been introduced.

In the present study, the discrimination of groups began with computation of all maximally complete subgraphs. Some subgraphs, those with too few points, and those insufficiently complete because they had few connecting points within them (Alba, 1973: 125) were then discarded.

Remaining subgraphs were used as input to the next step, the unit merger step. Two subgraphs were merged when one differed from the other by addition or deletion of one point. Subgroups produced by this step or remaining from the previous step were input for the final step, the overlap merger step. Two subgraphs were merged when the number of points in the intersection was greater than a percent of points in the smaller subgraph.

The statistics used to isolate groups have been applied flexibly in the present research. This is despite the argument by Boyle (1969), Nosanchuk (1963), and Philips and Conviser (1972) that a predefined use of the statistics avoids arbitrary discrimination of groups. The criteria of density of choices and degree of overlap have been varied in analysis to ensure that there were sizeable groups in each class.

Appendix B

Conditions and permit for research

GOLDTOWN STATE HIGH SCHOOL

Dear Sir,

After discussion of your proposed questionnaire and interviews, teachers have decided to grant your request to obtain information from Grade 9 students at this school. The dates of our end of Semester examinations are 18, 19, 20 June.

Please note the following criticisms:

(a) Teachers do not want to be 'named'.
(b) It does not seem to be wise to ask for the names of students as answers to questions.
(c) Interview in pairs may not be entirely satisfactory. Some students do not have any friends in the class.
(d) The teachers involved would like to discuss the proposed study before you begin.

I request that loss of time from classes be cut to the absolute minimum.

Yours faithfully,

PRINCIPAL

Appendix C

A girls' classroom note

The note reproduced below is longer than most. Otherwise it is a typical example of the innumerable notes that girls with active but immature sexual interests exchanged among themselves. It has been chosen for reproduction here because the use of this note was discussed at length in Chapter 4.

The alphanumerics on the left refer to the girl who wrote that part of the note. Double brackets within the text indicate an inserted comment by c3/31.

c3/32*   I don't believe what b5/16 said (about b5/32* liking me) but I wish it was true. I mean I've all of a sudden flipped over b5/32*.

c3/31   Yeah – he's a dream.

c3/33*   Well, he's not that good is he. I mean a guy like him with a girl! He may be a nice looker but gosh he's untouchable by girls.

c3/31   Gee I would soon change that I feel that b5/32* would be a goer at the flicks.

c3/32*   You shouldn't say things like that about him. You said he has a nice personality. How do you know he's untouchable by girls. HAVE YOU (cough cough) *TRIED* TO GET HIM?

c3/31   Yeah c3/33* how do you know?

c3/33*   Well I dunno! but he's never had a *real* girlfriend has he. ((INSERTED HERE BY c3/31) I don't know and you don't know). And anyway the only person I know who's FLIPPED OVER HIM (?) is you c3/31. If he's so nice why won't he talk to you, because he's not shy and you two need and suit each other.

c3/32*   You said he was shy!

c3/33*   Because I told you b5/16 probably only said it and also because I think c3/12* is the lucky one, he always talks to her.

c3/32*   c3/33* why do you keep on changing what you say about him?

c3/33*   c3/32* why do you always butt in I told you he was shy because he was at the time.

c3/31   She knows him better. Try falling over his feet or dropping a rock on his toe?

c3/32*   Don't be stupid! I can't he goes to cricket and besides I couldn't talk to him when c3/12* is around cos she told me to keep my eyes off him but . . .

c3/31   Alright I won't but cause I don't believe anything you say about so shove it up your asshole if you know where it is.

c3/33*   c3/31 What a break WHAT A BREAK MAN. WOW & BEAUTY.

          c3/32* Sorry but I'm trying to think.

c3/31   How do ya mean

c3/32*   MAD.

c3/33*   PLAY CRICKET & HIT HIM IN THE FACE WITH THE BAT.

Bibliography

Adams, R.A. (1970), Perceived teaching styles, 'Comparative Education Review', 14: 50-69.

Adams, R.A., and Biddle, B. (1970), 'Realities of Teaching', New York, Holt, Rinehart & Winston.

Ahier, J. (1974), Professions and Ideologies, in Ahier, J., and Flude, M., 'Educability, Schools and Ideology', London, Croom Helm, pp. 184-191.

Alba, R. (1973), A graph-theoretical definition of a sociometric technique, 'Journal of Mathematical Sociology', 3: 113-126.

Alba, R., and Guttman, M. (1971a), COMPLT. A program for the analysis of sociometric data and the clustering of similarity processes, mimeo.

Alba, R., and Guttman, M. (1971b), SOC. A sociometric analysis, mimeo.

Alexander, C., and Campbell, E. (1964), Peer influence on adolescent educational aspirations and attainments, 'American Sociological Review', 29: 568-575.

Anderson, D., and Western, J. (1970), State differences in authoritarian attitudes, 'Australian Journal of Psychology', 22: 261-264.

Anderson, D., Western, J., and Boreham, P. (1976), Conservatism in recruits to the professions, in Browne, R., and Magin, D., 'The Sociology of Education', Melbourne, Macmillan, pp. 402-408.

Atkinson, J., and O'Connor, P. (1966), Neglected factors in achievement oriented performance: social approval as an incentive and performance decrement, in Atkinson, J., and Feather, N., 'A Theory of Achievement Motivation', New York, John Wiley, pp. 299-326.

Atkinson, J., and Raphaelson, S. (1956), Individual differences in motivation and behaviour in particular situations, 'Journal of Personality' 24: 349-363.

Atkinson, P., and Delamont, S. (1976), Mock-ups and cock-ups, in Hammersley, M., and Woods, P., 'The Process of Schooling', London, Routledge & Kegan Paul, pp. 133-142.

Ausubel, D. (1970), 'Educational Psychology', New York, Holt, Rinehart & Winston.

Bakan, D. (1966), 'The Duality of Human Existence', Chicago, Rand McNally.

Bardwick, J. (1971), 'Psychology of Women', New York, Harper & Row.

Barker Lunn, J. (1970), 'Streaming in Schools', Slough, NFER.

Bates, R. (1973), Classroom, location learning and status, 'New Zealand Journal of Educational Studies' 8: 136-153.

Becker, H. (1958), Problems of inference and proof in participant observations, 'American Sociological Review', 23: 652-660.

Becker, H., Geer, B., and Hughes, E. (1968), 'Making the Grade', New York, John Wiley.

Bellack, A. (1966), 'The Language of the Classroom', New York, Columbia University Teachers' College Press.

Berger, I., and Bass, B. (1961), 'Conformity and Deviation', New York, Harper Bros.

Bernard, P. (1971), Stratification sociometrique et reseaux sociaux, 'Sociologie et sociétés', 5:127-150.

Bernstein, B. (1973), 'Class Codes and Control', London, Routledge & Kegan Paul, vol. 1.

Bernstein, B. (1977), Social class, language and socialisation, in Karabel, J., and Halsey, A., 'Power and Ideology in Education', New York, Oxford

University Press, pp. 437-448.

Bidwell, C. (1973), The social psychology of teaching, in Travers, R., 'Second Handbook of Research of Teaching', Chicago, Rand McNally, pp. 413-449.

Bird, C. (1980), Deviant labelling in school, in Woods, P., 'Pupil Strategies', London, Croom Helm, pp. 74-93.

Blau, P. (1962), Operationalising a conceptual scheme: the universalism-particularism pattern variable, 'American Sociological Review', 27: 159-169.

Blau, P. (1964), 'Exchange and Power in Social Life', New York, Wiley.

Blau, P., and Meyer, W. (1971), 'Bureaucracy in Modern Society', 2nd edn., New York, Random House.

Bledsoe, J. (1964), Self concepts of children and their intelligence, achievement interests and anxiety, 'Journal of Individual Psychology', 20: 55-58.

Blyth, W. (1960), The sociometric study of children's groups in English schools, 'British Journal of Educational Studies', 8: 127-147.

Boocock, S., and Coleman, J. (1970), Games with simulated environments, in Miles, M., and Charters, W., 'Learning in Social Settings', Boston, Allyn & Bacon, pp. 336-357.

Bossert, S. (1979), 'Tasks and Social Relationships in the Classroom', Cambridge University Press.

Bourricaud, F. (1981), 'The Sociology of Talcott Parsons', University of Chicago Press.

Boyle, R. (1969), Algebraic systems for normal and hierarchical sociograms, 'Sociometry', 32: 99-119.

Bradley, J. (1974), Clique membership and academic achievement, 'Sociology of Education', 18: 1-8.

Briody, O. (1960), The Nature and Functioning of the One-Teacher Schools in the West Moreton District, unpublished thesis, University of Queensland.

Brown, J., and Gilmartin, N. (1969), Sociology today: lacunae, emphases and surfeits, 'American Sociologist', 4: 283-291.

Brown, V. (1972), Social Relations in a Girls' Secondary School, unpublished dissertation, University of Birmingham, discussed in Shaw, J. (1973), Some implications of sex-segregated education, in Barker, D., and Allen, S., 'Sexual Divisions and Society: Process and Change', London, Tavistock, pp. 133-149.

Brown, W., and Bond, L. (1955), Social stratification in a sixth grade class, 'Journal of Educational Research', 48: 539-543.

Bycroft, P. (1973), 'The Architects Construct Schools', Brisbane Environmental Research and Development Group.

Campbell, J. (1964), Peer relations in childhood, in Hoffman, M., and Hoffman, C., 'Review of Child Development Research', New York, Russell Sage, pp. 289-322.

Campbell, W., Bassett, G., Campbell, E., Cotterell, J., Evans, G., Grassie, M. (1976), 'Some Consequences of the Radford Scheme for Schools, Teachers and Students in Queensland', Canberra, Australian Government Publishing Service.

Cantril, H. (1947), The place of personality in social psychology, 'Journal of Psychology', 24: 19-56.

Cheyne, J. (1972), Direct and vicarious reinforcements, 'Journal of Educational Psychology', 63: 63-68.

Cohen, E. (1973), Sociology and the classroom teacher-student interaction, 'Review of Educational Research', 42: 441-452.

Coleman, J. (1959), Academic achievement and the structure of competition, 'Harvard Educational Review', 29: 330-351.

Coleman, J. (1961), 'Adolescent Society', New York, Free Press.

Collins, R. (1979), 'The Credential Society', New York, Academic Press.

Corrigan, P. (1977), 'Schooling the Smash Street Kids', London, Macmillan.

Covington, M., and Beery, R. (1976), 'Self Worth and School Learning', New York, Holt, Rinehart & Winston.

Crandall, V., Dewey, R., Katkowsky, W., and Preston, A. (1964), Parents' attitudes and behaviours and grade school children's academic achievement,

'Journal of Genetic Psychology', 104: 53-66.
Criswell, J. (1949), Sociometric concepts in personnel administration, 'Sociometry', 12: 287-300.
Croft, I., and Grygier, T. (1965), Social relations of truants and juvenile delinquents, 'Human Relations', 9: 439-466.
Cusick, P. (1973), 'Inside High School', New York, Holt, Rinehart & Winston.
Dale, R. (1972), 'The Culture of the School', Milton Keynes, Open University Press.
Davey, G. (1981), 'Preface', in Lindsay, P. and Palmer, D., 'Playground Game Characteristics of Brisbane Primary School Children', Canberra AGPS, pp. v-xvi.
Davies, B. (1976), 'Education and Social Control', London, Methuen.
Davies, L. (1978), Deadlier than the male? Girls' conformity and deviance in school, in Barton, L., and Meighan, R., 'Schools, Pupils and Deviance', Driffield, Yorks, Nafferton Books, pp. 59-74.
Dawe, A. (1970), The two sociologies, 'British Journal of Sociology', 21: 207-218.
Deem, R. (1978), 'Women and Schooling', London, Routledge & Kegan Paul.
Demaine, J. (1981), 'Contemporary Theories in the Sociology of Education', London, Macmillan.
Deutsch, M. (1949), An experimental study of the effects of co-operation and competition upon group process, 'Human Relations', 2: 199-231.
Di Tomaso, N. (1982), 'Sociological reductionism' from Parsons to Althusser: linking action and structure in social theory, 'American Sociological Review', 47: 14-28.
Dreeben, R. (1968), 'On What is Learned in School', Reading, Mass., Addison-Wesley.
Dreeben, R. (1976), The organisational structure of schools and school systems, in Loubser, J. et al., 'Explorations in General Theory in Social Science', London, Free Press, pp. 857-873.
Edgar, D. (1974), Adolescent competence and sexual disadvantage, 'La Trobe Sociology Papers', No. 10.
Elder, A. (1967), Age integration and socialisation in an educational setting, 'Harvard Educational Review', 37: 594-619.
Emerson, J. (1969), Negotiating the serious import of humour, 'Sociometry', 32: 169-181.
Eng, E., and French, E. (1948), The determination of sociometric status, 'Sociometry', 11: 368-371.
Erben, M., and Gleeson, D. (1977), Education as reproduction, in Young, M., and Whitty, G., 'Society, State and Schooling', Guildford, Surrey, Falmer Press, pp. 73-92.
Fairbairn, K. McBryde, B., and Rigby, D. (1976), 'Schools under Radford', Brisbane, Queensland Department of Education and Board of Secondary School Studies.
Farber, J. (1972), The student and society, in Smith, G. and Kniker, C., 'Myth and Reality', Boston, Allyn & Bacon, pp. 14-23.
Freeland, J. (1979), Class struggle in schooling: Macos and Semp in Queensland, 'Intervention', 12: 29-62.
French, E. (1955), Some characteristics of achievement motivation, 'Journal of Experimental Education', 50: 232-236.
Furlong, V. (1976), Interactions sets in the classroom, in Hammersley, M., and Woods, P., 'The Process of Schooling', London, Routledge & Kegan Paul, pp. 160-170.
Galtung, J. (1967), 'Theory and Methods of Social Research', London, Allen & Unwin.
Garai, J., and Scheinfeld, A. (1968), Sex differences in mental and achievement traits, 'Genetic Psychology Monographs', vol. 77.
Gardner, E., and Thompson, G. (1956), 'Social Relations and Morale in Small Groups', New York, Appleton-Century-Crofts.
Giddens, A. (1979), 'Central Problems in Social Theory', London, Macmillan.
Glidewell, J., Kantor, B., Smith, R., and Stringer, L. (1966), Socialisation

and social structure in the classroom, in Hoffman, L., and Hoffman, M., 'Review of Child Development Research', vol. 2, New York, Russell Sage Foundation, pp. 221-225.

Gnagey, W. (1961) Effects of a deviant student's power and response to a teacher-exerted control technique, 'Journal of Educational Psychology', 51: 1-8.

Goode, W. (1963), 'Readings in the Family and Society', Englewood Cliffs, N.J., Prentice Hall.

Gordon, C. (1957), 'The Social System of the High School', Chicago, Free Press.

Gorman, A. (1969), 'Teachers and Learners', Boston, Allyn & Bacon.

Gould, L. (1964), Juvenile entrepreneurs, 'American Journal of Sociology', 74: 710-719.

Grant, A. (1979), Processes and Components in Curriculum for Adolescent Girls, unpublished dissertation, University of Queensland.

Gregersen, G., and Travers, R. (1968), A study of the child's concept of the teacher, 'Journal of Educational Research', 61: 324-327.

Griffiths, W. (1971), A daring educational experiment, 'New York Times Magazine', 30 May.

Gronlund, N. (1959), 'Sociometry in the Classroom', New York, Harper Bros.

Hallworth, H. (1953), Sociometric relations among grammar school boys and girls between the ages of eleven and sixteen years, 'Sociometry', 16: 39-70.

Hargreaves, D. (1967), 'Social Relations in a Secondary School', London, Routledge & Kegan Paul.

Hargreaves, D. (1972), 'Interpersonal Relations and Education', London, Routledge & Kegan Paul.

Hargreaves, D., Hester, S., and Mellor, E. (1975), 'Deviance in Classrooms', London, Routledge & Kegan Paul.

Harper, D. (1968), The reliability of measures of sociometric acceptance and rejection, 'Sociometry', 31: 219-227.

Henry, M., and MacLennon, G. (1978), Attacks on curricula in Queensland state schools, paper presented at the Conference of the Sociological Association of Australia and New Zealand.

Hibbins, R. (1974), Authority in the Classroom, unpublished dissertation, University of Queensland.

Hoffman, L. (1972), Early childhood experiences and women's achievement motives, 'Journal of Social Issues', 11: 33-41.

Holland, P., and Lienhardt, S. (1973), The structural implications of measurement error in sociometry, 'Journal of Mathematical Sociology', 3: 85-103.

Hollingshead, A. (1949), 'Elmtown's Youth: The Impact of Social Classes on Adolescence', New York, Wiley.

Holter, H. (1970), 'Sex Roles and Social Structure', Oslo, Universitetforlaget.

Hughes, E., Becker, M., and Geer, B. (1962), Student culture and academic effort, in Sandford, N., 'The American College', New York, Wiley.

Jackson, P. (1968), 'Life in Classrooms', New York, Holt, Rinehart & Winston.

Jennings, H. (1950), 'Leadership and Isolation', New York, Longman Green.

Johnson, D. (1970), 'The Social Psychology of Education', New York, Holt, Rinehart & Winston.

Jones, M. (1943), Adolescent friendships, 'American Psychologist', 3: 352-358.

Kahn, R., and Mann, F. (1952), Developing research relationships, 'Journal of Social Issues', 8 (3): 4-10.

Kandel, D., and Lesser, G. (1972), 'Youth in Two Worlds', San Francisco, Jossey-Bass.

Katz, L. (1953), A new status index derived from sociometric analyses, 'Psychometrika', 18: 39-43.

Keeling, B., and Nuthall, G. (1969), Changes in personal value-structure during early and middle adolescence, 'Australian Journal of Education', 13: 32-36.

Keeves, J. (1972), 'Educational Environment and Student Achievement', Melbourne, ACER.

Keeves, J., and Radford, W. (1969), 'Some Aspects of Performance in Mathematics in Australian Schools', Melbourne, ACER.

Kidd, J. (1958), Social influence phenomena in a task-oriented group situation, 'Journal of Abnormal and Social Psychology', 56: 13-17.

King, R. (1973), 'School Organizations and Pupil Involvement', London, Routledge & Kegan Paul.

Klinger, E. (1966), Fantasy need achievement as a motivational construct, 'Psychological Bulletin', 60: 291-308.

Knapp, M., and Knapp, H. (1976), 'One Potato, Two Potato', New York, Norton.

Kohl, H. (1976), 'On Teaching', London, Methuen.

Kolesnik, W. (1969), 'Co-Education', New York, Vantage Press.

Koneya, M. (1976), Location and interaction in row-and-column seating arrangements, 'Environment and Learning', 8: 265-282.

Kounin, J., Gump, P., and Ryan, J. (1967), Explorations in classroom management, 'Journal of Teacher Education', 12: 235-246.

Labov, W. (1972), The logic of nonstandard English, in Giglioli, P., 'Language and Social Context', Harmondsworth, Penguin, pp. 176-216.

Lacey, C. (1970), 'Hightown Grammar', Manchester University Press.

Lambart, A. (1976), 'The sisterhood', in Hammersley, M., and Woods, P., 'The Process of Schooling', London, Routledge & Kegan Paul, pp. 152-159.

Leeds, C. (1947), The construction of a scale for determining teacher-pupil attitudes, 'Journal of Experimental Education', 16: 149-157.

Leiter, K. (1980), 'A Primer on Ethnomethodology', New York, Oxford University Press.

Llewellyn, M. (1980), Studying girls at school, in Deem, R., 'Schooling for Women's Work', London, Routledge & Kegan Paul.

Lofland, J. (1971), 'Analysing Social Settings', Belmont, Cal., Wadsworth.

Loomis, L., and Beegle, J. (1957) 'Rural Sociology', Englewood Cliffs, N.J., Prentice Hall.

Lott, A., and Lott, B. (1960), Group cohesion and learning, 'Journal of Educational Psychology', 57: 1-10.

Luce, R., and Perry, A. (1949), A method of matrix analysis of group structure, 'Psychometrika', 15: 169-190.

Lukes, S. (1974), 'Power: A Radical View', London, Macmillan.

Lundgren, V. (1972), 'Frame Factors and Teaching Process', Stockholm, Almqvist & Wiksell.

Lynn, D. (1962), Sex role and parental identification, 'Child Development', 33: 555-564.

McArthur, J. (1981), 'The First Five Years of Teaching', Canberra, Australian Government Publishing Service.

McClelland, D., Atkinson, J., Clark, R., and Lavell, E. (1953), 'The Achievement Motive', New York, Appleton-Century-Crofts.

Maccoby, E., and Jacklin, C. (1974), 'The Psychology of Sex Differences', Stanford University Press.

McKennel, A. (1969), Self images and smoking behaviour, 'British Journal of Educational Psychology', 39: 27-39.

Macpherson, J. (1977), Classroom idiom, in Macklin, M., and Yeates, H., 'Australian School Reader', Brisbane, Norton Bailey, pp. 90-92.

McSweeney, R. (1971), Adolescent Values, unpublished dissertation, University of Queensland.

Mancini, D. (1972), An Investigation of the Relationship Between Self-Concept of Ability, Classroom Verbal Interaction, and Achievement of Seventh Grade Pupils in Biological Sciences in Two Suburban Schools, unpublished dissertation, State University of New York.

Marsh, P., Rosser, E., and Harré, R. (1978), 'The Rules of Disorder', London, Routledge & Kegan Paul.

Martin, J., and Harrison, C. (1972), 'Freedom to Learn', Englewood Cliffs, N.J., Prentice Hall.

Martin, R. (1971), Selected Aspects of Elementary School Structure and Students' Acceptance of the Norm of Universalism, unpublished dissertation,

University of Toronto.

Martin, S. (1972), The Student's Role in the Classroom, unpublished dissertation, Columbia University.

Mehan, N. (1979), 'Learning Lessons', Cambridge, Mass., Harvard University Press.

Mehrabian, A. (1968), Male and female scales of the tendency to achieve, 'Educational and Psychological Measurement', 29: 445-451.

Menzies, K. (1977), 'Talcott Parsons and the Social Image of Man', London, Routledge & Kegan Paul.

Meyenn, R. (1980), School girls' peer groups, in Woods, P., 'Pupil Strategies in the Sociology of the School', London, Croom Helm, pp. 108-143.

Milner, E. (1949), Effects of the sex role and social status on the early adolescent personality, 'Genetic Psychology Monographs', No. 40.

Möhle, C. (1978), The view from inside, in d'Urso, S., and Smith, R., 'Changes, Issues and Prospects in Australian Education', Brisbane, University of Queensland Press, pp. 131-138.

Montague, M. (1978), Internal Migration and an Australian Rural Community, unpublished dissertation, University of Queensland.

Moreno, J. (1952), Current trends in sociometry, 'Sociometry', 15: 146-163.

Muldoon, J. (1955), The concentration of liked and disliked members in groups and the relationship of the concentration to group cohesiveness, 'Sociometry', 18: 73-81.

Münch, R. (1981), Talcott, Parsons and the theory of action. I. The structure of the Kantian core, 'American Journal of Sociology', 86: 709-739.

Murdoch, G., and Phelps, C. (1972), Youth culture and the school revisited, 'British Journal of Sociology', 23: 478-487.

Musgrave, E. (1964), Role conflict in adolescence, 'British Journal of Educational Psychology', 34: 34-42.

Musgrove, F., and Taylor, P. (1969), 'Society and the Teacher's Role', London, Routledge & Kegan Paul.

Nash, R. (1976), 'Teacher Expectations and Pupil Learning', London, Routledge & Kegan Paul.

Northway, M. (1952), 'A Primer of Sociometry', Toronto University Press.

Nosanchuk, T. (1963), A comparison of several sociometric partitioning techniques, 'Sociometry', 26: 112-124.

Oetzel, R. (1966), Annotated bibliography of sex difference literature, in Maccoby, E., 'The Development of Sex Differences', Stanford University Press, pp. 233-351.

O'Hanlon, J. (1964), Student-Generated Classroom Group Atmosphere and Its Influence on Achievement, unpublished dissertation, University of Nebraska Teachers' College.

O'Leary, V. (1977), 'Towards Understanding Women', Monterey, Brooks/Cole.

Oppenheim, A. (1964), Social status and clique formation among grammar school boys, 'American Sociological Review', 29: 189-205.

Parsons, T. (1937), 'The Structure of Social Action', New York, McGraw-Hill.

Parsons, T. (1951), 'The Social System', Chicago Free Press.

Parsons, T. (1959), The school class as a social system, 'Harvard Educational Review', 29: 297-318.

Parsons, T. (1964), 'Social Structure and Personality', Chicago, Free Press.

Parsons, T. (1966), 'Societies', Englewood Cliffs, N.J., Prentice Hall.

Parsons, T. (1967), 'Sociological Theory and Modern Society', New York, Free Press.

Parsons, T. (1969), 'Politics and Social Structure', New York, Free Press.

Parsons, T. (1971a), 'The System of Modern Societies', Englewood Cliffs, N.J., Prentice Hall.

Parsons, T. (1971b), Evolutionary universals in society, in Desai, A., 'Essays on Modernisation of Underdeveloped Countries', Bombay, Thacker & Co., vol. 1, pp. 560-587.

Parsons, T. (1978), 'Action Theory and the Human Condition', New York, Free Press.

Parsons, T., and Bales, R. (1955), 'Family, Socialisation and Interaction

Process, Chicago, Free Press.
Parsons, T., Bales, R., and Shils, E. (1953), 'Working Papers in the Theory of Action', Chicago Free Press.
Parsons, T., and Platt, G. (1972), Higher education, changing socialisation and contemporary student dissent, in Riley, M. et al., 'Aging and Society', vol. 3, New York, Russell Sage, pp. 24-63.
Parsons, T., and Platt, G. (1973), 'The American University', Cambridge, Mass., Harvard University Press.
Parsons, T., Shils, E., Naegele, K., and Pitts, J. (1961), 'Theories of Society', Chicago, Free Press.
Parsons, T., and Smelser, N. (1956), 'Economy and Society', London, Routledge & Kegan Paul.
Pascoe, M. (1973), Radford upsets pupils, 'Brisbane Courier Mail', 7 May 1974: 4.
Pearce, R. (1953), Streaming and sociometric study, 'Educational Review', 10: 248-251.
Peay, E. (1974), Hierarchical clique structure, 'Sociometry', 37: 54-65.
Phillips, D., and Conviser, R. (1972), Measuring the structure and boundary properties of groups: some uses of information theory, 'Sociometry', 35: 235-254.
Phillips, D. (1971), 'Knowledge from What?', Chicago, Rand McNally.
Pink, W. (1972), Social Class, School Status, Student Commitment and the Educational Experience, unpublished dissertation, University of Oregon.
Polanksy, L. (1954), Group social climate and the teachers' supportiveness of group status systems, 'Journal of Educational Psychology', 28: 115-123.
Polk, K., and Pink, W. (1971), Youth culture and the school, 'British Journal of Sociology', 22: 160-171.
Potashkin, R. (1946), A sociometric study of children's friendship groups, 'Sociometry', 9: 47-80.
Power, C. (1972), The Effects of Communication Patterns on Student Surrounding Status, Attitudes and Achievement in Science, unpublished dissertation, University of Queensland.
Richardson, S., Dohrenwend, B., and Klein, D. (1965), 'Interviewing', New York, Basic Books.
Robinson, P. (1974), An ethnography of classrooms, in Eggleston, J., 'Contemporary Research in the Sociology of the School', London, Methuen, pp. 251-266.
Robinson, P. (1981), 'Perspectives on the Sociology of Education', London, Routledge & Kegan Paul.
Rosenberg, M. (1965), 'Society and the Adolescent Self-Image', Princeton University Press.
Sarup, M. (1978), 'Marxism and Education', London, Routledge & Kegan Paul.
Scarr, H. (1964), Measures of particularism, 'Sociometry', 27: 413-432.
Schachter, S. (1951), Deviation, rejection and communication, 'Journal of Abnormal and Social Psychology', 46: 190-207.
Schmuck, R. (1973), Social-Emotional Characteristics of Classroom Peer Groups, unpublished dissertation, University of Michigan.
Schwartz, F. (1981), Supporting or subverting learning: peer group patterns in four tracked schools, 'Anthropology and Education', XII: 92-121.
Scrupski, A. (1975), The social system of the school, in Shimahara, N., and Scrupski, A., 'Social Forces and Schooling', New York, McKay, pp. 141-186.
Sears, P. (1963), 'The Effect of Classroom Conditions on the Strength of Achievement Motivation and Work Output Among Elementary School Children', Co-operative Research Project A873, Stanford University.
Secord, F., and Bachman, C. (1968), 'A Social Psychological View of Education', New York, Holt, Rinehart & Winston.
Sharp, R., and Green, A. (1975), 'Education and Social Control', London, Routledge & Kegan Paul.
Shaw, J. (1976), Finishing school: some implications of sex-segregated education, in Barker, D., and Allen, S., 'Sexual Divisions and Society',

London, Tavistock, pp. 143-149.

Shaw, M., and McCuen, J. (1960), The onset of academic underachievement in bright children, 'Journal of Educational Psychology', 51: 103-108.

Sherif, M., and Sherif, C. (1961) 'Reference Groups', New York, Harper Bros.

Sluckin, A. (1981), 'Growing Up in the Playground', London, Routledge & Kegan Paul.

Smith, C. (1969), 'Achievement-Related Motives', New York, Russell Sage.

Smith, J., and Zopf, P. (1970), 'Principles of Inductive Rural Sociology', Philadelphia, P.A. Davis Coy.

Smith, R. (1978), Fundamentalism, in Macklin, M., Möhle, C., and Yeates, H., 'Intentions', Brisbane, Norton Bailey, pp. 51-55.

Smith, R., and Knight, J. (1978), The Politics of Educational Knowledge, paper presented at the Conference of the Sociological Association of Australia and New Zealand.

Sommer, R., and Becker, F. (1974), Learning outside the classroom, 'School Review', 82: 601-608.

Spreltzer, E., and Pugh, M. (1973), Interscholastic athletics and educational expectations, 'Sociology of Education', 46: 171-182.

Staines, J. (1963), The self-concept in learning and teaching, 'Australian Journal of Education', 7: 172-186.

Stebbins, R. (1973), Physical context influences on behaviour, 'Environment and Behaviour', 5: 291-314.

Stein, A., and Bailey, M. (1973), The socialisation of achievement orientation in females, 'Psychological Bulletin', 80: 346-366.

Stinchcombe, A. (1964), 'Rebellion in a High School', Chicago, Quadrangle Books.

Strasser, H. (1976), 'The Normative Structure of Sociology', London, Routledge & Kegan Paul.

Sugarman, B. (1968), Social relations in teenage boys' peer groups, 'Human Relations' 21: 41-58.

Sugarman, B. (1973), 'The School and Moral Development', London, Croom Helm.

Sykes, G. (1958), 'The Society of Captives', Princeton University Press.

Tempest, P. (1950), 'Lag's Lexicon', London, Routledge & Kegan Paul.

Thomas, C. (1981), Girls and counter-school culture, in McCallum, D., and Ozolins, U., 'Melbourne Working Papers 1980', Department of Education, University of Melbourne, pp. 125-156.

Turner, R. (1975), Rule learning as role learning, 'International Journal of Critical Sociology', 1: 34-48.

Tyler, F., Rafferty, J., and Tyler, B. (1962), Relationships among motivations of parents and their children, 'Journal of Genetic Psychology', 101: 69-81.

van Zeyl, C. (1973), 'Ambition and Social Structure', Lexington, Mass., Lexington Books.

Veroff, J., Wilcox, S., and Atkinson, J. (1953), The achievement motivation in high school and college age women, 'Journal of Abnormal and Social Psychology', 48: 108-119.

Vidich, A. (1955), Participant observation and the collection and interpretation of data, 'American Journal of Sociology', 60: 354-360.

Waller, W. (1965), 'The Sociology of Schooling', New York, Wiley.

Werthman, C. (1971), Delinquents in school, in Cosin, B. et al., 'School and Society', London, Routledge & Kegan Paul, pp. 39-48.

White, J. (1961), Management conflict and sociometric structure, 'American Journal of Sociology', 67: 185-199.

Willis, P. (1977), 'Learning to Labour', Farnborough, Hants, Saxon House.

Wilson, T. (1971), Normative and interpretative paradigms in sociology, in Douglas, J., 'Understanding Everyday Life', London, Routledge & Kegan Paul, pp. 57-79.

Woods, P. (1976), Having a laugh, in Hammersley, M., and Woods, P., 'The Process of Schooling', London, Routledge & Kegan Paul, pp. 178-187.

Woods, P. (1979), 'The Divided School', London, Routledge & Kegan Paul.

Wrong, D. (1961), The oversocialised concept of man in modern sociology, 'American Sociological Review', 26: 183-193.
Young, M., and Whitty, G. (1977), 'Society, State and Schooling', Ringmer, Sussex, Falmer Press.
Zander, A., and van Egmond, E. (1958), Relationship of intelligence and social power to the interpersonal behaviour of children, 'Journal of Educational Psychology', 49: 259-281.
Zelditch, M. (1962), Some methodological problems of field studies, 'American Journal of Sociology', 67: 566-576.

Index of students

This is an index of some of the students to whom multiple references were made in the text. It indexes only references which illustrate in single students, or, in a few cases, pairs of students, empirical continuities which are split in the text.

Students indexed have had an asterisk placed by their alphanumeric when it occurs in the text. They are arranged below in alphabetical and numerical order. They are thus ordered in a sequence of male and female classes, and within each sex from high to low stream. The students are then ordered in each class following a sequence of rows from the back of the room.

b1/17 claims to status are unacknowledged by classmates, 51; low
power is shown by failure in
competitive mucking around,
56; behaves well, is a crawler,
101; dependent style as
academic high achiever leads
to classmates denying him
status as brain, 126; is
accused of crawling for marks,
127; meets strong academic
competition from classmates
because he takes marks too
seriously, 127; his helping
teachers is interpreted by
classmates as crawling for
marks, 132; classmates debate
his right to be teacher's
favourite, thinks classmate is
improperly favoured by
teachers for unearned
academic status, 163f

b1/18 joins in pellet wars, 62;
competes with academically
ambitious classmate, 127; is
quiet and not recognised as
brain, 146; sits in corner away
from classroom action, 178;
corner seat allows him to work
without interruption, 187; only
student to refuse initially to
be interviewed, 202

b1/23 succeeds in competitive mucking
around, 56; is powerful and so
has few problems as captain,
119

b1/24 is competent with spitballs,
61; dobs as a joke, 109; independent academic style leads
to acknowledgment as brain,

b1/24 117; his academic help of
classmates is legitimate act of
brain, 145

b1/32 acceptance as mate shown by
competitive mucking around,
62; propriety of his crawling
for marks, 132; accepts
propriety of teachers favouring well-behaved students,
163

b1/45 classmates dissuade him from
talking to girls at school, 81;
jokes as clown enjoyed by
some classmates and teachers,
condemned by other class-
mates as crawling, 101; what
he claims is disinterested help
is condemned by classmates as
crawling, 127; favoured by
teacher because of good work,
132f; right to receive favour
contested by classmate, 163f

b1/58 is bested in competitive mucking around, 61; stirs classmates interested in girls, 81;
his being chosen to help by a
teacher is favouritism, 133;
sits at front, unworried by
teacher supervision, 180

b2/21 mucks around too much to work,
50; joins in competitive mucking around, 55, 57; knows
when to stop stirring, 93f;
stirs differently, is a clown,
96; acts well in serious and
comic roles, writes amusing
poems, 97; is bullied as a
clown, 98; stirs teachers who
do not share his definition of
a joke, 100; influences

b2/21 stirring but not recognised as leader because he lacks power, 108f; even serious dobbing by a clown is a joke, 109

b2/22 aspirant to power, and clown by association with seatmate, dominates weaker students, fails with stronger students, 36f; fails to overturn academic status of brain, 51; bullies classmates who do not reciprocate his competitive mucking around, 56; stirring is controlled by classmates, 93; his efforts to control stirring are illegitimate because his stirring causes trouble for classmates, 100; his stirring is influenced by the clown, 100f; dobs indirectly, 110; deserts the principal role in class play without ensuring its failure, thereby loses control status, 150f; tries without success to challenge teachers' definitions of his low academic status, 153; to draw attention to himself accuses teacher of victimising him, 170; his talking prevents people working in his vicinity, 182

b2/28 high academic commitment leads some classmates to see him mucking around enough to be sociable, others see him as not mucking around and therefore not sociable, and others see him as not mucking around but still sociable, 51; counters UFOs which he thinks childish, 61; disclaims any present interest in girls, 81; discounts classmate's academic performance, 145; is respected for acting, academic rival fails to discount his performance, 150f; discounts as teacher favouritism classmate's high academic status, 167

b2/35 can fight but has low power because of refusal to fight, 36f; his academic commitment precludes mucking around, 50; is labelled as weak because of not reciprocating competitive mucking around; his being a goody goody leads to classmates not associating with him because they fear stigmatisation, 56f

b2/56 is a goody goody, 94; is dominated by powerful classmate in defining time for stirring, 100; high marks are discounted because of alleged teacher favouritism, 167; is hit by student sat behind, 187

b3/24 is induced by money to make a fool of himself by incompetent stirring, 34; does not know when to stop stirring, 50; is threatened by classmates because his stirring disrupts work, 93; is punished by reciprocated real dobbing, 114

b3/26 creates power to counter labelling as homosexual, 35; his independent academic knowledge is praised by teachers and condemned as crawling by classmates, 128; his talking with teachers is condemned by classmates but not teachers, 136f; is teacher's favourite, 164

b3/45 and b3/46 are bullied as a joke, 35; clowning and creative writing, 96; b3/46's concern to produce good plays is shown by his choosing actors by ability, 96f; acts well before large audience, takes advantage of classmates, 97; is picked on as a joke by more powerful classmates, 97f; they stir a teacher by offering help, 131; condemn classmate who accepts subordinate diffuse relations with teachers, 136f; b3/46 tends not to sit in fixed place in classroom, 179; b3/45 is conscious of pressure to work at front, 180

b4/17 and b4/18 come to school because they enjoy mucking around, 50; are good but not top stirrers, 92; assert definition of propriety of stirring, 100; believe respect from classmates comes from high academic achievement and independence from teachers, 126; sit at back to avoid being caught with homework undone, 181

b4/23 is bested in competitive mucking around, 58; follows classmates throwing UFOs round room, 61; is topic of b4/23   girls' classroom notes, 73; classmates find him interested in girls and golf, 82; ends unwanted teacher favour by stirring, 167f

b4/31   powerful, breaks work norms with impunity, 30; picks on less powerful classmates, 39; starts throwing of UFOs, 61; stirs well because he thinks about what he is doing, 92; dominates class because of successfully resisting teachers' authority, 94; initiates and defines proper stirring, 98f; classmates approve his stirring when they understand its motivation, 99f; overrules less powerful captain, 120; believes high academic status and stirring requisite for peer respect, 127; because of power can boast about high academic status, 144, 145

b4/46   is picked on by powerful classmates, 39; resents powerful classmates who dominate him and resist teachers' authority, 94; sits at front to see blackboard, 180

b4/56   his unsuccessful attempts to control class are resented by classmates, 93; dominant classmates accuse him of offering help in order to curry favour with teachers, 132

b5/26   powerful classmate imposes a joke on him, 47; his initiation of competitive mucking around is accepted, 54; his initiation of competitive mucking around is rejected by dominant classmate, 59; his initiation of dobbing as a joke on the dominant clique is reciprocated by real dobbing, 110; dominant classmate limits and defines as poor his classroom discourse, 148; as a poor actor his election to the principal role in class play is ensured by dominant classmate so that the play should fail, 150; activates principle of equity in favour of classmates, 175f

b5/31   resents less powerful classmate calling him names he has called the teacher, 39; discounts dominant classmate's outside activities, claims

b5/31   dominant classmate's sporting prowess a source of association rather than prestige, 87; defines possible clown as would-be stirrer, 102; controls definition of situation to label subordinate student as dobber, 113f; is faced with alliance led by dominant classmate, 137; sees dominant classmate as justified teacher's favourite for academic excellence, 175; sits near back to indulge in competitive mucking around, 183

b5/32   is thumped by more powerful classmates, 40; is easily overpowered by dominant classmate, 56; is subject of admiring letter among immature but sexually active girls, 63f; discounts dominant classmate's outside activities, 87; accuses dominant classmate to his face of crawling, 132; sees dominant classmate as justified teacher's favourite for academic excellence, 175; sits near back to engage in competitive mucking around, 183; is subject of class note, 219

b5/41   initiates competitive mucking around, 59; ascribes dominant classmate's popularity to sporting prowess, 87; evaluates and condemns classmate's stirring, 92; advocates balance of work and mucking around, 99; a moralistic would-be dobber is too scared to dob him in, 111; job as captain is easy because of alliance with dominant classmate, 121; lets allies muck around while he quietens the rest of the class, 122

b5/42   reinforces and defines teachers' authority, 35f; suppresses classmate's challenge to his authority, 46; punishes classmate who gives him cheek, 47; his thumping an effective punishment, uses power to abuse others but stops reciprocal abuse, 47; defines less powerful students who do not return his violence as 'sooks', 48; initiates mode of competitive mucking around, supposedly as a joke, really b5/42 to hurt a friend of whom he is tiring, 58; can initiate and resist initiation of competitive mucking around, 59; skites about outside activities, 87; his high sporting prowess unimportant in classroom interaction, 87f; praises classmate's criminal and dangerous activities, 88; enforces teacher's discipline to get to lunch, 99; evaluates classmate's stirring, 102; dobs in seriously classmate who dobs as a joke, 110; a moralistic dobber is too scared of b5/42's power to dob him in, 111; condemns classmate's stirring which gets the class into trouble, 112; controls classmates engaged in unnecessary dobbing, 115f; controls class for captain, 121; warns class of teacher's approach, receives favoured treatment from captain, controls class elections, 122; monopolises self-interested help of teachers, is accused of crawling, 132; stigmatises classmate who helps teacher, 137; talks informally with teachers, 138; his marks, 146; monopolises classroom discourse, appropriates classmate's academic work, 147f; labels class brain a goody goody, 149; his control elections secures his reputation as an actor despite nonperformance, 150; discounts stirring and alleged victimisation of classmate, 170; teachers favour him, 174f; students perceive him a teachers' favourite, 175; appropriates attention gained by victimisation of classmate, 176

b5/47 is condemned for not resisting dominant classmate, 48f; condemns dominant classmate's praise of another classmate's dangerous act, 88; blames classmate for not hiding signs of fight, 110; too scared to publicise dominant classmate's appropriation of work, 147; is a low academic conformist pariah, 158

b5/51 is subject to unreciprocated competitive mucking around by dominant classmate, 59;

b5/51 evaluates classmate's stirring, 92; his dobbing as joke by less powerful classmate leads to real dobbing of that student, his not hiding signs of losing fight leads to his being labelled a dobber, 110; observes that captain's alliance with dominant classmate makes former's job easy, 121; to maintain alliance with dominant classmate helps teacher, 137

b5/55 his disrespect for dominant classmate dismissed as cheek, 39; believes small and weak boys unable to resist degradation by classmates, 40; accepts powerful student's claim to respect, 57f; works against classmate's mucking around, 61; discounts dominant classmate's sporting prowess, 88; accepts against prevailing opinion a classmate as clown, 102; is too scared to dob moralistically dominant classmates, 111; is blamed as dobber by powerful classmates for what was only ambiguously culpable, 113f; describes dominant classmate's enforcement of ban on dobbing, 115f; is prevented by classmate from joining in academic discourse, 147f; believes dominant classmate despite nonperformance is a good actor, 150

b5/57 subordinate brain, is prevented from finishing work by dominant classmate eager to go to lunch, 35; is aware of dominant classmate's power, 47; boasts of successful competitive mucking around, 57; is condemned by dominant classmate for helping the teacher, 137; superiority of academic discourse acknowledged by dominant classmate who prevents him joining in, 149; high academic status is acknowledged by dominant classmate who labels him a goody goody, 149

b6/13 competes for punishment, 92; typifies weaker classmate as dobber even while admitting to dobbing himself, 114; deters signification of his low academic status; denies b6/13   relevance of school knowledge and marks to performance on a job or getting a job, 155; is victimised fairly by teachers, 170

c1/11 and c1/12 have active and physical sexual life, 68f; their sexual activities intrude into the classroom, 69; defensively exercise high influence, define goody goodies in terms of classroom and sexual behaviour, 70; sex-related activities lead to conflict with teachers, 71; conflict with students with less developed sexual interests, 79; uneasy about classmate's high academic status, 142; teachers victimise them for their sexual interests and related classroom activities, 171

c1/13 and c1/14 consensual influence is shown in regard for subordinate classmate, 44f; are annoyed by low academic status conformist asking for help, 157; criticise adults' misuse of sexually active girls' reputation, 172; choose back of room to avoid inter-action with teachers, 180

c1/16   uses imposed influence, 40f; picks on less influential class-mates, 43f; chooses girls with same levels of sexual interest as work mates, but competes with them for boys, 69; her use of influence successfully countered by classmates of same level of sexual maturity, 70; does not notice less in-fluential classmate's dependent and diffuse relations with teachers, 136; activates pariah status of academic status conformist, 158

c1/17   her breaking of work norms is resisted, 30f; dislikes class-mates' use of conflictual influence, 44; acts as sexual intermediary for classmates, 60; when removed from back for talking about boys dislikes sitting next to girl who does not share her sexual interests, 79; annoys classmate by talking about boys to detriment of work, 157; prefers to sit at back because of freedom to talk, 183

c1/23   fails to redress her low influence by creating power, 42; fails because of low influence to resist victim-isation by influential class-mates, 43f; consensually influential classmate listens to her interest in pigs, 45; experiences problems of low academic status management, 156; her requests for help are resented, 156; does not always understand the lesson enough to work, is accused of laziness, argues classmates to work, 157; is a pariah because of low academic status conformism, 158; sexual minority do not see alleged bases of pariah status, 159; makes no use of victim-isation by teachers for low academic status, 171; sympathises with girls with active and mature sexual interests who are victimised by teachers, 171

c1/41   uses classroom notes to stir teacher, 63; sits at side of room, halfway between back and front to see the board, look out the window and avoid teacher supervision, 189

c1/51 and c1/52 unwillingly accept classmate's imposed influence, 40f; control subordinate classmate by selective activ-ation of commitments, 42; describe assertion of influence among mature and sexually active classmates, 70; condemn classmate as goody goody for rejection of expression of sexual interests, 80; accept legitimacy of low academic status conformist's skiting about occasional high marks, 156, 158; share classmate's opinion of pariah status of low academic status conformist, 158

c1/53   classmates signify her subordination by selective use of influence and activ-ation of commitments, 42; is treated kindly by consensually influential classmate, 45; manifestations and correlates of her being a goody goody are opposed to classroom expression of sexual interests,

c1/53   classmates condemn her style
of uniform, 78ff; her diffuse
and dependent relations with
teachers are ignored by
classmates, 136; former classmate moved away to avoid
close interaction with teacher
consequent on location of
desk, 182

c2/16   fights with moll over boyfriends, 67; uses sex
referents in verbal fights,
consensually influential classmate settles fight, 86; sits
towards back because of
opportunities to exchange
notes, 183

c2/18   creates control, 45f; is friends
with girls from higher grades,
has jobs, is criterion by
which classmates' sporting
and playground activities are
judged, 83; has respected and
wellknown sexual activities,
84; counsels classmates with
sexual problems, cares for
moll, 84f; sexual counselling
and care of classmates are
focus of contested control,
85f; is a clown and stirrer,
102f; imposes definition of
good stirring, 103; shared
attitudes to stirring and
clowning are not a condition
of membership in her clique,
instead a shared interest in
boys, 104; extricates herself
from problems associated with
having got the class into
trouble by activating norm
against real dobbing, 112f;
support for her over this
issue is not a condition for
membership of her clique,
113; as captain controls the
class easily, 120f; obtains the
respect of classmates because
she defines her control as in
their interest, 121; controls
class elections, 122; signifies
her maturity and stirs
teachers by talking to them
personally, 138f; stigmatises
classmate who talks to
teacher as goody goody,
teacher's pet and too eager
to gain high academic status,
but does not act against this
student, 139; classmates
believe she has high academic
status despite low marks, 146;
creates high academic status,

c2/18   146f; uses real and alleged
victimisation by teachers, 172f;
teachers' perceptions of
conditions for good relations
with her, 173f; obtains favoured
treatment from teachers, 174

c2/24   her real dobbing in class
interest of dominant classmate
leads to division of her group
and her stigmatisation as
dobber, 112f; conspicuously
offers teachers help, is labelled
by dominant classmate a goody
goody, teacher's pet, and too
eager for high marks but
experiences no pressure from
that quarter, 139

c2/27   supported in fight at dance by
dominant classmate, 84; shared
sexual interests and not shared
mucking around and stirring
are reasons for her membership
of dominant clique, 104;
disinterestedly helps teachers,
130; does not perceive how
dominant classmate limits
subordinate brain's participation
in classroom discourse, 143f,
147

c2/32   is easily influenced, 41; describes patterns of girls' fights,
42; alleged activities with boys
lead to fights and gossip, 66f;
tries at schoolwork, amenable
to discipline, 67f; chats with
class neighbours, classmates
condemn her uniform as im-
modest, 68; is seen to compete
for prestige with dominant
classmate, 83; when upset is
comforted by dominant classmate, 85; dominant classmate
arbitrates fight with another
girl, 86

c2/41 and c2/42 sexually mature
students who oppose dominant
classmate. c2/41 influences
moll's self-opinion, 41; c2/41
as aspirant leader fights
physically with and is beaten
by dominant classmate, 46;
c2/41 labelled a moll when
associated with class moll, 66;
support moll in fight over boy
with classmate, 67; talk with
moll so much that teacher
separates them, 68; classmates
see c2/41 aspiring to become
dominant, they assert dominant
classmate's popularity, 83;
c2/42's being counselled on
sexual matters by dominant

c2/41   classmate leads to fight between c2/41 and dominant
classmate over leadership,
85; fight lost by c2/41, c2/42
believes dominant classmate's
counselling helpful, 86;
c2/41 loses fight with
dominant classmate occasioned
by c2/41, 86; accept by imposition definition of value
of dominant classmate's
stirring, 103; ally them-
selves with dominant classmate by informing the latter
who dobbed her in, 112;
believe dominant classmate a
good captain, 121; dominant
classmate quells c2/42 by
selective activation of norm
of equitable opportunity to
join in academic discourse,
c2/41 asserts that dominant
classmate has false pre-
tensions to academic knowledge, 147; attribute
dominant classmate's
activation of subordinate
brain's problems of status
management to envy, 149

c2/46   dislikes teachers' public-
ising her high marks, 142;
dislikes classmates advertising
her high marks, 142f; dominant
classmate prevents her joining
in academic discourse, 147;
dominant student activates
her problems of academic
status management, 149

c3/11   and c3/12 c3/11 competently
runs down dominant classmate,
44; c3/12 has a coveted boyfriend, 64; define sexually
immature classmates' approaches
to boys as stupid, 72; c3/12
as captain blamed because
she cannot keep class quiet,
116; c3/12 blamed because
she and her friends misbehave
while trying to keep others
quiet, 118; dominant classmate defines c3/12's efforts
as captain to keep class
quiet to be improper dobbing,
120; debate with dominant
classmate propriety of latter
helping teacher, 133; although
shifted around by teacher
because of constant talking
revert to back corner, 179

c3/14   classmates accept propriety
of her doing extra work, 30;
her rival for control dis-

c3/14   comforts her with competent
verbal attack, 44; limits interaction with sexually immature
girls whom she generally
despises, 74; denies propriety
of rival for control using
position of captain to control
her, defines captain as dobber
when trying to control others,
keeps class quiet and thereby
asserts claim to captaincy,
120; debates with control rivals
the propriety of her helping
teacher, 133; although she
helps teachers and does extra
work, she stigmatises less
influential conformists as
teachers' pets, is herself seen
as unjustified favourite because
she is not punished and rewarded
as other students, 164f; feels
unable to end unwanted status
as unjustified teacher's
favourite, 166; sees herself
as victimised by some teachers,
168

c3/23   friends argue that she is not
intelligent enough to be a
lesbian, 41; contests ably
friends who run her down, 44;
classroom interaction of girl
with active immature sexual
interests, 71f; shifts to back
to avoid trouble from teachers,
182; dobs for a joke friend
sat in front, 186

c3/32   and c3/33 competently deride
friends, 44; pass class notes,
63f; outside activities,
approaches to boys, 71f; boys
are subject of their class notes,
73; varying work habits of girls
with active immature sexual
interests, 74; allege that goody
goody girls against expression
of sexual interests are lesbian,
78f; c3/32 deplores substitution
of dobbing for verbal fights,
114; help teacher to manipulate
her, 130f; c3/32 is victimised
by teachers despite doing good
work, 143; c3/33 successfully
manages low academic status
and commitment, 153f; prefer
to sit at back to avoid dobbing
by friends, pick on subordinate classmate in front, 186;
write long letters about boys,
218f

c3/51   and c3/52 work norms are
activated against c3/51 for
doing too much work, 30;

c3/51   fear boys, 78; do all schoolwork, 79; cannot talk with
classmates who want to talk
about boys, 79f; their dress
shows lack of interest in boys,
80

c4/23   is target of conflictual
influence, 44; pariah because
low academic status conformist, 158f; is shifted to back
by teacher who could rely on
her to behave, 179

c4/31 and c4/32 have cohesive
relations with other goody
goodies with weak or no public
sexual interests, 75; refuse
to publicise sexual interests,
76; do not muck around,
c4/31 despite academic ability
is prevented by influential
classmates from joining in
classroom discourse, have
diffuse friendly relations with
teacher, 76; have childish
playground activities, uniforms
denote lack of sexual interests,
77; influential classmate
activates c4/31's problems of
high academic status management, 144; c4/31 is accused
of taking too much satisfaction
in high marks, 145; c4/31,
although prevented by classmates, would prefer place at
front to see blackboard and
to interact with teachers, 180;
influential classmate uses
position at front to let c4/31
see that she is being talked
about unfavourably, 186

c4/43 and c4/44 dismiss as childish
the playground activities of
goody goodies against
expression of sexual interests,
77; moralistically and secretly
dob in stirrers, 111; classmates praise c4/44 for ability
to talk to teachers as equal,
135f; use front to competently
signify classmates' failings,
186

c4/47 and c4/48 competently derogate
low academic status conformist, 44; throw lollies across
room, 62f; attempt initiation
of talk about boys with goody
goody girls, 76; c4/48 can be
relied on to stir when the
lesson requires it, 93; classmates dob them moralistically
for their harsh stirring, 111;
although c4/48 was noisy, she

c4/47   blames captain for not keeping
class in order and letting it
get into trouble, 117; c4/48
activates subordinate brain's
problems of academic status
management, 144; c4/48 is
favourite of only teacher who
can control her, 166; c4/48
acts effectively against her
selective punishment for
offences also committed by
classmates, 170; stir goody
goodies in front, 186

c4/56   asserts her ability to fight
physically a classmate but
sees no point in exercising
or creating power, 43;
effectively signifies low
status of style of uniform worn
by goody goody, 77; refuses
to associate with sexually
immature girls, 77f; incites
dominant stirrer to stir, 93;
categorically opposes real
dobbing, 107; joins classmates' isolation of low academic
status conformist, 159

c4/57 and c4/58 form with similar
students cohesive goody goody
clique, 75; activities of goody
goodies without public
expression of sexual interests,
accused of lesbianism by
sexually maturer students,
78f; c4/58's talking with
teachers is that of a subordinate goody goody, 135f;
c4/58 rejects classmates'
definition of aspects of pariah
status of a low academic
status conformist, 159; are
annoyed by stirrers sat behind
them, 186

Subject index

academic commitment, 27f, 50f, 65f,
70, 74f, 79, 92f, 99, 104, 135,
141, 155-9, 179f, 184-6, 187
academic competition, 29f, 127, 139,
144, 145, 151f, 156, 163f, 165, 167
academic discourse, 46f, 156, 164,
165, 173, 174
academic performance, 7, 8, 12, 14,
20, 22, 141-60; see also Academic
discourse; High academic status;
Low academic status
academic streaming, 13, 23f, 60, 81,
92
activation of commitments, 116-22,
128f, 138, 201

calling out, 140f
captaincy, 116-22, 128f, 138, 201
Christianity, 23, 42, 78, 89, 192
classroom as unit of analysis, 2
classroom location, 25f, 62, 68, 90,
178-91
clowns, 95-102, 107-9, 139, 178f,
193, 215
competitive mucking around, 52f,
107, 183, 192; see also Dobbing
control, 2, 5, 9, 16, 32f, 45f,
52-61, 94, 113f, 118-22, 123, 133,
139, 141, 146-51, 171-7, 191-200,
215; see also Activation of
commitments; Inducement;
Influence; Power

dobbing, 36, 106-11, 119f, 186
dress, 15, 43, 68, 71, 75, 77, 80,
86, 158-9

elections, 120, 122, 149f
ethnography, 1f, 204f
extracurricular activities, 10, 16,
38f, 69f, 71f, 81, 83, 87f, 161,
166-8, 175, 194

fighting ability, 37, 192; see also
Physical fights; Verbal fights

goody goodies, 38, 61, 70, 75-80,
93, 95, 111, 126, 131, 139, 149,
164, 166, 180, 184f

help for teachers, 128-33, 137-9,
150f, 161, 163, 164, 174f
homosexuality, 35, 41, 65, 78f, 158

independence, 8f, 27f, 72, 76, 94,
126-8, 133-5, 139, 141, 143, 153,
155-9, 170-6, 179-85, 189, 193,
205
inducement, 33f
industrial societies, 3, 22, 154, 155,
198f, 202f, 205f
influence, 40f, 45f, 65, 77, 83f,
100f, 102f, 106, 184, 186, 194-6

Jew, 34, 59
jokes, 45, 54, 55, 60, 66, 93f, 96,
97, 107-10, 131, 134f, 144, 145,
151f, 153, 156

low academic status, 44, 74f, 145,
151-9, 189

Marxist studies, 1, 3, 106-7
money, 33f, 83, 86
mucking around, 9f, 38, 49-64, 76,
95f, 120, 121, 122, 141, 153, 156,
167, 182f; see also Competitive
mucking around

norms, 4f, 48, 191-97; see also
Control
notes, 63f, 65, 67, 73f, 183, 185,
217-18

particularism, 6f, 12f, 89f, 123, 132,
161-77, 194-6, 216; see also
Universalism
pedagogy, 25f
peer group, 8-11, 198-9
performance, 7, 23, 192-3; see also
Academic performance; Clowning;
Competitive mucking around;
Influence; Mucking around;
Power; Stirring; UFOs
physical fights, 9, 42f, 46, 54f, 62,
84, 85f, 110f, 114f, 137, 192-3;
see also Fighting ability
picking on by students, 37, 43, 56,
57, 119
playground, 60, 72, 75, 77, 82, 83,

playground, 89, 111, 157, 198-9
power, 9f, 35f, 46f, 57f, 87, 98f,
   101f, 155, 184, 191-4
pushing around, 39f, 46, 56, 57,
   119

schooling, 6-11, 198-9
scunge, 33f, 127
sexual interests, 13, 60f, 63f, 65-90,
   104, 113, 125, 179, 183, 186, 188,
   194-6, 219-20
sexual minority, 29, 159
size, 36, 40, 43
skiting, 144f, 151f, 156
social class, 15f, 21f, 89
socio-sexual differences, 2f, 11f,
   32f, 62f, 142, 191-6
specificity/diffuseness, 7, 15f,
   124-50, 214f; see also Help for
   teachers; Talking with teachers
stirring, 9, 34, 49f, 63, 71, 81, 87,
   91-105, 109, 112, 124-40, 149,
   153, 161, 165, 166, 167f, 173,

176, 178, 179, 184, 185, 192;
   failed stirring, 9, 34, 49f, 95,
   102, 168, 170f, 194f

talking with teachers, 133-7, 161,
   165, 175
teacher's pets, 101, 102, 130, 132f,
   138, 161-8
thumping, 35, 36, 39, 46f, 58f, 119,
   148

UFOs, 61-3, 184, 185
universalism, 7f, 11, 123, 147f,
   216; see also Particularism

verbal fights, 16, 42f, 46, 65, 67,
   69, 85, 114f, 116, 194-6
victimisation, 143, 168-76, 184

work noms, 29f, 50f, 153-5, 157;
   see also Academic competition;
   Low academic status